COST BENEFIT ANALYSIS AND ENVIRONMENTAL PROBLEMS

To my mother

Cost benefit analysis and environmental problems

PETER ABELSON
*Macquarie University,
New South Wales*

SAXON HOUSE

British Library Cataloguing in Publication Data

Abelson, P
Cost benefit analysis and environmental problems.
1. Environmental policy 2. Cost effectiveness
I. Title
301.31 HC79.E5

ISBN 0-566-00267-1

Published by
SAXON HOUSE, Teakfield Limited,
Westmead, Farnborough, Hants., England

Printed by
Itchen Printers Limited, Southampton, England

ISBN 0 566 00267 1

Contents

Acknowledgements		vi
Introduction		vii
1	Economic analysis and environmental problems	1
2	The method of cost benefit analysis	26
3	Why cost benefit analysis?	57
4	Cost benefit analysis of a soil conservation project	80
5	Cost benefit analysis of sand mining	105
6	Cost benefit analysis of airport location	124
7	Aircraft noise and the use of cost benefit analysis	154
8	Property prices and the value of amenities	174
Concluding comment		197
Index		199

Acknowledgements

A large number of people have influenced the thoughts and the projects that make up this book and I regret that it is not possible to do justice to them all. I should like, however, to thank those who have reviewed and commented on one or more of the draft chapters, including Andrew Abelson, Robert Clarke, Michael Cook, Tony Flowerdew, Peter Forsyth, David Henderson, David Hensher, Ian Heggie, David James, Ed Linacre, Anil Markandya, Greg McColl, Les Stein and David Throsby. I am also most grateful to Cathy Charlton, Muriel Kyle and Lucy Koonaporntum who performed the unrewarding task of typing drafts. My thanks are also due to the journals, *Transportation Research* and *Environmental Economics and Management* and to the Bureau of Transport Economics in Canberra for permission to use extracts from published papers. Finally, but most important of all, I am grateful to my wife Jeanne who has painstakingly reviewed the whole book.

Needless to say in making these acknowledgements I do not mean to impute any guilt by association. The author alone is responsible for the opinions and errors that remain.

Peter Abelson

Introduction

The principal aim of this book is the practical one of showing how economic analysis can be usefully applied to typical environmental problems of the sort which regularly confront decision makers. These include such problems as the desirable rate of exploitation of scarce natural resources, the management of wilderness areas, soil conservation, policies towards various kinds of pollution, notably noise, and appraisal of major environmental changes occasioned by large investments such as an airport. In order to obtain satisfactory solutions, it is necessary to evaluate the costs and benefits of alternative decisions. This applies to decisions not to disturb the environment as well as to those which sanction a major change. For while there may be benefits from an undisturbed environment, there are frequently also costs in terms of benefits foregone.

In using money as the unit of measure of costs and benefits, the economist is simply being practical. Any other weight or measure would be as acceptable if it were as convenient. The real issues for the analyst to resolve are the relative amounts of money that should be associated with each cost and benefit and the method of aggregation of these amounts so that the decision maker(s) can determine the most beneficial course to society. This is essentially what cost benefit analysis, and therefore this book too, is all about. Needless to say, the formulation of socially desirable policies (even if possible) does not provide any guarantee of their adoption. But discussion of the efficiency of political institutions, important as this is, is beyond the scope of this book.

The book has two main parts. The first part, consisting of the first three chapters, deals with various broad environmental and economic issues. These are the nature of environmental problems and an economic assessment of them, the method of cost benefit analysis and the justification for its use. The first task, of course, is to define what we mean by environmental problems. Following the normal practice of the discipline of economics, these are defined as problems whose origins lie in the constraints imposed on us by the natural environment in which we live. In particular, productive and amenity resources are scarce and there are limits to the amount of waste which the environment can absorb without harm to mankind. Given the technological resources of society, these constraints appear to us to be important but not insuperable barriers to improvements of social welfare. The greater threat to our well-being is seen as our possible inability to manage technological advance in such ways as would enhance our welfare. However, the essential point is that whatever the nature of the constraints, given that all decisions have costs and benefits, we need to develop a rational way of reaching the correct ones.

Our description of the method of cost benefit analysis has two main components – the first comprises a discussion of how costs and benefits may be evaluated and the second is concerned with the decision related features of cost benefit analysis. These include decision criteria, the choice of discount rate, the treatment of uncertainty and methods of dealing with distributional issues. The discussion is intended to be useful to the reader with little economic background, but I have also tried to take account of the more important controversies in the recent literature, for example those concerning the relative value of consumption and investment and the treatment of equity issues.

As is well known, there are various evaluation methods other than cost benefit analysis, for example, environmental impact statements, goal achievement matrices and planning balance sheets. The choice of criteria by which to assess their theoretical and practical value is inevitably subjective. Those used in this book are the comprehensiveness of the evaluation method, its philosophical coherence and ethical acceptability, the extent to which it takes account of individual preferences or can justify departures from them, and the usefulness of the method to decision makers. The purpose of the discussion is not to provide a blank cheque for the use of cost benefit analysis. Indeed the limitations of the method, notably with respect to the analyst's ability to quantify everything in monetary units and to resolve distributional issues in a definitive way, are stressed. But other evaluation methods suffer these and other limitations as well and do not appear to offer a satisfactory alternative.

The second part of the book, consisting of chapters 4 to 8, is mainly concerned with applications of cost benefit analysis. Although the general theory and the case studies are thus separated, I have attempted throughout to illustrate the close relationship between the theory and the practice of cost benefit analysis. The first and simplest of the case studies is an analysis of a soil conservation programme in Victoria, Australia. This illustrates a number of evaluation principles, for example the evaluation of non-marketed output and the importance of the hypothetical alternative with which the project is compared. But the main aim of this discussion is to illustrate the basic procedures of cost benefit analysis. The second case study deals with the exploitation of mineral sands, drawing on examples from several Australian studies. The issues discussed in this study arise in many projects involving choices between resource exploitation and conservation.

The costs and benefits associated with alternative airport locations are discussed with illustrative material from the Roskill Commission on the proposed third London airport and from the second Sydney airport study. Special attention is paid to questions of airport management and the need for a new airport, to traffic forecasts, and to problems of uncertainty and distributional effects, as well as to methods of estimating the basic costs and benefits. Aircraft noise, however, is discussed separately in order to bring out the problems that arise in any analysis of policies to reduce environmental pollution. These problems include the development of a measure of the pollution, estimation of its cost and the cost of reducing it, and determination of the preferred set of policies. This determination is based on the minimisation of the sum of pollution and abatement costs, taking into account other factors, such as equity, which might affect the choice of policy. The last study in the book is concerned with the relationship between property prices and the values which households place on amenities like freedom from aircraft or traffic noise, good views, spacious streets and access to shops. Although the estimated amenity values depend on the prevailing demand and supply conditions in Sydney where the research was undertaken, the results from this type of research provide a basis from which environmental values to be used in cost benefit analysis can be estimated.

There is finally a very brief conclusion summarising the main arguments of the book. Similar arguments can of course be found in the many books on cost benefit analysis and on environmental economics. Despite a considerable literature on these subjects, many students of economics apparently complete their studies with little idea how to apply the economic theory they have learned. Also many highly qualified non-economists who work in areas related to economics show a lack of appreciation bordering on scepticism of the possible role of economics. It is hoped therefore that this book will prove a useful addition to the literature for some undergraduate students of economics in their second or third year and for some graduate students in multi-disciplinary courses. Possibly too, it may be of use to those public servants and consultants who regard economics more as an academic theory than as a tool for practical men.

1 Economic analysis and environmental problems[1]

This chapter outlines an economic approach to environmental problems. Given that each choice in the use of the environment involves various costs and benefits, it is necessary to establish a framework for considering these costs and benefits so that decisions may be consistent with social objectives. In the first section, environmental problems are defined as those which arise from the limitations of the natural environment. The second section discusses how social objectives may be formulated in such a way as to be helpful to decision making. The third and fourth sections outline an economic approach to the problems of limited productive resources and environmental pollution respectively. Finally, the main points are summarised in the conclusion.

1.1 Environmental problems

The word 'environment' is used here, as is the convention with economists, to refer to the natural environment. This is of course a much narrower view of the environment than that expressed in the Shorter Oxford English Dictionary which describes the environment as 'the condition or influence under which any person or thing lives or develops'. Likewise Australian legislation defines the environment as including 'all aspects of the surroundings of man, whether affecting him as an individual or in his social groupings'. [2] Such all embracing definitions are not very useful, however. When nothing is non-environmental, the word 'environmental' has no meaning. Thus many 'Environmental Inquiries' in Australia, for example, could as easily be described as 'Planning Inquiries' or simply 'Inquiries'. [3]

Although I emphasise the natural environment, I do so only in so far as it provides services, or fails to provide them, to man. It follows that no value is attached to the environment for its own sake. [4] Environmental change is seen as neither good nor bad, but may be accounted so only after consideration of man's interests. Nor is any value attached to such concepts as ecological stability or diversity for their own sake, unless instability or lack of diversity can be shown to be harmful to man's interests.

The natural environment may be seen as providing four main services namely (a) extractive resources for the production ultimately of consumer goods and services, (b) natural amenities for recreational use, (c) space to live in, and (d) space for productive wastes. As there is often a choice between (a) and (b), the extraction of resources and the maintenance of a natural environment, it is convenient to consider them both under the general topic of the limitations of the environment as a supplier of resources. Likewise congestion and pollution problems (c) and (d) are related through the concept of externalities, which suggests that the major cause of both problems is the ability of one individual to impose costs on someone else without paying for them. [5] The separation of the two main subjects – scarce productive resources and pollution – helps to clarify the environmental issues but they are often of course interrelated problems. It is beyond the scope of this book to attempt the grand synthesis of all possible environmental interactions, which for instance *The Limits to Growth* [6] attempted, but some of the important relationships between resource exploitation and pollution are mentioned below.

The major elements of environmental economics are shown in simplified form in figure 1.1. Despite our emphasis on the natural environment it is not possible, as figure 1.1 and the discussion following it show, to ignore the relationship between the natural and the socio-political or man-made environments.

In brief, environmental problems may be seen to arise because economic markets and political institutions do not provide the goods and services that man demands, including environmental goods like clean air and water, given the supply constraints imposed by the environment and by man's ability to exploit it (i.e. by technology). In the rest of the chapter I argue that to satisfy man's demands, much can be achieved, despite supply constraints, by way of improvements in the working of economic markets and in governmental decisions.

1.2 Social objectives

Households have so many objectives that it is difficult to formulate a measure of social welfare which is simple enough to be operational but not so simple as to be meaningless. The measure of social welfare proposed here with qualifications is the estimated aggregate value of social consumption. This is the estimated value of the consumption of all goods and services, including non-marketed goods such as clean air and water, enjoyed by all members of society. Other things being

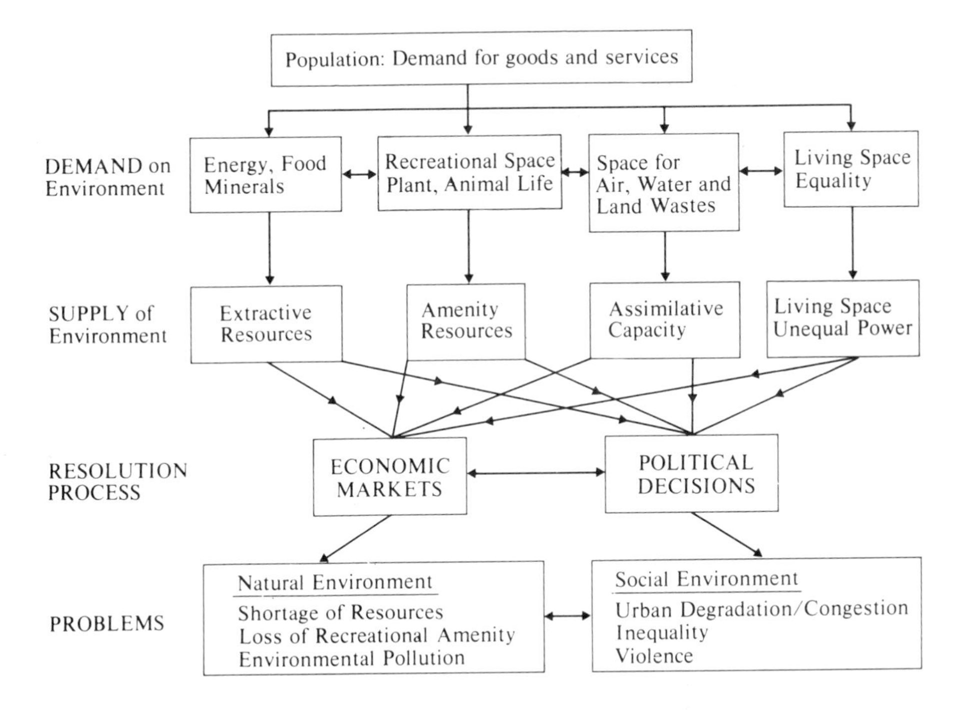

Figure 1.1 An overview of environmental problems

equal, an increase in the value of aggregate consumption represents a desirable welfare position.

The value of aggregate consumption over time can be expressed as follows,

$$w_1 x_1 + w_2 x_2 + \ldots w_n x_n \quad (1)$$

where the x's are the values of aggregate consumption in each period and the w's are the weights attached to that consumption. The values of aggregate consumption in each period can usefully be re-written as

$$x_i = \sum_{i=1}^{n} Q_i (WTP_i - C_i) \quad (2)$$

In equation 2, the Q_i are the goods consumed, including non-marketed goods, in period i. The WTP_i are the prices individuals are willing to pay for goods in period i, and the C_i are the marginal costs of producing the goods in period i. In graphical terms, the net consumption benefit from any good may be represented by the area 'Z' between the demand and supply curves as shown in figure 1.2.

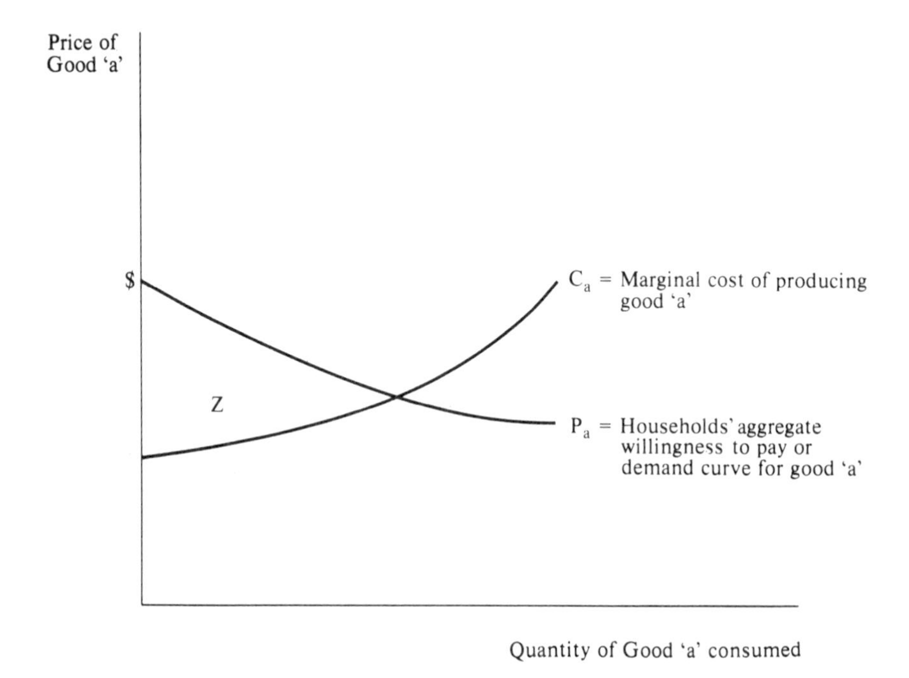

Figure 1.2 The value of a good

It is also convenient to re-write the consumption weights, w_i, as follows:

$$w_i = \frac{1}{(1 + r)^i} \tag{3}$$

where r, known as the social time preference rate (STPR), is the rate per period at which future consumption is discounted, and i is the number of periods, usually measured in years. Generally future consumption is regarded as less valuable than present consumption (i.e. r is positive) both because households appear to behave as if this were so and because future generations are expected to be more affluent than present generations and to have a lower marginal utility of consumption. The nature of the STPR and possible values for it are discussed in more detail in the next chapter.

A major strength of the aggregate consumption criterion of social welfare is that it provides an operational way of including a number of apparently distinct objectives such as better food, better housing and better transport in one measure of welfare. It also incorporates a number of primarily economic objectives such as increasing foreign exchange, investment or employment. Each of these objectives is desirable mainly as a means to achieving a higher level of consumption. There are, to be sure, situations when a premium, an 'accounting' or a 'shadow' price as it is called in the literature, should be attached to an increase in exports or in employment etc., but this premium is calculated essentially with reference to the contribution the extra foreign exchange or employment would make to aggregate consumption.

On the other hand, there are perhaps three major questions about the aggregate consumption measure of social welfare. The first concerns issues related to demography. Should we aim to maximise the aggregate value of consumption or the per capita value of consumption, or some other alternative like aggregate consumption subject to the constraint that additions to the population would not reduce the consumption of existing members? These questions are important because if population can be controlled, a fall in total consumption is compatible with, and may even cause, a rise in per capita consumption. Generally, economists are reluctant to make the value judgements necessary to choose between these kinds of maximands, though they have shown their economic and demographic implications. [7] Fortunately, the great majority of projects, including those discussed in this book, have a negligible effect on population levels so that the problem can be ignored in these cases.

Secondly, it is generally agreed that the marginal consumption of all households should not carry equal weight. Extra consumption by the poor is worth more than extra consumption by the rich. There is however major disagreement whether to weight consumption according to the characteristics, especially the income level, of the consuming households, as Little and Mirrlees argue [8], or whether to account for distributional gains and losses separately from aggregate consumption as Harberger argues. [9] It should be emphasised that the issue is not whether to take account of distribution, but *how* to do so. In the next chapter, I argue in favour of the Harberger view that aggregate consumption and its distribution should be considered as separate welfare criteria.

Thirdly, it may be questioned whether everything can be valued in monetary terms. The principles of valuation, including the value to be placed on uncertain future consumption (or conversely on the loss of options due to irreversibility), are discussed in the next chapter and various examples of valuation are given in later chapters. Our general conclusion is that most non-marketed goods such as peace and quiet or recreational pleasures can in principle be given a monetary value, but it will not always be practical to do so. There are however some social objectives which virtually no amount of ingenuity would bring within the measuring rod of money. Increasing employment, for instance, may be desirable not only because it increases consumption, but also because an individual may prefer to work rather than be unemployed, or because fuller employment reduces social tensions. Also considerations like national culture and prestige or individual freedom may not be measurable in money terms. As Pigou remarked [10], we might well prefer the early nineteenth century Germany of Goethe, Schiller, Kant and Fichte to the materially advanced Germany of the early twentieth century.

But, as Pigou went on to argue, all is not lost. It is true that the estimated aggregate value of consumption is not an index of total welfare. Nevertheless, other things being equal, more consumption of goods and services, including non-marketed goods, is preferable to less, since total welfare would rise. Maximising the aggregate value of consumption therefore is a sensible objective providing due weight is given to social considerations, notably distributional equity, which are not allowed for in the aggregate consumption measure.

1.3 The environment as a supplier of resources

The general problem

Productive resources can be grouped conveniently into four classes, namely renewable and non-renewable material resources and renewable and non-renewable energy resources. The distinction between renewable and non-renewable resources is a fine one, depending on whether the resources 'exhibit economically significant rates of regeneration'. [11]

Renewable material resources include agricultural resources and animal and fish life. Normally such resources expand by biological reproduction sometimes aided by careful husbandry. They require management so that the preferred pattern of consumption over time is achieved. Depending on the circumstances, the preferred policy may turn out to be consumption of the whole stock of resources now, the maximisation of the growth of the stock by partial or total abstention from current consumption, or it may involve some compromise strategy (see the fishery management problem below).

Non-renewable material resources, such as copper or tin, are in fixed supply. However, as we know from the first law of thermodynamics, matter is not destroyed, it is merely dispersed. Virtually all material resources that are in the earth remain available to man even after they are consumed and the technology exists to reconvert most wastes, at a cost, into useful products providing the energy is available. Indeed, in the United States and Western Europe, some 40 per cent of all lead, 35 per cent of copper and 25 per cent of tin, aluminium and zinc were being recycled in the early 1970s. [12] The critical issue is not the quantity of resources *per se* which is available to man but the economic and social costs of exploiting them.

Certain energy sources, such as coal and oil, are also in non-renewable fixed supply. Unlike non-renewable material resources, however, they cannot usually be recycled after use. When used the energy is converted into heat which radiates away from the earth, so that although it is not destroyed it is virtually impossible to recapture. The question in this case is conceptually straight forward – at what rate should the fixed stock of energy sources be used? But the problem is greatly complicated when we consider that breeder reactors using uranium or nuclear fusion based on heavy hydrogen are both potentially capable of providing virtually limitless energy. This point is further emphasised when we consider the flow of energy resources. Every 100 minutes the earth receives as much energy from the sun as mankind uses in a year. Wind and water energy flows also greatly exceed the use that is currently made of them. The critical question for all these sources of energy is therefore not their availability but, once again, the economic and social costs of exploiting them.

To be sure, as resources become less accessible, they may become more costly to exploit and living standards may fall. Much depends on whether technological progress enables us to raise the productivity of increasingly inaccessible resources or to find substitutes for them. For example, the amount of coal required to produce one kilowatt hour of electricity fell from about 3 kilo-grams in 1900 to less than half a kilogram in the 1960s. The first electronic digital computers produced around 1950 weighed about 30 tonnes; modern ones which are faster and more efficient weigh one thousandth of the original versions. Since 1900, totally new materials, for example synthetic fibres and plastics, have been developed and productivity has risen dramatically in resource discovery and extraction, exploitation of low grade materials and recycling of scrap materials.

Unfortunately as Peterson and Fisher [13] point out, there is no very satisfactory way of measuring scarcity. Both real unit extraction costs and material and energy prices have drawbacks as measures of scarcity. The former are not easily observable and the latter often include government taxes and royalties and monopoly rents. Nevertheless, the authors conclude that 'virtually all the evidence, drawing on a variety of measures of cost and price, points in the same direction: we have not been running out (of resources) in an economic sense . . . . Though stocks are obviously being run down in a physical sense, technical change, economies of scale, and product and factor substitution have largely prevented erosion of the resource base of the economy. On the contrary, it appears that extraction commodities have become less scarce, in terms of the sacrifices required to obtain them, over the past hundred years or so'.

It is sometimes argued that there is one resource at least – untouched natural environments used for recreation – the supply of which by definition cannot be extended by man. The increase in population, income and leisure time is also said to create a fast rising demand for such environments. Not all this argument can be accepted. Many environments, such as areas subject to flooding may be improved and distant or mountainous areas made more accessible. The effective supply of natural environments is not fixed. Nevertheless the popular subjective judgement, with which I am inclined to agree, is that the value or relative price of accessible natural environments is rising as environments become scarce relative to the demand for them.

It is not sufficient, however, simply to trade off the declining accessibility of resources against technological progress without considering the critical issue of resource management. As we noted in the Introduction, such vital social questions as whether society can manage modern technology like nuclear energy, or whether society can cope with the international competition for resources, are beyond the scope of this book. But management is also very important to the efficient exploitation of resources over time, and in the next sections the contribution of economics to some particular management problems is discussed.

Economic responses to some resource exploitation problems

Economic responses to four fairly typical exploitation issues are outlined below. Firstly, fishery management is used to illustrate the genre of problems arising in connection with renewable resources such as forests and water supplies. Secondly, a mine management problem exemplifies the issues associated with non-renewable resources like oil and gas. Thirdly, recycling is discussed and, finally, the problem of resource development versus conservation for recreation is examined. The treatment here is necessarily sketchy and for further detail the reader is asked to refer to the relevant chapters of this book and more especially to the general references given in note [1] at the end of this chapter, especially the volume by Herfindahl and Kneese.

The four problems have one important aspect in common. In each case the objective is to exploit the resource to achieve the desired amount of consumption over time. Subject to the reservations noted in section 1.2, this objective can be expressed as maximising the present value (PV) of the resource as follows:

$$\text{Max PV} = \text{Max} \sum_{i=1}^{n} \frac{Qi\,(WTP_i - C_i)}{(1 + r)^i} \qquad (4)$$

Often PV is written as NPV, meaning net present value, since it is the difference between the benefits of consumption and the costs of production (i.e. consumption benefits foregone) which is maximised.

The fishery problem The starting point for the fishery analysis is the premise that the rate of growth of a given stock of fish, dx/dt, depends on the size of the fish population, x, as shown in figure 1.3. Given a biological growth function of this type, the stock is in natural equilibrium at Q_1 and Q_3, i.e. there is no change in the size of the stock at these population levels. Any consumption when the stock is close to Q_1 will risk extinction. At higher stock levels, the effect of consumption depends on the relationship between the amount of consumption and the ability of the fishery to replenish itself. The maximum sustainable level of consumption is given by dx/dt at the stock level Q_2.

The management problem is two-fold, namely (a) to determine the optimum rate of fish production over time and (b) to regulate the industry so as to obtain this pattern of production. With respect to the first of these problems, the essential points are: the level of consumption in one period affects stock size in the next; and the size of the stock affects both its rate of growth (as we have seen) and also the cost of fish production since this falls with increases in population size. Maximisation of the net returns to society from the fishery therefore involves a complicated dynamic problem the solution of which calls for mathematical techniques such as the calculus of variations or dynamic programming. It is often argued, and even embodied in statutes [14], that the optimum fish catch is equivalent

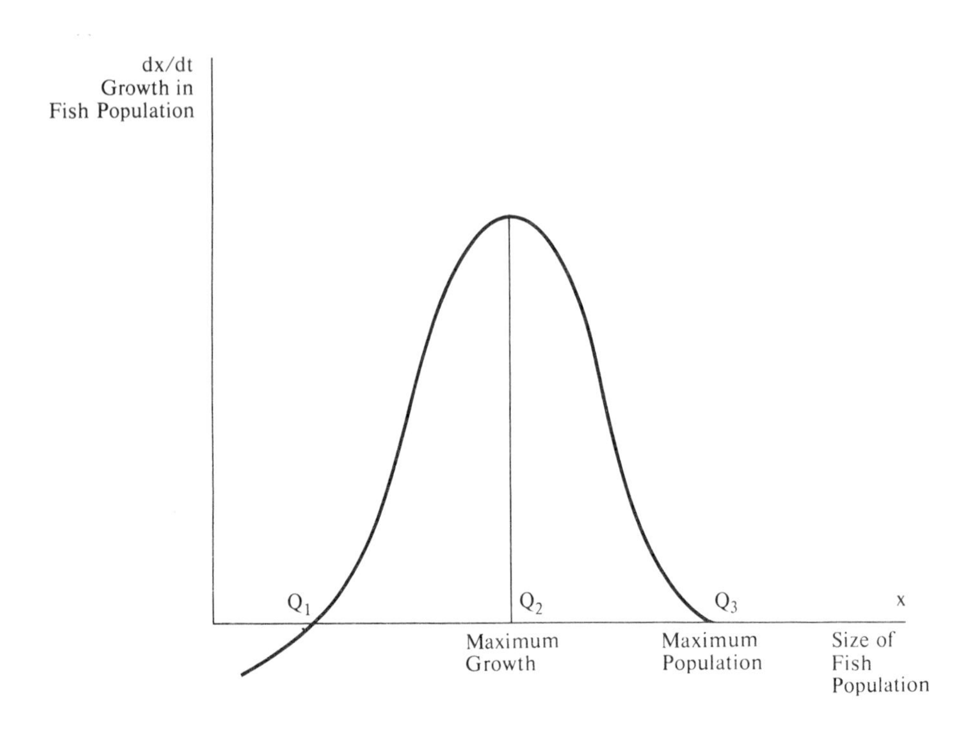

Figure 1.3 Growth of fish population as a function of population size

to the maximum sustainable consumption level. That this is not necessarily the case can be seen by considering the implications of a radical fall in fish prices or of a sharp rise in the costs of catching fish. In either case, future production of fish by the fishery may not be worthwhile and current consumption need not be reduced in order to ensure survival of the fish population. Conversely, if prices are expected to rise or production costs to fall sharply, then present consumption should be sacrificed to future consumption.

The need to regulate fishery production arises because competitive fishing is unlikely to bring about the preferred rate of fishery exploitation. The value to society of a fish caught is \$ (WTP – C) – U, where U is the productive value of the fish. This is sometimes called the 'user cost', and is the amount by which the present value of the fishery is reduced when an additional fish is removed from it. Since the individual fisherman is not much concerned with this user cost, the private returns to fishing exceed the social returns and fisheries tend to be over-exploited. [15] It is normally desirable therefore that the government take steps to manage the rate of exploitation. For example, it can tax the catch, in which case the tax should equal the user cost thus internalising the social cost incurred in excessive fishing, or it can impose quotas on the amount of fish caught.

The mine problem The way to maximise the net present value of consumption from a mine can be seen most easily by assuming that there are no marginal costs of production, i.e. C = 0 in equation 4. The NPV is then maximised if the price of the mined resource rises in real terms (that is relative to the consumer price index) at a rate equal to the social discount rate. The quantity consumed in each period will vary but the *marginal* benefit from consumption in each period, B_i, will be equal.

$$\text{i.e. } B_i = \frac{P_i}{(1 + r)^i} = K \text{ where K is some constant} \qquad (5)$$

If equation 5 holds, the present value of consumption cannot be increased by transferring a unit of consumption from one period to another. If the marginal costs of production are positive, then, irrespective of whether costs fall, remain constant or rise over time, the net profit $(P_i - C_i)$ should grow at a rate equal to r. [16]

An example taken from Herfindahl and Kneese [17] may illustrate the theorem. 'Consider the following case:

unchanging demand curve $P = a - bq = 10 - 1.q.$

cumulative cost curve $L = c + \beta x = 2 + .08\,x$

where P is market price, L is marginal cost per unit and x is output cumulated from t = 0,' (t is time). To maximise the net social gain, 'the solution, using a discount rate of 10 per cent, results in a rising market price and cost at first rapid and then with an asymptotic approach to the maximum price of 10 permitted by the demand curve. The rate of production is initially high but falls off rapidly as it approaches zero. The net price (the social gain on each unit produced) falls rapidly at first and approaches zero.' These results are shown in figure 1.4.

The theorem that net price should grow proportionally with the rate of interest has been described by Solow [18] as 'the fundamental principle of the economics of exhaustible resources . . . if the net price were to rise too slowly, production would be pushed nearer in time and the resource would be exhausted too quickly because no one would wish to hold resources in the ground and earn less than the

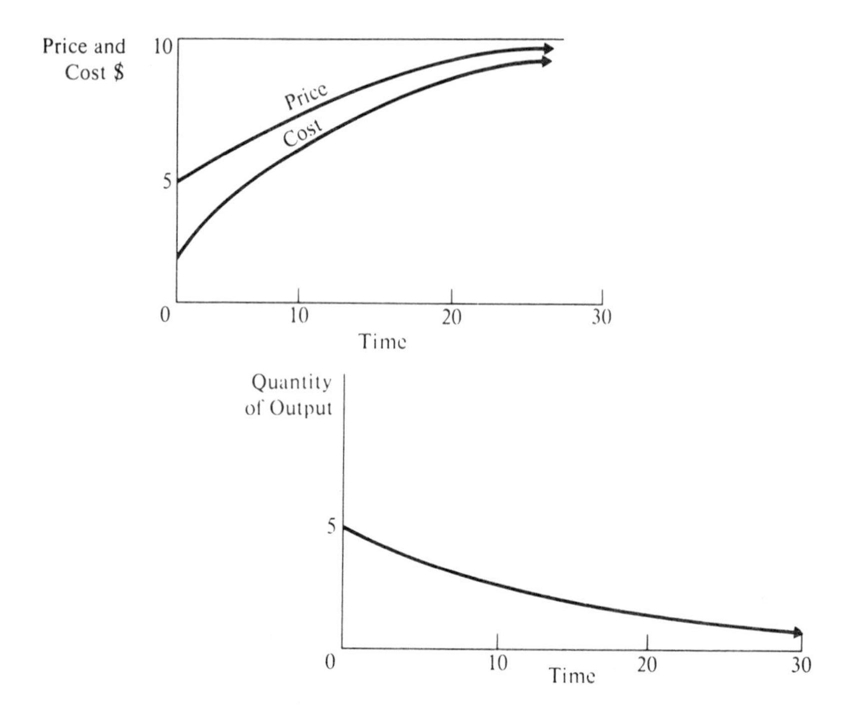

Figure 1.4 Solution to mineral price and output

going rate of return. If the net price were to rise too fast, resource deposits would be an excellent way to hold wealth, and owners would delay production while they enjoyed supernormal capital gains'. Note that an exponential rise in *net* price does not mean that market prices to users necessarily rise. If extraction costs are a significant part of net price and if they fall over time, market prices are likely also to fall.

The critical questions are whether market forces do create the preferred patterns of consumption of scarce resources over time and whether consumption is fairly distributed between different groups in society. Under certain very restricted conditions – including an absence of uncertainty and of monopoly, and perfect capital markets in which the riskless borrowing rate equals the social discount rate (r) – it can be shown that a competitive economy would exploit resources efficiently over time. [19] Profit maximising businesses, indifferent between a unit of profit now and (1+r) units in a year's time, would take account of the demands of future generations. High prices would signal shortages. Businesses would innovate in response to scarcity, substitute abundant for scarce materials and develop new techniques of recycling and production. These conditions would not guarantee, however, an acceptable distribution of resources between social groups.

Although perfect market conditions are not generally fulfilled, their non-fulfilment does not necessarily accelerate the rate of resource exploitation. Uncertainty, for example, tends to discourage exploration and development. Borrowing rates higher than the social discount rate also discourage investment. And monopolies generally raise prices and reduce the amount produced and sold. [20] On the other hand, businessmen who are unsure of the level of future demand or of their continued right to exploit resources may press for rapid resource exploitation. Present generation consumers too are often keen to see resources developed rather than conserved for future generations. In summary, it appears that investment in resource discovery and development may be lower than is socially optimal but that the rate of extraction from resources ripe for exploitation may be faster than is optimal. To take a concrete example, businesses have probably spent less capital exploring for and developing oil resources than society would like, but developed resources, especially low cost ones like Saudi Arabian oilfields, are probably being depleted too fast. The net effect of these contrary influences on the rate of resource exploitation as a whole is difficult to assess.

The general policy implications following from this analysis are that exploration and investment should be encouraged and rapid extraction rates discouraged. However, the net effect of giving to businesses with one hand and taking away with the other is not clear. Better defined policies will emerge only when the relationship between competitive markets, market imperfections and resource exploitation are more thoroughly understood.

Optimal recycling A private firm will recycle materials if recycling is cheaper than the use of virgin materials. But from the social viewpoint, pollution costs and the benefits of conserving resources should also be taken into account. For a given level of output it is desirable to recycle materials if

$$\sum_{i=1}^{n} \frac{(C_R + P_R - B_R)_i}{(1+r)^i} < \sum_{i=1}^{n} \frac{(C_V + P_V)_i}{(1+r)^i} \qquad (6)$$

where C_R and P_R are the production and pollution costs of using recycled materials, B_R is the benefit from extending the resource life of materials, and C_V and P_V are the production and pollution costs of using virgin materials.

The production costs of recycling, which include the collection and separation of waste materials, can be energy intensive and expensive compared with the use of virgin materials. Pollution costs include the value of the land taken up in waste disposal as well as air and water pollution. Thus recycling often reduces pollution costs, but not always. For example, bleaches added to paper to restore it to its original quality involve a bleaching plant, which can add obnoxious chemicals to the atmosphere. Of course, benefits of extending the life of raw materials favour recycling but when discounted to the present these benefits are generally small and may not justify the other costs involved.

As we have seen, businesses do recycle certain materials in quite significant amounts. The recycling may, however, be less than the socially desired amount if businesses lack secure property rights to raw materials and thus have an incentive to exploit them rapidly or if the pollution costs of using virgin materials are high. In principle, public ownership and exploitation of resources could obviate these difficulties, but public ownership may be inefficient in production and may deter desirable private investment. A combination of taxing the use of virgin materials and providing secure property rights to private investors may be preferred governmental policy. It is also important that businesses pay for the resources used in waste disposal and for the harmful effects of pollution. If businesses have to minimise pollution costs as well as production costs, they are more likely to produce the optimal amount of recycling which, for some materials, might mean an increase from present levels and, for others, a decrease.

Amenity resources Often, a resource with extractive value also has value as an unspoiled natural amenity and it is necessary to compare the benefits of development with those of conservation as shown in equation 7. In this example the following assumptions are made: the capital costs of development are incurred in the base year; net development benefits grow at an annual rate b, from year 1 to n, and are consumed in the year in which they occur; development creates irreversible changes to the environment so that no benefits of any kind can be obtained after year m. Without development, amenity benefits would grow at an estimated annual rate a, for n years.

Development would therefore be chosen if,

$$\sum_{i=1}^{m} \frac{B_1(1+b)^i}{(1+r)^i} - C_o > \sum_{i=0}^{n} \frac{A_o(1+a)^i}{(1+r)^i} \qquad (7)$$

where B_1 = net benefits of development in year 1
b = rate of growth of project benefits (which may be zero)
C_o = capital costs of project
r = social time preference rate
A_o = amenity benefits in year o
a = rate of growth of amenity benefits.

Equation 7 allows the benefits of development and conservation to grow at different rates because amenity value may grow faster than the value of other goods. Allowance could of course be made for more complicated sets of costs and benefits, including pollution costs.

As is well known, private enterprise tends to exploit natural environments for raw materials at the expense of amenity benefits because it is usually easier to obtain revenues from extraction of minerals than it is from provision of recreational services. This tendency is exacerbated when businesses are allowed to set up industries and pollute the environment without penalty. It is therefore normally considered necessary for governments to manage national parks and to regulate land uses within them.

Concluding comments We have looked at four resource exploitation problems, a fishery (the renewable resource problem), a mine (the non-renewable resource problem), recycling and amenity resources. In each case the objective was to maximise the value of consumption over time. And in each case either the lack of effective property rights or the mal-allocation of property rights was an important part of the problem. However, there was no one simple way to achieve the preferred consumption pattern: sometimes taxation, sometimes regulation of private industry, and sometimes public ownership would be the preferred policy. But whatever the instrument of policy, it was shown that formulation of a rational decision depends on an appraisal of the costs and benefits of the case. To be sure not all costs and benefits can be nicely measured. And we have not so far given much weight to distributional issues. Nevertheless cost benefit analysis, as argued in chapter 3 and demonstrated elsewhere, provides a reasonable method with which to evaluate most government policies.

1.4 Environmental pollution [21]

The problem

Pollution is not a new phenomenon. Urban environments everywhere in the nineteenth century suffered from far worse sanitation, noise and air pollution than is usual today in all except a few of the largest and poorest cities in the world. [22] However, it is generally agreed that (a) as incomes rise, households are prepared to spend an increasing amount of their incomes on environmental goods; (b) growth in production increases the amount of waste and the potential for pollution, although improvements in technology also enhance our ability to control it; (c) the harmfulness and persistence of pollutants are increasing. Examples of persistent pollution include nuclear radiation wastes, the accumulation of jet fuel ash in the upper atmosphere which may alter the earth's weather, and long lived heavy metals such as mercury or synthetic organic chemicals like DDT.

One way to measure the magnitude of the pollution problem is to estimate the cost of providing satisfactory environmental standards. Of course, 'satisfactory' is a subjective concept, but the OECD has calculated that most Western countries would need to increase pollution control expenditures by less than 1 per cent of their annual national product to achieve reasonable environmental standards. [23] For example, pollution control investment expenditure in Japan would rise from 1.2 to 2.1 per cent of gross national product (GNP). In the USA which has more stringent environmental aims than most OECD countries, investment expenditure would rise from 1.6 to 3.2 per cent of GNP. It was estimated that this would slow down the average yearly growth in GNP in the USA by 0.7 percentage points between 1972 and 1976.

It may be concluded that even if the OECD estimates prove to be significantly too low, the technical capacity exists to solve most pollution problems at fairly modest cost. What is required is effective allocation of that small percentage of GNP, which involves setting satisfactory standards for pollution control and establishing market or political mechanisms to achieve these standards.

Principles of pollution control

To maximise the present value of consumption, pollution should be reduced if the marginal cost of so doing is less than the marginal cost of the pollution itself. The principle is illustrated in figure 1.5. The marginal cost of pollution abatement, line FBD, is assumed to fall with higher levels of pollution. While it is generally possible to reduce

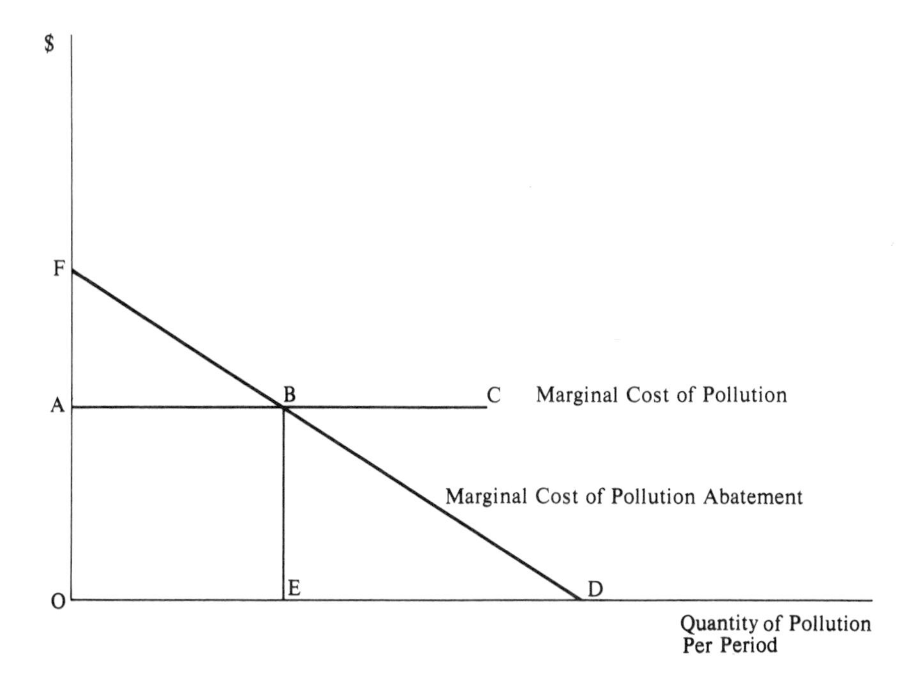

Figure 1.5 Pollution costs and pollution abatement costs

pollution a little at quite low cost, further reductions tend to become progressively more costly. The marginal cost of each unit of pollution is assumed in this case to be constant and is given by line ABC.

Total social costs are minimised (and this is equivalent to maximising the value of consumption) at the pollution level given by point E. When the amount of pollution exceeds E, the marginal cost of abatement is less than the marginal cost of pollution. Consequently pollution should be reduced. When pollution levels are between O and E, pollution abatement is not justified as the marginal abatement costs exceed the marginal pollution costs. In other words, the value of goods foregone in reducing pollution would be greater than the benefits.

The process for estimation of pollution costs can be outlined simply as shown in figure 1.6.

The difficulties involved in estimating pollution costs should not, however, be underestimated. It is not easy, for instance, to model the relationship between the wastes of a project and existing ambient conditions in order to estimate the change in environmental

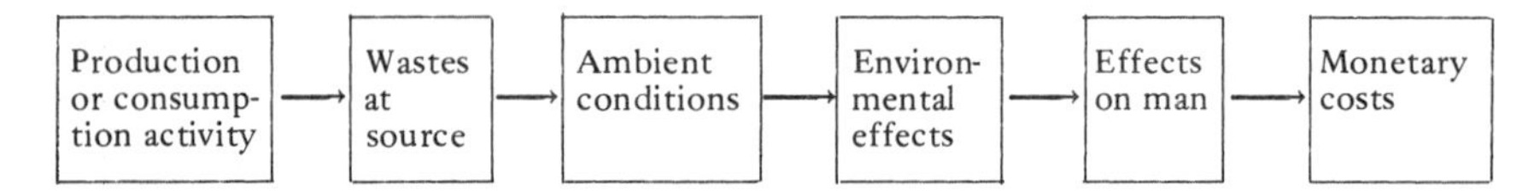

Figure 1.6 From production to pollution costs

conditions. Some wastes interact in a biological synergism so that the total effect is greater than that of the parts, as when DDT and chlorinated hydrocarbons occur together and exceed the absorptive capacity of the environment. In other cases, antagonistic effects occur, for instance, particulates from power stations may neutralise nitrogen and sulphur oxides. Indeed, not all interactions are fully understood. [24]

Moving to the next step in the costing process (see figure 1.6), many environmental effects on man or his products can be estimated. For example, property damage from air or water pollution can be calculated. However, the relationship between air pollution and health has not been firmly established. Nor is it clear how far man can successfully adapt to adverse environments like aircraft or traffic noise. The situation concerning estimates of monetary costs is similar. The costs of property damage due to air pollution, or the costs of crop loss due to soil erosion can be estimated with reasonable accuracy (see chapter 4). Adverse living conditions caused by noise or air pollution can also be costed, though with less accuracy (see chapter 7). Other costs, for example, those concerned with the loss of recreational facilities or of life itself are still more difficult to estimate, although attempts have been made. [25]

The quantification of pollution abatement costs is also complicated because abatement may be achieved by a variety of means, including the reduction of product output or of harmful emissions per unit of output, the redirection of emissions or the insulation of property. Thus, suppose that pollution may be reduced either by cutting output (which has a cost in terms of lower profits and employment and reduced consumer benefits) or by introducing a costly process of production. The marginal cost of pollution abatement would then in principle coincide with the cheaper of the two options and would follow the dotted line in figure 1.7.

It is important to note that figure 1.7 is drawn on the assumption that economies of scale exist in pollution abatement methods. Consequently in this example there is a straight choice between introducing technology to reduce pollution and reducing product output. This choice depends upon the demand for pollution abatement: if

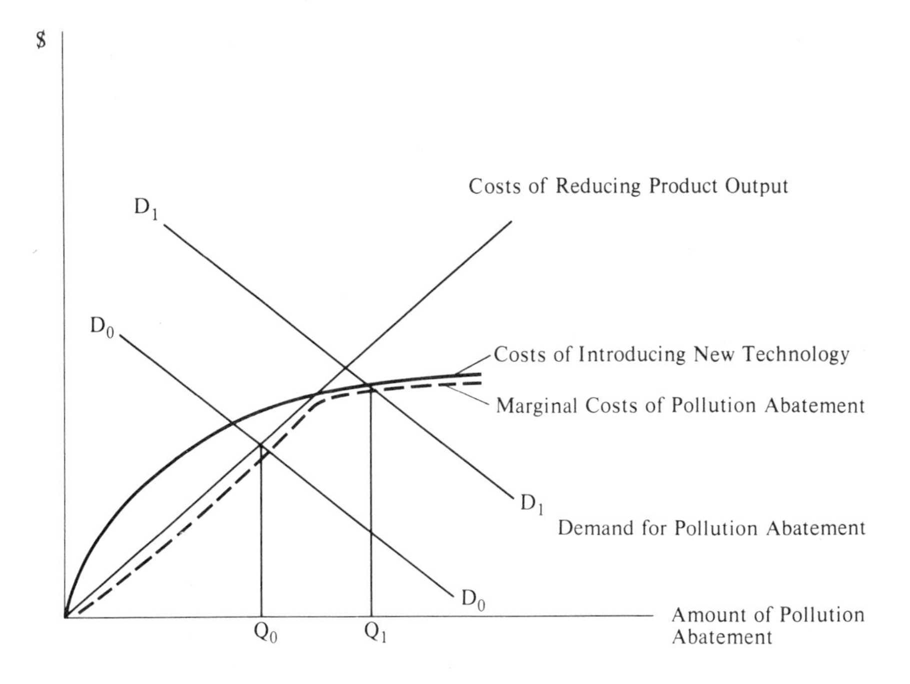

Figure 1.7 Demand and supply for pollution abatement

demand is high (D_1D_1 in figure 1.7) the former would be the cheaper solution, whereas, if it is low (D_0D_0) the latter would be less costly. On the other hand, if for all relevant methods of pollution abatement, the marginal costs of abatement increase rather than decrease, the optimum policy is to use all methods simultaneously so that the marginal costs per unit of pollution abatement are equal by each method.

The above analysis has been conducted essentially in what is known as a partial equilibrium framework, that is, it has been based on the polluting activities of one firm, with the activities of other firms and the ambient conditions taken as given. A more comprehensive systematic approach to pollution problems may, however, be required for at least two important reasons, namely (a) the pollution damage caused by one plant depends critically on the activities of other neighbouring plants, and (b) improvements in one environmental element may cause deterioration in another element. Improved air quality, for instance, may be achieved at the expense of reduced water quality or harmful solid wastes. Looked at in a different way, reduced pollution from one industrial operation may be associated with increased pollution from another. For example, reductions in rutile sand mining may reduce beach pollution but increase pollution from the paint production industry which has to switch from rutile to ilmenite (see chapter 5).

Various attempts have been made to create comprehensive input-output tables which depict not only inter-industry relationships but all residual emissions and those economic environmental relationships implied by (a) and (b) above. [26] According to Kneese [27] the most detailed input-output model to date is the American model by Resources for the Future which is used to estimate residual emissions in 1970 and to predict emissions for 1980 and 2000 under 4 scenarios reflecting alternative assumptions about population and economic growth. Kneese also instances input-output analyses on a sub-national scale, for example, the model of the Norwegian sulphite pulp industry and what is known as the Russell-Spofford model of the Delaware region. The essential difference between these general equilibrium models and the partial models discussed earlier in this section lies in the complexity of the data and the scale of the system under study. The evaluation of pollution abatement would in both cases be based on a balancing of its respective costs and benefits.

Policies for environmental protection

The absence of fair and effective property rights is probably the major cause of environmental pollution, as it is of excessive exploitation of extractive resources. When resource ownership is clearly defined and backed up by an accessible litigation process, resource owners can normally be relied upon to manage their property efficiently, if only to maintain its sale value. If someone else wishes to use or pollute it, he will have to pay to do so. This ensures among other things that the marginal costs of pollution will not exceed the marginal costs of reducing pollution. In practice, however, much of the environment is treated as common property which can be freely used and abused. Typically, pollution costs are not borne by producers or consumers who might adjust their behaviour in the light of these costs but by third parties who have little influence on the level of pollution.

Given this diagnosis of the problem, one possible solution would be to extend property rights to include such things as air, waterways, parks, etc. and concurrently to provide efficient and cheap litigation to implement the system of rights. Mishan [28] has indeed suggested that pollution problems could be resolved by giving individuals a charter of amenity rights. The political and practical difficulties of any radical expansion of property rights seem, however, to rule out such policies except in modest form. For example, managers of a factory which pollutes the atmosphere cannot easily negotiate with thousands of property owners of clean air. Even were the government to act as a negotiating body, the administration costs, sometimes called transaction costs, of operating such a market would generally be prohibitive. Most emphasis has therefore been placed on (a) the regulation of producers and (b) pricing policies.

Typically, regulations prevent individual producers or consumers from emitting more than a certain amount of waste either in total or per unit of output. Motor vehicles usually have to conform to certain emission standards, for example. A major problem with regulations is that they generally impose uniform conditions on all producers regardless of their ability to reduce pollution or of the real pollution costs to the community. It is often more economic to achieve a given level of pollution abatement by reducing pollution substantially in one business and a little in another rather than equal amounts in both. Moreover, damage from emissions depends upon the relationship between individual producer wastes and ambient conditions. The emissions of a few producers in some locations may not cause any pollution damage.

In general, as we have seen, the optimal pollution level varies with the cost of, and the demand for, pollution abatement. Thus it varies from Q_0 to Q_1 in figure 1.7 as the demand for pollution abatement rises. The authorities, even if they have the information on which to base rational policies, are rarely able to produce regulations sufficiently flexible to achieve the optimal social result or anything very close to it. On the other hand, regulations are well understood in the community and practical, though not necessarily cheap to implement, and for these reasons they are an essential part of any pollution abatement programme.

The pricing approach generally involves charges for emitting pollutants or subsidies for reducing pollution. Charges and subsidies have the same effect on pollution levels from existing plants but subsidies encourage investment in less costly, more polluting factories and so charges are generally preferred for this as well as for equity reasons. The appropriate charge would be given by OA in figure 1.5. Any charge higher than OA would mean more pollution abatement than could be justified, i.e. the costs of pollution abatement would exceed the costs of pollution. The effect of pollution charges is to make the cost of pollution part of the cost of production which businesses aim to minimise. Producers who can reduce pollution at low cost will do so, and those who cannot reduce pollution so easily will not. Charges therefore achieve given levels of pollution abatement at lower total cost than do regulations. [29]

An important caveat, based on what in the technical literature is described as the non-convexity problem, should however be noted. [30] If the marginal cost per unit of pollution is higher at lower levels of pollution, the optimum policy will sometimes involve plant closure rather than charges equivalent to the marginal pollution cost. In this case, the option of plant closure should be assessed with the aid of cost benefit analysis.

Pricing policies can also be extended to include compensation for producers and households affected by pollution. Compensation may be a low-cost way of combating pollution. For example, paying for noise insulation for property owners may be cheaper than reducing noise by cutting output. Adequate compensation also has the important advantage that compensated households would be less inclined to oppose developments that are generally in the public interest.

1.5 Summary

The environment supplies productive resources, including amenity resources, and receives the wastes of production. Left to itself, the environment would not satisfy man's wants so that it has to be managed to meet his objectives. Many of these can be measured in terms of the estimated aggregate value of consumption, which includes an estimate for non-monetary goods. The value of aggregate consumption is not an index of total welfare, since it normally does not take into account a number of important social conditions such as the distribution of consumption and equality before the law. Nevertheless, the maximisation of the aggregate value of consumption is a sensible objective providing that due weight is given to social considerations not included in the aggregate consumption measure.

Resources may become less accessible but they rarely disappear. Indeed, in economic terms, technological progress has been such that resources have been increasingly available. Similarly, technological progress has enabled us to resolve most pollution problems at modest cost, though it has also given us the means to destroy the environment as we now know it. The most critical problem is therefore man's willingness to control modern technology. Another important problem is the lack of effective property rights or controls over environmental resources, which causes over exploitation of some resources and excessive pollution of common property. Unequal property shares within and between nations also mean that some social groups suffer critically and unnecessarily from shortages of resources and from pollution of all kinds.

The solutions to environmental problems are not grand and simple, like stopping all economic growth. They are many and mundane. They include better defined property rights, encouragement of exploration and investment, pricing or regulating the destructive uses of the environment, more public provision of amenity goods and a more equitable sharing of environmental goods. But it is necessary of course to descend from this level of generality in order to be useful. Thus the costs and benefits of fishery management, mine operation, recycling, conservation of natural resources and pollution abatement have also been discussed in this chapter. Cost benefit analysis would seem to provide the most rigorous way of determining rational use of the environment. It can of course be effective only if it is allied to a profound scientific understanding of environmental relationships and if its application is not inconsistent with the prevailing ethical beliefs of society.

Notes

[1] For good introductory books on economics and the environment, the reader is referred to *Economics and the Environment* by Kneese A.V., Penguin 1977 and *Environmental Economics* by Pearce D.W., Longman 1976. An excellent but more advanced book is *Economic Theory of Natural Resources* by Herfindahl O.C. and Kneese A.C., Resources for the Future, 1974. Excellent summaries of the literature and extensive bibliographies are contained in two journal surveys by Fisher A.C. and Peterson F.M. They are 'The Environment in Economics. A Survey', *Journal of Economic Literature*, vol.XIV, no.1, March 1976, pp 1-33 and 'The Exploitation of Extractive Resources: A Survey', *Economic Journal*, no.348, vol.87, December 1977, pp 681-721.
[2] *Environmental Protection (Impact of Proposals) Act 1974-75*, Australian Government Publishing Service (AGPS).
[3] For example, both the *Ranger Uranium Environmental Inquiry, First Report*, AGPS, 1976, and the *Fraser Island Environmental Inquiry* (on sand mining), *Final Report*, AGPS, 1976, quote the definition of the environment given in the 1974-75 Act, op.cit. Both inquiries interpreted their task to include *all* relevant considerations.

[4] The weight, if any, to be given to animals is highly subjective. Note, for example, the comment in the Introduction to *The Thames Transformed* by Harrison J. and Grant P., Andre Deutsch, 1976, 'Let us remember that conservationists are not cranks. A goose does not appreciate that it is being conserved. It is being conserved by us for our enjoyment'. Economic analysis can show some of the costs and benefits to man of conserving animals, but it obviously cannot ascribe costs and benefits to the pains and pleasures of animals.

[5] In *Social Limits to Growth*, Cambridge University Press, 1976, Hirsch F., argues that the benefits of economic growth are also highly constrained by 'positional goods'. These are goods the enjoyment of which depends upon their being owned by a minority and the supply of which, so it is argued, cannot be increased. I ignore this issue here because it is not primarily a problem associated with the natural environment.

[6] Meadows D. et al, *The Limits to Growth*, Earth Island, London 1972. For some critical comments on this book, see Pearce D.W. op.cit., pp 188-91 or Kneese A.V. op.cit., pp 117-20.

[7] See Herfindahl O.C. and Kneese A.V. op.cit., pp 105-8.

[8] Little A.D. and Mirrlees J. *Project Appraisal and Planning for Developing Countries*, Heinemann 1974.

[9] Harberger A.C. 'Three Basic Postulates for Applied Welfare Economics: An Interpretative Essay', *Taxation and Welfare*, Little, Brown and Company, 1974, pp 5-20.

[10] Pigou A.C. *Economics of Welfare*, Macmillan 1920, p.13.

[11] Peterson F.M. and Fisher A.C., op.cit., 1977, p.681.

[12] Pearce D.W. op.cit., pp 169-70.

[13] Peterson F.M. and Fisher A.C. op.cit., 1977, pp 705 and 711.

[14] US Laws, Statutes, etc. *Statutes at Large*, vol.74, p.215; 'The Multiple – Use Sustainable – Yield Act of 1960', *Public Law*, pp 86-517.

[15] If the fishery were wholly owned by one firm, the incentive to over-exploit it would be greatly reduced (the firm's rate of discount might still exceed the social discount rate).

[16] This theorem is demonstrated more rigorously by many writers. See for example Pearce D.W. op.cit., pp 162-3 or Weinstein M.C. and Zeckhauser R.J. 'The Optimal Consumption of Depletable Natural Resources' in *Quarterly Journal of Economics*, vol.89(3) 1974, pp 371-92.

[17] Herfindahl O.C. and Kneese A.V. op.cit., pp 130-1.

[18] Solow R.M. 'The Economics of Resources or the Resources of Economics', *American Economic Review*, Papers and Proceedings, May 1974, pp 1-14.

[19] See Pearce D.W. op.cit., pp 149-50 or Weinstein M.C. and Zeckhauser R.J., op.cit.
[20] For elaboration of this point see Stiglitz J.E. 'Monopoly and the Rate of Extraction of Exhaustible Resources', *American Economic Review*, September 1976, pp 655-61. Note the exception to the monopoly conservation hypothesis. If the estimated elasticity of demand falls over time, monopolies may exploit resources faster than would competitive businesses.
[21] To simplify the exposition, I concentrate here on environmental pollution rather than congestion. An analysis of urban congestion can be found in Richardson H.W. *The Economics of Urban Size*, Saxon House 1973. Transport congestion is analysed in any standard transport economics text, e.g. Harrison A.J. *Transport Economics*, Croom Helm 1976.
[22] See for example, some fascinating descriptions of pollution in nineteenth century London quoted by Beckerman W. *In Defence of Economic Growth*, Jonathan Cape 1974.
[23] OECD Environment Directorate, *Survey of Pollution Control Cost Estimates made in Member Countries*, Paris 1972.
[24] As Fisher A.C. and Peterson F.M. remark op.cit., 1976, 'Natural scientists are uncertain, for instance, about the effects of hydrocarbon emissions on the creation of photochemical smog of the type that plagues Los Angeles and Washington. Hydrocarbon may limit photochemical reaction rates in some cities and nitric reactors may be the rate limitors in others'.
[25] Layard R. (ed.) *Cost Benefit Analysis*, Penguin 1972, pp 25-9. See also chapter 5 in this volume for a method for estimating the value of recreation.
[26] Victor B.A. *Economics of Pollution*, MacMillan 1972, pp 51-72.
[27] Kneese A.V. op.cit., pp 56-94 and 146-50.
[28] Mishan E.J. *The Cost of Economic Growth*, Pelican Book 1967, pp 102-6.
[29] An application of this approach with respect to aircraft noise is discussed in chapter 7.
[30] Slater M. 'The Quality of Life and the Shape of Marginal Loss Curves', *Economic Journal*, no.340, vol.85, December 1975, pp 864-72.

2 The method of cost benefit analysis [1]

Cost benefit analysis (CBA) attempts to quantify the social advantages and disadvantages of alternative courses of action in terms of a common monetary unit. The unquantified effects, often known as intangibles, should also be described.

In order to compare costs and benefits which occur at different times, it is necessary to discount them to present value equivalents. The difference between the discounted benefits and discounted costs is described as the net present value (NPV) and may be positive or negative. If the alternative to a project is to do nothing, a project with a positive NPV would normally be considered viable. Usually, however, there are many possible alternatives, including notably the possibility of postponing the project. [2] In this case, the project with the highest NPV, other things being equal, is preferred. But whatever the alternative(s), the project decision would probably depend on an assessment of the distribution and reliability of the quantified costs and benefits and on consideration of the intangibles as well as on the estimated NPV.

CBA is a versatile evaluation method which may be used to appraise a project or a programme (which is really a combination of projects), to optimise project design, to assess policies and regulations, and indeed to evaluate any decisions entailing (more or less) measurable economic consequences. The complexity of the evaluation may change with the circumstances, but the basic evaluation method does not alter. It may be noted especially that in each case there is likely to be a 'do-nothing' or 'base case' alternative. For convenience, I generally refer to CBA in the context of project appraisal, although it should be understood that CBA can be used in other contexts.

The chapter consists of two main parts, A and B. In part A, the valuation of costs and benefits is described. This consists of three sections, which treat the role of prices in CBA and the valuation of costs and benefits. In part B, decision related features of CBA – including decision rules, the choice of discount rate, uncertainty and distributional issues – are discussed in four sections. These are followed by a brief conclusion.

2.A THE VALUATION OF COSTS AND BENEFITS

2.1 The role of prices

The three main interrelated issues that surround the role of prices in CBA are discussed below. These are the use of market prices or accounting prices which allow for market imperfections, changes in general and in relative prices, and discrepancies between domestic and international prices. But first the main costs and benefits to be valued and some principles of valuation are outlined.

Costs, benefits and valuation

The total social costs of a project are all the incremental costs associated with it. These include the cost of resources employed by the project and the indirect costs (the external costs) imposed by the project on the community. The smoke from a factory or noise from an airport are typical examples of external costs. Costs which do not vary with the project should not influence the project decision and should not be included in the CBA.

The real cost of the resources used by the project are the social sacrifices involved in taking them away from alternative uses, which is often described as their opportunity cost. External costs are valued at the minimum amount required by businesses and households to compensate them for the imposition of the cost. This amount, if it was paid, would ensure that those exposed to external costs would be no worse off then they were in the ex-ante situation.

The total social benefits of a project are the advantages to users of its output plus any indirect (or external) benefits. A dam for example provides user benefits to farmers who obtain irrigation water and to households who enjoy the recreational facilities of the reservoir. It may also provide external benefits to farmers and others who benefit from reduced flood damage (see chapter 5). In practice, the distinction between user and external benefits is not always clear cut, and any benefit from the *output* of a project should count as part of the project's benefits. It is, however, important to distinguish between these and secondary benefits which follow from the expenditures or profits of a project. Secondary benefits should not normally be counted as a benefit in CBA (see section 2.3).

The estimated stream of costs and benefits determines the assumed economic life of a project. If an arbitrary end to a project is assumed, say 20 years for a dam, the project may be assigned a residual value.

In principle this value should, of course, be equivalent to the forecast flow of net benefits after the arbitrary end of the project.

Market prices and accounting, or shadow, prices

Domestic market prices normally form the basis of the evaluation for two reasons. First, they provide a unit of account, sometimes called a numeraire, for the evaluation, in the same way as kilometres provide a numeraire of distance. Secondly, they are the basis upon which costs and benefits are valued. They are not however, a sufficient basis as the following quotation shows:

> The market price would represent the true value of goods and services if the law of supply and demand operated freely, under perfect competitive conditions, with full employment of all resources and complete mobility of all factors. If because of any interference, obstacles or regulations these conditions do not exist, then the price system will be distorted, it will not correspond to that ideal system of equilibrium nor represent the value of the factors from the point of view of the community as a whole. It is therefore considered necessary to correct market prices in order to obtain what has been termed the social cost of the factors. [3]

Correcting for the divergence between market prices and social costs or, in other words, establishing the appropriate 'accounting' or 'shadow' prices for project evaluation, is an important part of the method of CBA.

General and relative price changes

Costs and benefits are normally valued on the assumption of a constant general price level, say 1978 prices. Inflation will not affect the real return to the project if all prices rise equally, for the value of the output from the project would always be worth the same amount of real resources. The assumption of constant prices is made therefore because it avoids the unnecessary complication of forecasting rates of inflation. However, it is important to note the following points.

(a) If constant general prices are assumed for the CBA, an inflation-free rate of discount should be used.

(b) Even assuming constant general prices, allowance should be made for expected changes in relative prices reflecting changes in the relative values of goods and services. If food or energy, for example, is expected to be in scarce (or plentiful) supply relative to demand, its estimated price should rise (or fall) relative to other prices used in the CBA.

(c) Any estimate of cash flows or of loan requirements would, of course, require a forecast of the general price level.

Domestic and international prices; the accounting price for foreign exchange

If a currency is protected by import controls, such as tariffs and quotas, or by export subsidies, the domestic prices of goods will generally be higher than the international prices when the currencies are converted at the official exchange rate. This has led commentators such as Little and Mirrlees [4] to suggest that international prices are a better unit of account in CBA than are domestic prices, because they make bureaucrats and politicians more aware of the gains from trade. But as Little and Mirrlees also point out, the choice of numeraire cannot affect the CBA results (it cannot for instance change a positive NPV into a negative one) and for most analysts, domestic prices provide a more practical and convenient numeraire than international prices. However to avoid underestimating the real value of foreign exchange, allowance should be made in the accounting price of foreign exchange for any divergence between domestic and international prices due to an overvalued, protected exchange rate. [5]

The generally accepted procedure for calculating the accounting price of foreign exchange is 'to estimate the likely pattern in which incremental dollars would be distributed over the various categories of goods'. [6] For example, suppose that half of all goods imported by Australia face a 50 per cent tariff, that the other half of imported goods face no tariff, and that one Australian dollar is exchanged officially for one US dollar. Assuming also that the patterns of marginal and average expenditures were similar, then an extra US dollar would enable Australians to purchase foreign goods worth 1.25 Australian dollars at Australian prices.

It is, of course, the responsibility of the government's central planning office, or its equivalent, to estimate the way in which incremental foreign exchange is likely to be distributed over imports and hence the accounting price of foreign exchange. The cost benefit analyst would be responsible for identifying the resources imported by the project. In theory, the imported components of goods bought from other domestic producers should be taken into account, but in practice allowance is usually made only for goods imported directly for the project.

Finally, it should be noted that important market imperfections other than an over valued exchange rate can occur. For example, domestic oil prices in the United States and in Australia are held below the international oil price. When a project uses relatively cheap local resources and thus obliges another producer to import the resource from a more expensive source, the real resource cost is the cost of the marginal imported good.

2.2 The valuation of costs

Accounting prices for labour

In a competitive market economy, the opportunity cost of labour is the wage required to attract workers to the project. This wage compensates the worker for the wage foregone in alternative employment (which also reflects output foregone) and for any disadvantageous change in his lifestyle.

In a non-competitive or non-market economy, the opportunity cost of labour has a direct and an indirect component. The direct cost is the sum of the value of output foregone plus any cost associated with the change in the worker's lifestyle. The real cost of employing an otherwise under-employed worker is therefore the wage required to compensate him for his loss of leisure. [7] The situation is complicated if there is widespread unemployment. If a project draws off an otherwise under-employed person whose place is then taken by an unemployed person, there is again no opportunity cost in terms of output foregone, although there may be a cost associated with the changes in lifestyle.

Indirect costs of employing labour occur if the social time preference rate (STPR) is lower than the return on investment and if the employment of labour rather than machines increases the consumption and reduces the reinvestment of project surpluses. For example, suppose that an investment in period 1 returns a surplus of $110 in period 2, and that the STPR is 5 per cent per period. The present value of that surplus is $\frac{\$110}{1.05}$ which is approximately $105. But if the $110 were reinvested at say 10 per cent per period and became $121 in period 3, its present value would be $\frac{\$121}{(1.05)^2}$ which is approximately $110. In words, the lower rate of reinvestment reduces the present values of the surpluses and hence the NPV of the project – and this fall in NPV is an indirect cost of employing workers who will not reinvest their savings.

Despite the attention of recent literature [8] to these indirect labour costs, they are rarely included in CBA. Their exclusion is probably more justified in developed than in less developed countries where savings are especially scarce and the difference between the STPR and the return on capital may be considerable. More generally, the indirect costs of labour should be included in the CBA only if other implications of the differences between the return on capital and the STPR are also taken into account. But I argue below (in section 2.5) that for most practical purposes this difference can be ignored.

It is important to note two other features of accounting prices for labour. First they would usually be below market prices only for groups whose future output is expected to be low or non-existent. It is the predicted, not the present employment level, which largely determines the accounting prices for labour in projects lasting many years. Market wages are generally satisfactory measures of the costs of employing skilled labour. Secondly, the relative cost of all labour rises over time with increasing real wages unless these increases are offset by continuing productivity gains. Such gains are unlikely if the project technology is fixed at the outset of the project.

Accounting prices for inputs of material

Prominent among the reasons why market prices of materials may exceed their real social costs of production are the existence of monopolies, indirect taxes and unemployment. Given this divergence between material prices and their true production costs, the question is, at what accounting price should materials be charged to a project? The general answer is that if materials are supplied by diverting them from other users, market prices represent their social costs because they reflect their value in alternative uses. If materials are supplied from increased production that would not otherwise take place, the accounting price is the marginal production cost. This should exclude monopoly mark-ups and indirect taxes, which reflect the transfer rather than the consumption of resources, and should include the appropriate accounting price for labour involved in the production of the materials. Examples where these principles might be applied include the cost of rail transportation (for say agricultural products) or the cost of steel (a monopoly product in the UK and in Australia) to a project.

Accounting prices for land

The market price for land gives some indication of its value to the community but it may need to be modified in at least two ways to represent the real social value. First, the price may be affected by subsidies which represent transfers from the government to landowners rather than any real productive value in the land. Such subsidies should be excluded from the CBA. Second, the price may fail to reflect externalities from certain land uses, such as the air pollution which industrial users may inflict on local residents. A negative externality of this kind would reduce the accounting price for land beneath its market price. If the market price has to be extensively revised, it may be preferable to ignore it and to value the land by estimating the net benefits foregone in the best alternative use.

Valuing land in public ownership may be even more difficult. It must be emphasised, however, that although land may cost nothing financially to the government, it still has an opportunity cost. This is seen most readily when the private sector is allowed to compete for the land, in which case private sector bids, modified as described above, would indicate the accounting price for the land. When land is not marketed, its net value is the difference between the gross benefits of services provided to businesses and households and the costs of providing these services.

External costs

Typical examples of external costs imposed by a project on other producers would be a plant which pollutes the water and raises the cost of water to downstream producers, or a farmer who over-grazes thus causing soil erosion and a consequent loss of productivity on neighbouring farms (see chapter 4). It may be difficult to estimate these external costs, but the principle that they be debited as a cost to the project in the same way as any other resource cost is clear enough.

Estimating the external costs imposed by the project on households is generally much more difficult for two main reasons. One is that there may be no explicit market for the 'bad' imposed on households. For example, no such market may exist for a stretch of water used for recreational purposes which becomes polluted or for an atmosphere disturbed by aircraft noise. However, there are often implicit markets which enable us to infer what households are willing to pay for non-marketed goods. In the next section, methods of estimating the value of non-marketed goods are outlined. And in the following chapters, various valuation problems are discussed: amenity values from improved pastures in chapter 4, recreational goods in chapter 5, aircraft noise in chapter 7, and various environmental goods related to properties in chapter 8.

Accepting for the time being that willingness to pay values for non-marketed goods can be estimated, a second problem arises because the household has not willingly sold or foregone its asset, the right to recreation, peace and quiet or whatever. (Other resources acquired by a project on the open market are, of course, purchased from willing sellers). To ensure that at least in principle households losing assets are not worse off, the household's loss is valued at the amount required in compensation rather than the amount it would willingly pay for the asset.

But why, it might be asked, should compensation values differ from, and indeed generally exceed, willingness-to-pay values? The answer lies in the assumption that the marginal utility of consumption rises with any fall in income. To take an example, a household with an annual income of $10,000 and a quiet house might require $1,000 per annum to compensate it for the loss of quiet, but if it has $10,000 and a noisy house, it might be willing to pay only $400 per annum to purchase quiet. This is illustrated in figure 2.1 where quiet is worth 'x' units of utility to a household.

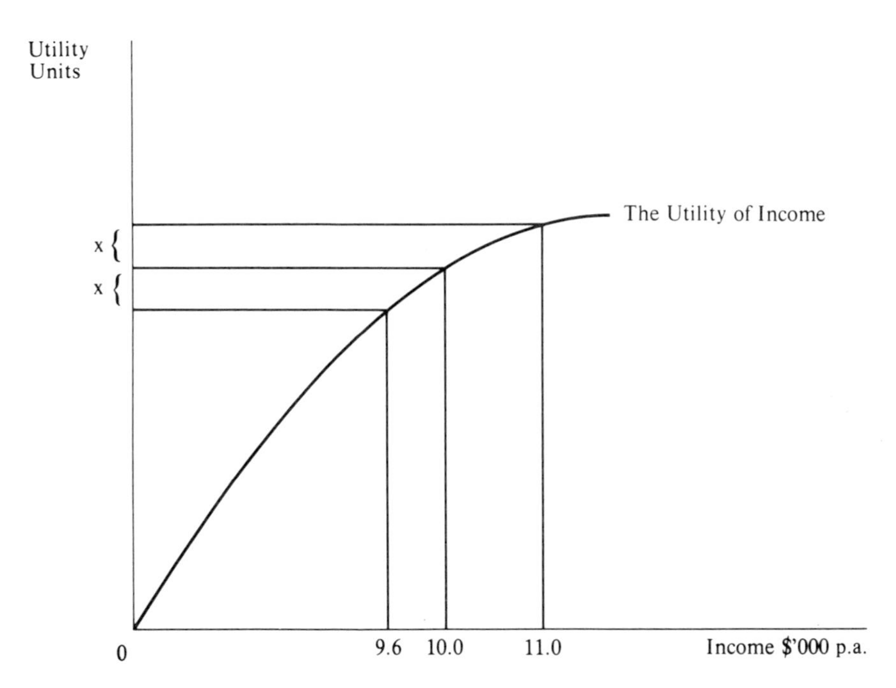

Figure 2.1 The declining marginal utility of income

So long as an external cost is a small fraction of a household's income it can be assumed, for the purposes of CBA, that compensation and willingness to pay values would be similar. But the assumption cannot be maintained if the household loses a major asset like peace and quiet. Broadly then, there are two possible approaches to assessing compensation values. One is to estimate an average marginal utility of money which can be used to convert willingness-to-pay values into compensation values. For example, Frisch [9] estimated that the elasticity of the marginal utility of money averaged -2, i.e. the marginal utility of consumption falls two per cent for every one per cent change in total consumption. His method of estimation relied, however, on the contentious assumption that the utility obtained from one good is independent of the quantity of other goods consumed. Other methods of estimating the marginal utility of money also tend to involve dubious assumptions. For instance, the marginal utility of income might be derived from decisions to insure against loss, since most individuals prefer a certain loss (the insurance premium) to an uncertain larger loss (the risk of theft etc. against which they have insured). But it is not easy to separate attitudes towards absolute levels of consumption from attitudes towards risk and uncertain consumption levels.

The second approach to estimating compensation values involves assessment of the prices at which households will forego particular assets. Suppose, for example, that P_0 in figure 2.2 is the market price for a standard house to be demolished because of a road project, and that the SS curve shows the prices at which owners would willingly sell their houses. The area ABC is the householder surplus lost if the project compulsorily acquires Q_1 houses at the market price. The loss of surplus is normally estimated through surveys, in which owners are asked the price at which they would be willing to sell their house. Thus Roskill estimated householder surplus to average 52 per cent of house price. [10] It must be emphasised, however, that as discussed in the next section, surveys provide only approximate data on the values attached to goods by households.

Finally, when should compensation values be used? If the CBA is concerned with the costs and benefits of any change from the present, as it usually is, it is legitimate to estimate compensation values for the loss of those current assets which form a significant part of a household's income. (As noted above, compensation values need not be estimated for minor external costs). This does not, however, resolve problems surrounding assets which households may expect to have in the future, especially public property rights to such benefits as parks and beaches. In these cases, the cost benefit analyst may attempt to be 'neutral' and estimate both conservation and development benefits on the basis of willingness-to-pay measures, but this is not a value-free judgement. [11]

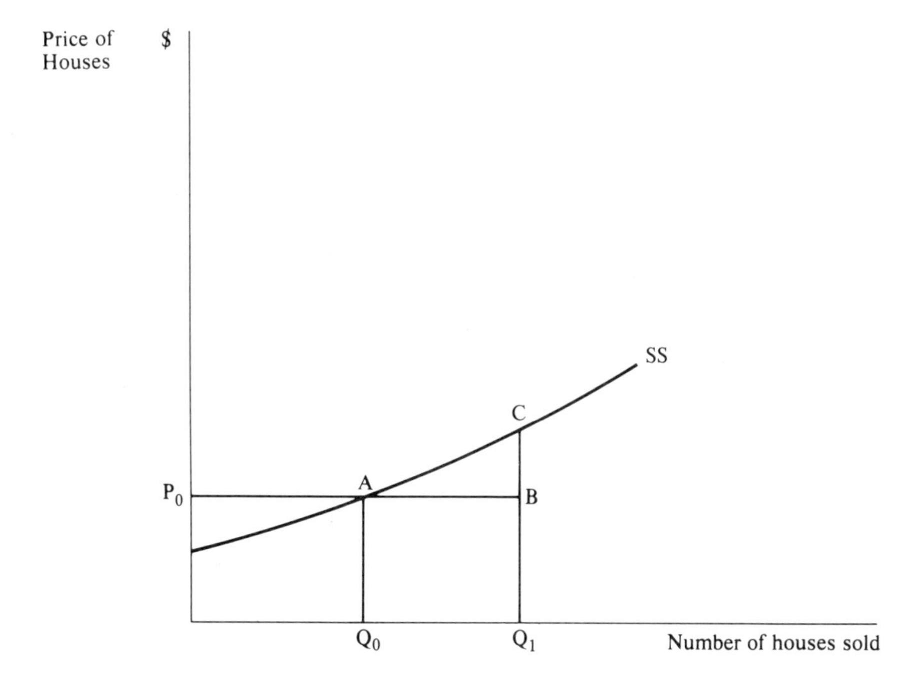

Figure 2.2 House prices and householder surplus

2.3 The valuation of benefits

The output from a project, including the output consumed by users and the external benefits, may conveniently be considered in three categories, namely (a) the fall in production costs, (b) the value of marketed goods and (c) the value of non-marketed goods. Any fall in the resource costs of production is clearly a benefit as resources are released and additional goods and services provided. In situations of joint works, a project may also generate external benefits by reducing another producer's costs. Dredging off-shore areas for airport development may reduce the costs of port development, for example. Or the soil conservation practices of one farm may reduce the work of neighbouring farms. The valuation of these cost savings follows the principles outlined in the previous section for estimating costs and does not call for further comment. We turn therefore to the valuation of marketed and non-marketed goods respectively. Subsequently we consider the valuation and role of secondary benefits in CBA.

The value of marketed goods

The value of marketed goods is illustrated in figure 2.3 where Q_0 goods are bought at price P_0. The gross value of the Q_0 goods is given by the whole area (A+B) between the willingness-to-pay demand curve and the horizontal axis. The net value of the goods is shown by area A between the demand and marginal cost curves.

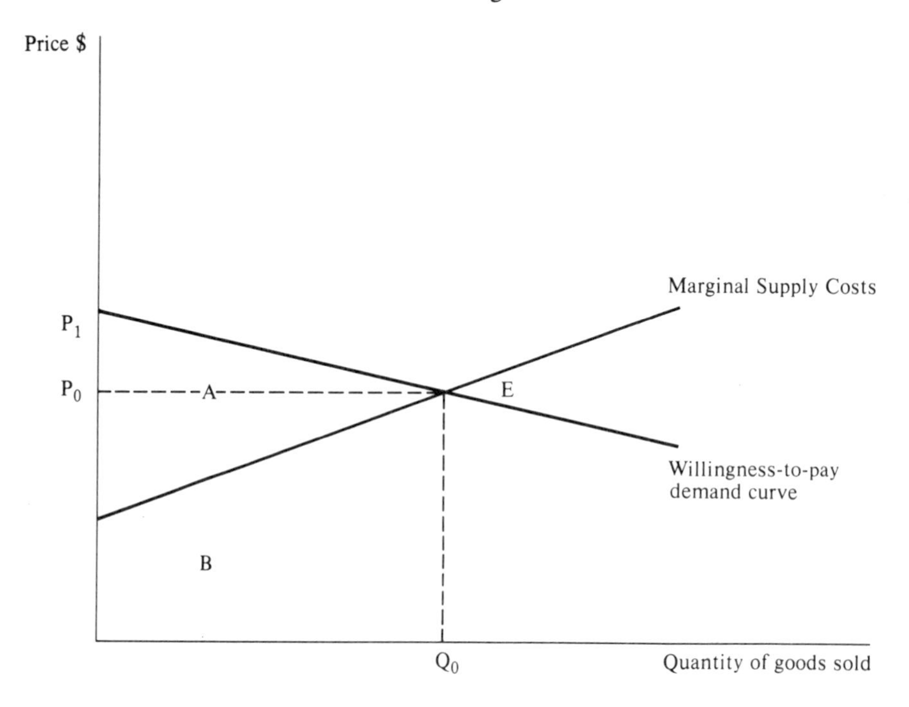

Figure 2.3 Project benefits

To estimate the gross value of marketed goods, the cost benefit analyst is therefore concerned with (a) predicting the output which will be sold at various prices and (b) assessing whether market prices reflect willingness-to-pay prices or need to be adjusted in order to express household values.

Demand forecasting is of course a very large subject, but following Harberger [12], 'certain general statements can be made:

(a) The potential market for the product must be ascertained (local, regional, national, international).

(b) Factors influencing the intensity of demand for the product in this market must be isolated and projected.

(c) On the basis of (b), the overall level of demand for the product must be projected.

(d) The prospects of expansion of existing alternative sources of supply must be examined and corresponding projections made.

(e) The prospects of new sources of supply appearing in the future must be evaluated, and if they are likely to appear, supply from these sources must be projected'.

Price predictions, which would be based on the demand and supply relationships (a) to (e), are of course intimately bound up with output predictions. It is particularly important for both price and output predictions to take account of future reactions of competitive suppliers and not to extrapolate too far from any present excess or deficiency in supply. [13] It is also important to allow for any technological progress, which may reduce the relative price of the product in the future.

In a free competitive market, forecast domestic market prices, inclusive of indirect taxes, may be taken to measure the value of goods to households. However, four exceptions to the principle that market prices reflect the amounts which households are willing to pay for goods should be noted. (a) If prices are controlled or goods rationed as, for example, housing rental prices are sometimes controlled, accounting prices should attempt to measure the full price that households would be willing to offer for the good. (b) Alternatively, if goods are subsidised, like some of the European Common Market's agricultural products, the price consumers are willing to pay is below that received by the producer. (c) When goods are sold internationally, the relevant price is normally the export price, even if the output from the project itself is sold only locally. This is because the export price represents the marginal revenue obtained. For instance, if wool from a project is sold locally and another producer is thereby obliged to export (rather than sell at home) the real value of the wool from the project is given by the export price, adjusted by the foreign exchange premium if any is required.

The fourth exception (d) arises when a non-marginal project produces a new type of goods or causes prices to fall. [14] In both these cases, additional consumption is generated and a consumer surplus, shown by the triangle $P_1 E P_0$ in figure 2.3, created. An assumption often made in CBA studies is that the demand curve is linear. The consumer surplus from generated consumption may therefore be estimated by the formula $\frac{1}{2}(\Delta Q.\Delta P)$, where ΔQ is the increase in consumption and ΔP is the change in prices. Applying this formula to the case of a new product is, of course, more of an approximation because the initial price at which the first unit would be sold is not known. However suppose that Q_0 in figure 2.3 represents a million new (or extra) units consumed each year, that P_1 is the maximum price the consumer would pay for one new (or extra) unit and equals \$1.50, and that P_0 represents \$1. Then the consumer surplus would equal $\frac{1}{2}(\$1.50 - \$1.0)$ 1.0 million = \$250,000 each year. Consumer surplus may be important for new goods or when large price changes occur and significant additional consumption is generated. However, it is generally not important for small or even medium sized projects in a competitive environment, when the demand curve for the product is fairly elastic. In these cases, market prices, subject to those exceptions previously noted, are a reasonable measure of the gross value of the product.

The value of non-marketed goods

In this section we shall be concerned chiefly with the value of non-marketed goods to those who use them directly or indirectly. For example, a park has recreational value to users and may have aesthetic, relaxation value to households who live close by. However, reference is often made in the literature, without precise definition, to three other types of benefit, which should be mentioned first. (a) Option benefits are benefits attributed to the availability of a capital asset over and above those actually accruing from its use. Since option benefits depend for their value, if any, on attitudes towards an uncertain future, they are discussed below in section 2.6. (b) Interdependent benefits occur when people derive pleasure, for selfish or altruistic reasons, from the pleasures enjoyed by others. Thus a mother may be happy that her children are enjoying a peaceful walk in the park. In principle interdependent benefits might be worthy of inclusion in CBA, but they are virtually impossible to measure, except in so far as the third party encourages a particular activity with financial support. Moreover, all goods, be they football matches or national parks, generate interdependent benefits. It would be necessary to plead a special case that the interdependent benefits associated with the particular project were especially important. Consequently, such benefits are generally ignored in CBA studies. (c) Existence benefits are values attached to the environment in its own right and without reference to human use. They are normally ignored in CBA in line with the philosophy expressed in the first chapter that only benefits to man matter.

The benefits from non-marketed goods are represented by the whole area under the demand curve, A + B in figure 2.3. In the absence of market price information, the two main methods employed to estimate what individuals would be willing to pay for non-marketed output are surveys and a technique which economists describe as revealed preference analysis. Individuals may be questioned, for example, tofind out how much they would be prepared to pay to use a park at the weekend or what annual increase in rates they would pay for continuous access to the park. In order to elicit realistic answers, surveys should generally simulate real choice situations, such as whether an individual would prefer an *additional* $1,000 to be spent on sports fields or on parks. It is important to emphasise the use of additional expenditures. It is not sufficient simply to ask the tax-payer whether he prefers sports fields or parks. But there are problems even with a well prepared survey. If questions are hypothetical, the answers may not accurately reflect behaviour; if questions are not hypothetical, it may be in the respondant's interests not to reply truthfully.

Revealed preference analysis is the study of market behaviour to deduce individual values. A simple example of revealed preference is the toll road where it can be observed how many travellers will pay the toll to save travel time on other longer routes. Much study has also now been done on the value of commuting time. Following Layard [15], let the costs (C) of bus and underground (rail) journeys be given by the following expressions:

$$C_B = a_B + bT_B + M$$

$$C_u = a_u + bT_u + M_u$$

where a_B and a_u are parameters reflecting the intrinsic pleasures of bus and underground respectively and T and M are the time and money costs involved. The difference in these costs (ΔC) depends on where a person lives and turns out to be a good predictor of the probability (P_B) of his travelling by bus rather than underground. One can for example fit a function such as the following:

$$\log \frac{P_B}{1-P_B} = B \, \Delta \, C = B \, (a_u - a_B + b \, \Delta \, T \dagger \Delta \, M)$$

From it we can estimate b and hence the cost of commuting time in terms of its money equivalent. Such studies . . . have found costs of commuting time at around 25 per cent of the traveller's gross wage rate'. Other examples of revealed preference analysis to obtain households' valuation of environmental goods through studies of implicit markets are given, as previously noted, in the following chapters.

Surveys and revealed preference analysis should be used as complementary rather than as competitive techniques. Answers to hypothetical survey questions about consumer preferences are much strengthened if they are consistent with observed market behaviour, but statistical inferences from market behaviour are also strengthened if they conform with individuals' expressed beliefs.

Secondary benefits

Project expenditures and surpluses generate demands for goods and services which may lead to the creation of a second order of value added. A farm machinery business, for example, would generate additional expenditures (a) by its employees if they were paid higher wages than previously, (b) by businesses who sell equipment and materials to the project insofar as they profit from the sale and do not reduce their sales elsewhere, and (c) by disbursing its own profits. Assuming that accounting prices for labour and materials are used in the project evaluation and that there are no worker or consumer surpluses, the estimated project surplus represents these potential additional expenditures resulting from the project.

The total benefit, B, of a project, including secondary benefits, may therefore be estimated approximately as

$$B = SM \qquad (1)$$

$$\text{and} \quad M = \frac{1}{1 - (C-I)} \qquad (2)$$

where S is the project surplus, M is the secondary expenditure multiplier [16], C is the proportion of marginal income consumed and I is the proportion of marginal income spent on imported goods. From a national viewpoint, C is typically around 0.85. But from a regional viewpoint, local expenditure is reduced by central government taxation, so that to obtain M in equation 2, (C–I) is multiplied by (1–T) where T is the proportion of income and profit taxed by the central government.

The value of M is very sensitive to the value of I. In a fully employed economy, all *marginal* consumption will be imported, i.e. I = C and M = 1. This corresponds to the traditional assumption that the level of aggregate demand and output in the economy is independent of project choice and that secondary benefits are irrelevant. On the other hand, given significant local unemployment, I may fall below 0.5. How far it falls depends partly on the size of the local area, since I is, of course, higher for small areas.

The prediction that a project would generate secondary benefits still does not mean that such benefits should count in project evaluation since alternative projects may also generate secondary benefits. It is only the *differences* in secondary benefits which can affect the national aggregate NPV. If a $10 million investment in area A or B would generate say $2 million of secondary benefits in that area, the benefits are essentially a transfer from one location to the other. This would be important for the distribution of income, but aggregate consumption would not be affected by the choice of area.

To sum up, for the purposes of CBA, secondary benefits can be ignored if aggregate demand is independent of project choice. One example of this is the fully employed economy. Even with unemployed resources it is often not unreasonable to assume that secondary benefits are essentially transfers which affect the distribution of consumption but not its aggregate value. It must be emphasised, however, that the conclusion that secondary benefits can normally be excluded from CBA is based on the assumption that they do not alter the total value of consumption. This assumption will not always hold, especially when either capital or labour resources are substantially under-employed in an area from which they cannot move without considerable cost, and for which there are few viable alternative projects. Secondary benefits may be important, for instance, in areas of less developed countries with unexploited resources but few alternative projects, or in declining towns in developed countries where there is a high unused infrastructural capacity.

2.B COST BENEFIT ANALYSIS AND DECISION MAKING

2.4 Decision guides

The two main guides to decision making used in CBA are the net present value of consumption (NPV) and the internal rate of return (IRR). The NPV may be defined as follows,

$$NPV = \sum_{i=1}^{n} \frac{B_i}{(1+r)^i} - C \qquad (3)$$

where B = the expected net annual benefits
C = the expected capital investment
r = the social discount rate per annum
n = the number of years of project life.

If the discounted net annual benefits exceed the capital investment (the latter should also be discounted to the base year if it is made over more than one year), the NPV is positive. [17] This means that the aggregate value of consumption in present value terms is higher with the project than without it. On the criterion of aggregate consumption (disregarding such things as the distribution of income), the project is preferred to the alternative of doing nothing. If there are several alternative projects, the one with the highest NPV, other things being equal, would be preferred.

The internal rate of return is obtained by solving for r in the following equation,

$$C = \sum_{i=1}^{n} \frac{B_i}{(1+r)^i} \qquad (4)$$

where the symbols are as before. For example, the internal rate of return is 14 per cent per annum in equation 5.

$$\$329 = \frac{\$200}{(1+r)} + \frac{\$200}{(1+r)^2} = \frac{\$200}{(1+.14)} + \frac{\$200}{(1+.14)^2} \qquad (5)$$

If r exceeds the social discount rate, the project, judged on the criterion of the aggregate value of consumption, is acceptable.

It will be seen that the NPV is necessarily positive when the IRR is higher than the social discount rate. However, when projects are compared, the NPV and IRR methods may rank them differently. Table 2.1 gives an example where project A would be preferred with the IRR criterion and B would be chosen with the NPV criterion.

The difference in the ranking of projects A and B can be overcome by calculating the rate of return on the *differences* between A and B (-120, 136). This gives an IRR of 13 per cent which is higher than the 10 per cent discount rate and justifies project B. However this procedure makes the IRR more complex to perform than the NPV and it illustrates that 'it is not the intrinsically correct rule'. [18] The NPV is a measure of the total gain of the project, but the IRR has no economic meaning in that the surpluses cannot necessarily be reinvested at the internally determined discount rate. The point is not just academic: the IRR criterion encourages projects which at the start use little capital and earn high rates of return, but which may generate relatively low net present value. On the other hand, contingent factors may strengthen the case for the IRR. Some readers of the report may find the IRR more comprehensible than the NPV; also international institutions, like the World Bank, may find the IRR helpful in comparing projects in different countries. Thus, although the NPV is objectively superior, the IRR is also quite frequently used.

Table 2.1
Project criteria compared

Project	Year 1 capital	Year 2 net return	Year 3 net return	IRR %	NPV with 10% per annum discount rate
A	$100	$120	0	20	9
B	$100	0	$136	17	12

A third possible decision guide, the benefit cost ratio (BCR), also has a use in certain circumstances. The BCR is defined as follows:

$$BCR = \sum_{i=1}^{n} \frac{\frac{B_i}{(1+r)^i}}{C} \qquad (6)$$

where the symbols are as before. The BCR, like the IRR, may rank projects differently from the NPV criterion. Indeed it fails generally to maximise present values because, again like the IRR, it is biased towards low capital projects. However, the BCR is relevant if the capital available to an agency is limited, so that its marginal return on capital exceeds the marginal return available elsewhere to the government. In this case, 'projects should be selected in the order of their present value per unit of constrained cost until the cost constraint is exhausted.' [19] Even so, at the margin a small project with a high BCR should not displace a large one with a lower BCR unless 'the sum of its present value and that of the new project admitted to take up the new funds is greater than that of the larger project'. [20]

2.5 The choice of discount rate

The choice of discount rate is often critical to the acceptability of a project even when the choice lies between such apparently similar rates as say 7 and 10 per cent per annum. Suppose that $500 invested in year 1 returns $700 in constant prices in year 5. Discounted at 7 per cent per annum, the $700 would be worth $532 in year 1, while at 10 per cent it would be worth $483 in year 1. With the former discount rate, the estimated NPV would be positive; with the latter it would be negative. In general, the higher the discount rate, the more important are costs and benefits close to the present.

At first sight it may appear that this is no problem: project surpluses would be discounted according to the weights attached to consumption in different periods which would be given by the social time preference rate. Unfortunately quite apart from the difficulty of estimating the STPR, it also turns out that the STPR is generally lower than the social return attainable on alternative investment (the social opportunity cost of capital, the SOC). It is necessary therefore to decide which rate to adopt in CBA studies, or whether indeed to use a combination of the two discount rates.

The relevant measure of the SOC in many circumstances is the expected total pre-tax return on marginal private capital. This includes not only the return to the private investor, but also the revenue through direct and indirect taxes received by the government. If the market is not perfect, the social return on private investment will also include any payments to workers and to suppliers of materials over and above accounting wages and prices, as well as external benefits or costs, although these are not easy to measure. The total return on private investment is the appropriate measure of the SOC if the government is borrowing its marginal funds from the private sector, or if it is trying to maximise aggregate consumption over time, in which case it should attempt to equalise the marginal social returns to private and public investment. In some circumstances, of course, the marginal public investment would generate a higher surplus than would marginal private investment. Also a government may sometimes consider its investment more socially valuable than private investment and be unwilling to see funds transferred back to the private sector, although the marginal return on public investments (in terms of its estimated NPV) might be lower than that on private investment. In these cases, the SOC is the marginal return on public investment.

It is sometimes argued that the SOC of investment financed from taxation or reduced welfare payments, which involve a reduction in current consumption, should be measured by the social time preference rate. [21] This ignores the fact that generally, whatever the source of the funds, there are alternative investment opportunities which are sacrificed if the project is adopted. Since these alternatives foregone represent the opportunity cost of the capital, the source of the funds is not normally relevant to the choice of discount rate in CBA studies. It should be noted, however, that if foreign loan capital is provided to a project when it would otherwise not be made available to the country, the appropriate discount rate is the cost of servicing the foreign capital.

An additional refinement sometimes made is to forecast the change in SOC over time, or at least to distinguish between the SOC applicable in the immediate future and over the rest of the life of the project. This may be necessary to optimise the timing of the project. Also, as noted above, the SOC should be estimated as a real rate of return, not as a monetary rate. From a practical viewpoint, the cost benefit analyst can take comfort that the SOC should be determined by some central government economic department, since the government is generally best placed to make the decision and since consistency between studies is important. In my experience, the SOC is normally estimated at between 8 and 12 per cent per annum. [22]

The two main ways to attempt to estimate the STPR are by observation of individual market behaviour and by what may be described as taking a social approach to the problem. In a perfect market, lending and borrowing rates would be equal and the individual time preference rate would equal the marginal SOC. But taxation, amongst other factors, makes the market imperfect. If marginal company tax is say 50 per cent, then, even if there were no tax on dividends, the monetary return to lenders would be half the monetary return on capital. [23] Moreover, the private lending rate does not reflect only a re-ordering of consumption patterns over time; it reflects also uncertainty about the future. The effect of this on preferred consumption patterns is unclear. Traditionally, it was argued that uncertainty makes individuals short-sighted (i.e. they would have a high time preference rate) but offsetting this, uncertainty probably increases the demand for savings as insurance against hard times. Accepting in advance the argument of the next section that social decisions should not depend on individual attitudes to risk, it is the time preference rate under certainty which is relevant to CBA, and this cannot be known. A final problem with deriving the STPR from observed market lending rates is that these rates are largely determined without reference to the wishes of future generations.

The 'social approach' to estimating the STPR attempts to measure the marginal utility of consumption over time and is generally based on the assumption that the marginal value of consumption falls with increases in total consumption. Thus, the STPR would be defined as the product of the expected rate of growth of per capita income and the elasticity of the marginal utility of per capita consumption. If this elasticity were say 1.5 and expected per capita income growth 3 per cent per annum, the STPR would equal 4.5 per cent per annum. This approach suffers of course from the considerable difficulty noted above of deriving a marginal utility of consumption from individual behaviour. But a number of tentative estimates [24] put the marginal utility of per capita consumption at between -1 and -2, so that the societal STPR is generally estimated as lying between 2 and 6 per cent per annum.

The difficulty must now be faced however that any estimated STPR is likely to be significantly below the estimated SOC. If the higher SOC rate is adopted to calculate the NPV, more emphasis is placed on present consumption than can be justified by the STPR. On the other hand, a low rate of discount may encourage inefficient capital expenditures and undervalue the reinvestment of project surpluses, for as we saw in considering indirect labour costs, the NPV can be increased by reinvesting surpluses and discounting the new surpluses at the STPR. Some authorities, including the authors of the UNIDO Guidelines and Little and Mirrlees, recommend therefore that a shadow price should be attached to all investment funds and that annual net benefits available for consumption should be discounted at the STPR. [25] Though this approach is correct in principle (indeed it is often used to evaluate Australian sand mining projects – see chapter 6), its general adoption is not recommended here for mainly practical reasons. First, if the reinvested surpluses from the project are of similar magnitude to reinvested surpluses on alternative projects, it is not necessary to distinguish between reinvested and consumed surpluses. Second, it may be difficult to predict the amounts reinvested. Third, calculating the shadow price for investment is a complex procedure, so that consistency in appraisal method will be hard to obtain. The normal procedure in CBA studies is therefore to follow the NPV approach, as expressed in equation 3, which does not distinguish between investment and consumption expenditure.

Furthermore the discount rate most often chosen is the SOC. One reason is that the SOC rate of discount broadly balances the capital required for projects with the capital available to them. It is simply not possible to do all projects satisfying the STPR. Second, and most important, use of the SOC makes it easier to avoid inefficient projects, for example projects with a 5 per cent return when others with returns of 10 per cent and higher are available. Inefficient projects reduce future as well as present consumption. Third, the use of the SOC is consistent with attempting to maximise the aggregate value of consumption, which I argue in chapter 3 provides the basic rationale for CBA. The use of the STPR, especially if it is based on the 'social approach' described above, implies an attempt to maximise aggregate utility. This latter objective, apart from being outside the scope of CBA, involves an inconsistency if allowance is made for differences in marginal utilities of consumption over time but not for differences at a given point in time. (This is further discussed under distributional analysis, section 2.7). Of course, sensitivity tests with different discount rates should be made, but these tests will not necessarily obviate the need to choose between discount rates.

2.6 The treatment of uncertainty

Uncertainty lies both in the state of the world and in our perception of it. Thus the number turning up on the throw of an unweighted die will be uncertain, although we know that there is a 1 in 6 chance of each number turning up and that the mean value is 3½. But if the die is weighted in some unknown manner, we can neither predict the distribution of the outcomes of a throw nor their mean value. What this means for CBA is that (a) most costs and benefits have a range of possible values and (b) the real mean values of the costs and benefits and their probability distribution are unlikely to be known. How should these problems be resolved?

First, a general point can be made: the difference between a quantified and an unquantified variable reflects the degree of uncertainty surrounding it rather than the kind of cost or benefit which it represents. If the distribution of values attributable to a variable is sufficiently uncertain, the variable should be considered an intangible item.

Concerning the quantified items, the commonest and simplest form of uncertainty analysis is sensitivity testing. This shows the variation in NPV as a function of changes in the values attached to particular variables, such as forecast prices or output. A sensitivity test has the advantage of simplicity, but the major disadvantage that it makes no allowance for the probabilities of occurrence of high or low values of the variable. Often, too, it fails to take into account the interdependence between the independent variables. A reduction in output, for example, may be offset by higher prices. Over and above this, it can be questioned, as we shall see, whether sensitivity tests are really necessary.

The form of uncertainty analysis generally favoured by economists is the expected value method. The expected value of a variable is the 'weighted average of all possible values of the variable, each weight being weighted by the probability of occurrence. It is not necessarily the value we expect to occur; indeed in some cases the expected value is one which can never occur. For example, the expected value in throwing a die is 3½. Although its value cannot occur, it is the average of the numbers which turn up when the experiment is repeated many times.' [26] It is important that the estimation of expected values be done carefully. As Heggie [27] points out, for example, if $y = x^2$, expected y is the average of x^2, it is not (average $x)^2$. The expected net present value (ENPV) is therefore the product of the expected values of all relevant variables.

The question now arises whether a project with a higher ENPV than another is always superior to it. For example, is a project with an ENPV of $1.5 million, with a 50 per cent chance of a NPV of $4.0 million and a 50 per cent chance of a NPV of -$1.0 million, better than a project with a certain NPV of $1.0 million? The answer is 'yes generally but not always'. Generally, the law of averages ensures that with a reasonable number of projects such as a government has, projects exceeding expectations will balance those which underperform. (It is assumed that the expectations have an informed, rational basis). Project selection based on ENPV's would result therefore in a higher aggregate return to society than would project selection based on risk avoidance principles.

There are however two main cases where some risk avoidance may be justified. One concerns the value households attach to preserving assets which may be lost forever when change is irreversible. This concept, which may be called the option value of a good, can be defined as the difference between the total present value of an asset, measurable in principle by the sum of the capital amounts individuals would be willing to pay for the asset, and its expected value in use. [28] As Cicchetti and Freeman [29] have shown, this difference is equivalent to the risk aversion premium which individuals will pay for an option. There are however problems with allowing for such a premium in CBA. First, although individuals may be risk averse, when the risks are spread out over many individuals, by the law of averages the cost of risk bearing is low. Second, there are risks attached to nearly all decisions. There is a risk that people may die if hospital services are not improved or if remote areas are not developed for energy production. Development may therefore have as large an option value as preservation.

From a social viewpoint, therefore, the value of an asset is the expected value of its use even if change is irreversible, subject to one exception which Arrow and Fisher [30] have termed a 'quasi-option value': 'If the development involves some irreversible transformation of the environment, hence a loss in perpetuity of the benefits from preservation, *and* if information about the costs and benefits of both alternatives realised in one period results in a change in their expected values for the next, the answer is yes – net benefits from developing the area are reduced and, broadly speaking, less of the area should be developed'. The reason is that with increasing knowledge, underinvestment can be remedied, whereas irreversible mistaken overinvestment cannot and its consequences may entail long term disadvantages. This asymmetry means that the 'expected benefits of an irreversible decision should be adjusted to reflect the loss of option it entails'.

The second possible case for a risk aversion premium occurs when a project is so large a part of the national or regional economy that the law of large numbers is not applicable. It is then desirable to estimate the distribution of net present values as well as the ENPV. Various methods for deriving a full distribution of a project's outcomes are described by Heggie. [31] Probably the most common method is the Monte Carlo simulation, which draws on a sample of the distribution of inputs. The probability distribution of the relevant variables is fed into a computer and a simulation programme selects the values of the variables on the basis of their probability of occurrence. The process may be likened to the throw of a die to select a value from 1 to 6 when the chance of each value really occurring is 1 in 6. From a sample of simulations, the programme estimates the true distribution of outcomes for the project. As software simulation packages become more available, the main constraint on Monte Carlo and other similar programmes will be the generation of the inputs. When these cannot be generated, CBA will normally adopt sensitivity tests to show the effect of high or low values of important variables. Despite their limitations, these tests can be illuminating.

It must be emphasised, however, that estimation of the distribution of net present value of a project does not finally resolve the project's viability. That resolution depends on the decision maker's attitude towards risk. Nevertheless I believe that the technical advice would be at fault if it failed to point out the advantages of the EPNV criterion.

2.7 Distributional analysis

Traditionally, CBA was used to maximise the value of aggregate consumption regardless of the groups to whom benefits and costs accrued. [32] The rationale for this was twofold. First, if this criterion were generally applied, most households would be better off than if projects with negative NPV's were adopted. Projects would tend to generate sufficient surpluses to compensate those who lost from them (ex-post NPV's may not, of course, always match ex-ante NPV's). Second, a strong case may be made for the view that distributional objectives can be achieved more effectively and at less cost with a combination of taxation, expenditure and monetary policies than through individual projects, especially projects with a negative NPV. Unfortunately in practice the losers from projects are often not compensated and macro-economic policies alone may be considered insufficient to effect a fair distribution of income. For these as well perhaps as for more self-motivated reasons, decision makers are undoubtedly interested in the distribution of the costs and benefits of a project.

Two main components of distributional analysis can usefully be distinguished. One is analysis of the incidence of costs and benefits on selected community groups, sometimes called incidence analysis. This involves determining (a) what data is required in addition to that collected to calculate the NPV, (b) which groups matter and (c) how costs and benefits are borne or passed on between groups. The second more controversial component of distributional analysis consists in showing how the incidence of costs and benefits might affect the project decision.

The incidence analysis will, of course, include all costs and benefits involved in the calculation of the NPV as well as additional data. Exactly what extra data will be required depends on the information sought from the incidence analysis. It may or may not be important, for example, to estimate the project's cash flow implications for the government. But at least three things are likely to be important. The first of these is the distribution of the estimated surplus. Some of the surplus will go to workers on the project and to businesses providing materials to the project who are paid more than the accounting price for their labour and materials. Most of the surplus will, however, be divided between the owners of the project and the consumers of the project's output, the division depending largely on the pricing policy used. To be sure, prices affect the amount of output produced by the project, and therefore its NPV, but generally pricing policy is of greater importance to distributional analysis.

Secondly, transfers affect the incidence of costs and benefits, although they do not affect the value of aggregate consumption. These transfers will be chiefly the effects of indirect taxes and subsidies. Thirdly, there is the magnitude and distribution of secondary benefits and costs. Quite likely it will not be possible to determine the secondary effects with much accuracy as they tend to spread quite diffusely in the area of the project. It should be noted however that the beneficiaries of competitive projects may lose out if the project under investigation proceeds. One example, a road transport project, may illustrate the above points. Unlike the estimate of NPV, the incidence study would be concerned amongst other things with the distribution of benefits from lower transport costs, the incidence of fuel tax, and the development benefits to areas close to the road, while areas close to alternative roads may suffer a loss of development.

The second main issue in incidence analysis, though intimately tied up with the first, is: whose costs and benefits matter? It is impracticable to show the costs and benefits to every household, so that the important social groups must be selected. The kind of socio-economic characteristics that might be considered relevant to group selection would be nationality, area of residence, occupation, income, age, number of dependents and length of residence in an area, to mention but a few. Choosing the discriminating factor(s) is often difficult. For example, the poor households affected by the project may be young and live in a generally prosperous area or rich ones may be old and unable to move to avoid the adverse impacts of the development. Clearly, the choice of discriminating factor will vary from study to study and it must be emphasised that it will be a subjective choice which inevitably involves the use of value judgements.

The shifting of costs and benefits between groups is important because final incidence effects may be quite different from initial ones. For example, if an irrigation project reduces the cost of water to farmers, the initial benefit is in their favour. But in the final analysis, if competition leads to a fall in food prices, local consumers may receive much of this benefit. Alternatively, if the government taxes foreign manufacturers resident in the country, local consumers will pay a proportion of the tax in higher prices for foreign manufacturers' goods, the proportion depending amongst other things on the amount of competition from domestic manufacturers. Second, we are generally concerned with the costs and benefits of households rather than of entities like 'businesses' or 'governments'. Tracing the effects of a change in business profits or in government revenues on households according to their income is however very difficult and the shift from initial to final incidence can rarely be quantified with accuracy. (The relationship between initial and final incidence in the case of airport development is outlined in chapter 6).

The relationship between the incidence analysis and the project decision also raises major problems. Economists are divided between those who believe that the costs and benefits to different groups should be factored to give greater weight to benefits accruing to disadvantaged groups and hence obtain a weighted NPV and those who believe that, after the incidence analysis has been made, the decision maker should take over. The use of weights may clarify the effects of distributional choices and the trade-offs of costs and benefits between groups. Also if the weights are determined by a central authority, their use could improve the consistency of decision making. One weight which in particular should be mentioned because it is so widely used, is a zero weight for foreigners' costs and benefits, which implies that the effect of the project on foreigners can be ignored.

There are however several important objections to the use of weights. Perhaps the most important of these is that no objective and scientifically derived set of weights exists. Governments are likely to be reluctant to provide weights explicitly. And although marginal tax rates may reflect a government's view of fairness, they may also be designed so as not to affect the supply of labour. Weisbrod [33] has attempted to discover weights by inference from government decisions favouring social groups, but this approach presupposes a consistency in public decision making which is unlikely. Little and Mirrlees [34] simply attempt to simulate weights which they believe some less developed countries would accept. A second major objection to the use of weights is that they are inconsistent with the idea that CBA is essentially concerned with the value of aggregate consumption rather than with aggregate utility. To be sure, aggregate consumption is neither a necessary nor a sufficient criterion for project acceptability, but the use of weights obscures this important criterion. It can therefore lead to inefficient projects being unwittingly adopted or efficient ones not being adopted. Thirdly, even if the objective of CBA were to maximise aggregate utility, the introduction of weights could still be consistent with the adoption of projects in which the rich get richer and the poor poorer. Thus low social time preference discount rates which attempt to maximise aggregate utility over time have the effect of passing resources from the poor (today's generation) to the rich (future generations). Fourthly, there is the practical problem that there is not always an exact correspondence between the costs and benefits counted in a CBA and those identified in incidence analysis.

To summarise, a good case can be made for dealing with distributional problems through a combination of taxation, expenditure and monetary policies rather than through projects, but this is not always sufficient because some households cannot be compensated adequately for losses from projects. Consequently, estimates of NPV should generally be supplemented by an analysis of the incidence of costs and benefits, at least of the initial effects of the project. There are however compelling reasons, I believe, why weights should not be used to factor the costs and benefits according to the marginal utility derived by consuming households in a vain attempt to measure the aggregate utility achieved by a project.

2.8 Conclusion

The chapter has described the CBA method with the emphasis on the valuation of costs and benefits and on decision making. However if the CBA is to be efficient, it is also important (a) to generate a reasonable set of alternative projects and policies to be considered, including the option of postponing the project and (b) to bring out the more important implications for project implementation such as the cash flow requirements.

The detail required for each cost benefit study varies, of course, with the nature of the problem and the study resources available, but many studies can be useful with only a few man months work and no great expertise. The minimum requirements for a useful CBA would probably be something like the following. Costs and benefits would be valued in terms of constant domestic market prices, with an allowance for expected changes in relative prices of important commodities and an accounting price for foreign exchange, as advised by the relevant economic department of the central government. Approximate accounting prices should also be used for inputs of labour, materials and land. Where possible, the major external costs should be quantified, probably at willingness-to-pay prices, unless the costs are a large part of household income when a compensation premium may be allowed. Even in a relatively simple study, it is essential to forecast the project output with care. Market prices generally provide a reasonable approximation of the value of marketed output in a competitive economy. In addition, some attempt should be made to value non-marketed output in order to show the sensitivity of the result to non-marketed benefits. The annual costs and benefits would be discounted with a government advised discount rate to obtain a NPV of aggregate consumption and the IRR would also be calculated. In addition, the study would probably include an analysis of initial incidence effects, sensitivity tests to show the effect of uncertainty in key variables, and a description of the most important intangibles.

It would be wrong to strive for greater analytical complexity or numerical precision (is the IRR really 9 per cent or 11 per cent?) when rational decisions can be derived from simple analysis, or when projects are too small to justify a costly decision making procedure. On the other hand, the simplified synopsis of the previous paragraph would not provide an adequate basis for evaluating complex, multi-million dollar projects. When a decision is likely to have far-reaching consequences, rigorous, detailed studies are required to get the decision right.

Notes

[1] Useful books on cost benefit analysis in roughly ascending order of complexity include: Pearce D.C. *Cost Benefit Analysis*, Macmillan, 1971; Layard R. (ed.) *Cost Benefit Analysis*, Penguin, 1972; Harberger A.C. *Project Evaluation* (chapter 2 is recommended), Macmillan, 1972; Little I.M.D. and Mirrlees J.A. *Project Appraisal and Planning for Development Countries*, Heinemann, 1974; and the UNIDO *Guidelines for Project Evaluation* by Dasgupta P., Sen A. and Marglin S. United Nations Publication, 1972. The books by Pearce and by Little and Mirrlees also contain useful bibliographies.
[2] Project identification and definition and the generation of alternatives are an important part of any CBA. See for example chapter 6 on airport location. Since these tasks are not unique to the CBA method of evaluation, they are not discussed in this chapter. A useful discussion on them can be found in Heggie I.G. *Transport Engineering Economics*, McGraw Hill, 1972, pp 125-46.
[3] United Nations Economic Commission for Latin America, *Manual on Economic Development Projects*, United Nations Publication Sales no.64, II.B.1, p.203.
[4] Little I.M.D. and Mirrlees J.A. op.cit., 1974, pp 358-62. It may be noted that Little and Mirrlees changed their proposed numeraire from aggregate consumption in domestic prices in 1968 (see reference below) to uncommitted social income in international prices in 1974. The latter numeraire highlights public investment but the two numeraires were shown by the authors to give equivalent results (op.cit., 1974, pp 358-62). The choice of numeraire should not be confused with another Little and Mirrlees argument, used in 1968 and in 1974, that any good that might potentially be traded should be valued as if it was traded, even if it was not. The adoption of this valuation principle can affect the CBA result. See Little I.M.D. and Mirrlees, J.A.

Manual of Industrial Project Analysis, OECD Development Centre, 1968.
[5] Domestic and international prices may also diverge because employment in certain industries is protected even though there may be no shortage of foreign exchange. This is the general case in Australia, for example.
[6] Harberger A.C. op.cit., p.53. See also UNIDO Guidelines, op.cit., p.216, 'the shadow price of foreign exchange is a weighted average of the ratios of market clearing prices to official CIF prices, the weights reflecting the content of the marginal import bill'.
[7] One cost a worker may incur in taking up employment is the loss of unemployment pay, but this is offset by the benefit to those who no longer have to fund the unemployment pay. Such unemployment pay is a transfer payment rather than a resource cost; it is not included in CBA.
[8] The UNIDO Guidelines, op.cit., for example, emphasise the importance of indirect labour costs. They also show how they should be calculated (pp 205-7).
[9] Frisch R. 'Dynamic Utility', *Econometrica*, vol.32, no.3, 1964, pp 418-28.
[10] Roskill, Commission on the Third London Airport, Report, HMSO, 1971, pp 274-5.
[11] This 'neutral' procedure appears to be at the root of many bitter conflicts between economists and conservationists, who apparently believe that property rights in public goods belong to them rather than to the party which is willing to pay the most for the rights.
[12] Harberger A.C. op.cit., pp 42-3.
[13] The vital importance of this can be seen from the spectacular collapse of the nickel price during the 1970s owing partly to the general over-investment in nickel mines in the early 1970s. See also the demand for mineral sands (chapter 4).
[14] If a country has a strong market position and is an international price maker rather than price taker, a project can also cause international prices to fall. See for example the wool and mineral sand markets in chapters 4 and 5 respectively.
[15] Layard R. op.cit., p.24.
[16] See UNIDO Guidelines, op.cit., pp 80-1, for the derivation of the multiplier formula.
[17] Costs and benefits are normally discounted to the first year of the project. Discounting them to other years changes the magnitude but not the sign (positive or negative) associated with the NPV. For further discussion of this point, see chapter 4, note 11.
[18] Layard R. op.cit., p.51.

[19] Feldstein M.S. and Fleming J.S. 'The Problem of Time Stream Evaluation: Present Values vs Internal Rate of Return Rules', *Oxford Institute Economic and Statistical Bulletin*, 26, 1964, pp 79-85.
[20] Layard R. op.cit., p.53.
[21] Pearce D.C. op.cit., pp 45-9.
[22] Little I.M.D. and Mirrlees J.A. make a similar judgement about the value of the SOC, op.cit., 1974, pp 296-7.
[23] Note the 'monetary' return. Suppose that the expected monetary return on capital is 18 per cent, the marginal tax rate 50 per cent and the expected inflation rate 10 per cent. The total real return to capital would be $(18 - 10) = 8$ per cent, but the expected real return to lenders would be $(18 \times 0.5) - 10 = -1$ per cent!
[24] Layard R. op.cit., p.43 and Dasgupta A.K. and Pearce D.N. *Cost Benefit Analysis*, MacMillan, 1972, p.144. See also Frisch R. note 9 above.
[25] See UNIDO Guidelines op.cit., pp 173-200 and Little I.M.D. and Mirrlees J.A. op.cit., pp 246-54.
[26] Makower M.S. and Williamson E. *Operational Research*, Hodder and Stoughton 1975, p.26.
[27] Heggie I.G. op.cit., p.226. See also chapter 6 in this book on the problem of estimating congestion costs which are a non-linear function of forecast air traffic. As congestion costs rise faster than forecast traffic, the expected congestion cost is *not* the cost experienced at the mean forecast traffic level.
[28] The concept of option value is defined precisely by Schmalensee R. 'Option Demand and Consumer's Surplus: Valuing Price Changes under Uncertainty', *American Economic Review*, vol.LXII, no.5, December 1972, pp 813-24.
[29] Cicchetti C.J. and Freeman A.M. 'Option Demand and Consumer Surplus: Further Comment', *Quarterly Journal of Economics*, 85(3), August 1971, pp 528-39.
[30] Arrow K.J. and Fisher A.C. 'Environmental Preservation, Uncertainty and Irreversibility', *Quarterly Journal of Economics*, 88(2), May 1974, pp 312-29.
[31] Heggie I.G. op.cit., pp 234-40.
[32] The US Flood Control Act (1936) authorised federal participation in flood control schemes, 'if the benefits to whomsoever they accrue are in excess of the estimated costs'.
[33] Weisbrod B.A. 'Income Redistribution effects and benefit cost analysis' in Chase S.B. Jr. (ed.) *Problems in Public Expenditure Analysis*, The Brookings Institution, 1968, pp 177-209.
[34] Little I.M.D. and Mirrlees J.A. op.cit., 1974, pp 238-41.

3 Why cost benefit analysis?

This chapter provides a critique of CBA and other major eva
methods in terms of four criteria. These are (a) comprehensiv
the extent to which the evaluation method deals with the vario
requirements of the whole evaluation process, including the selection of alternatives, assessment and valuation of the effects of these alternatives and the determination of collective decisions; (b) philosophical coherence and ethical acceptability; (c) the ability of the evaluation method to take account of individual valuations of costs of benefits or to justify departures from such valuations; and (d) the practical usefulness of the method to decision makers. In the light of these considerations, I conclude that CBA meets more of the requirements of the evaluation process and more nearly satisfies the other criteria than does any other evaluation method. Other methods may complement CBA but rarely substitute for it.

Various major evaluation methods are identified and their contributions to the evaluation process are discussed in section 1. The implications of the other three criteria, with most emphasis being placed on criterion (c), are considered in the next three sections. In order to demonstrate some of the points made in the chapter, the relationship between a CBA and an environmental impact statement (EIS) and some problems of an EIS are described in the Appendix with reference to the Sydney Airport Study.

3.1 Evaluation methods

Grouping the many evaluation methods discussed in the literature is a necessary but inevitably slightly arbitrary procedure. The following groups appear to be among the more important:

(a) Planning with no valuation of the costs or benefits, e.g. EIS [1] or trade off matrix (TOM)

(b) Planning with valuation of the costs and benefits, e.g. goal achievement matrix (GAM) or environmental standards planning (ESP)

(c) Cost effectiveness (CE)

(d) Cost benefit analysis

(e) Mixed solutions based on CBA, e.g. planning balance sheet (PBS)
(f) Systems analysis (SA)
(g) Collective choice rules (CCR).

Planning with no valuation of costs and benefits

Planning without valuation involves identifying, measuring and describing the consequences of an action, but it does not explicitly attach values to them. Of course, refraining from valuation is not the same thing as refraining from value judgements. The analyst's choice of what to describe and what to ignore and his method of presenting the findings will reflect his value judgements. More importantly, it is not possible to derive a policy recommendation directly from a description of consequences as in an EIS or TOM. Normative policy conclusions can be reached only when these consequences have been valued, at least implicitly but preferably explicitly.

Planning with valuation of costs and benefits

An extreme view of the role of planning judgement in valuation is expressed by Self [2] who argues that planning should consist of the views of experts. Subject to some public debate, the elite planners, somehow chosen, determine appropriate community values and the relative merits of proposals. The role of planning judgement in valuation is less explicit in the goals achievement matrix described by Hills [3] : 'By determining how various objectives will be affected by proposed plans, the GAM can determine the extent to which specific standards are being met.' The choice of objectives, the measurement of the extent to which they are achieved and the trade-off between objectives may be determined by planning judgement or derived from studies of individual values. In the latter case, the GAM could approximate quite closely to CBA. However, in origin, GAM was proposed as an alternative to CBA and it is normally associated with the view that individual preferences cannot be accurately measured and compared.

Another form of planning valuation would be the use of environmental standards, based on the view, and sometimes the law, that certain standards should be met. For example, the construction of houses may not be permitted close to heavy industry. Sometimes these standards will be determined by cost benefit considerations but often they are imposed as a matter of planning judgement as 'good things' regardless of the cost of providing them.

Cost effectiveness

The cost effectiveness method normally measures inputs in monetary units and outputs in physical units. It may be used for instance to determine the least cost way to save lives. It is a satisfactory method when competing projects produce similar outputs, but less so when they produce numerous, dissimilar outputs such as traffic speeds, traffic noise and air pollution. Arising from the diversity of environmental effects, it is sometimes suggested that an index of environmental quality should be developed but such an index implies that environmental effects can be weighted. It is then only a small step to valuing them in monetary units.

Cost benefit analysis

CBA may be considered to have two major distinguishing features. First it attempts to value costs and benefits as far as possible in monetary units, so that they can be summed together and compared. The intangibles would however also be considered. Thus, in order to rank alternative airport sites for London, the Roskill Commission [4] considered the CBA results and the unquantified results, especially the regional planning implications, in separate chapters. Second, CBA incorporates a decision guide such as the net present value (NPV) or internal rate of return (IRR). Both features have brought heavy criticism against CBA and are discussed at some length below.

Mixed evaluation methods

The PBS, like CBA, measures costs and benefits in monetary units as far as seems reasonable. However, the practitioner of PBS is probably more sceptical of the accuracy of the valuations than is a cost benefit analyst. Also, PBS rejects the second major feature of CBA, namely, a single figure of net present value or a rate of return which sums up the worth of a project. Rather 'it [PBS] evaluates the alternative from the point of view of the benefits and costs accruing to homogeneous sectors of the community from each alternative to see which would promote the maximum net advantage (benefit).' [5]

Systems analysis

Some writers also propose systems analysis as an alternative evaluation method. [6] SA is alleged to substitute for CBA on the grounds that it measures the effects of all options and objectives whereas CBA is a partial analysis which constrains the options and objectives of a project. However, CBA and SA are more suitably treated as complementary. Many inputs to CBA, such as traffic speeds in a road feasibility study, are obtained with the use of systems analysis. SA is essentially a method for describing and predicting events; it does not offer any tools for valuing those events. Thus it can aid CBA but cannot substitute for it.

Collective choice rules

Collective choice rules provide a means of deriving a collective ranking of social alternatives from individual rankings. Majority voting is probably the most commonly used CCR. At this stage, it may be noted simply that the CCR does not generate any information on which to base a decision; it is only a decision procedure (see section 3.4).

Conclusions

From this brief review of evaluation methods, it can be seen that CBA covers more stages of the evaluation process than any other method. No other method provides both a means to value costs and benefits and a decision rule. On the other hand, some critics argue that the valuation procedures and decision rules are unsatisfactory and have sought substitutes or complements. Thus sometimes the best approach is perceived to be some combination of evaluation methods rather than reliance on one single method.

3.2 The philosophy of the evaluation method

An evaluation method should clearly be oriented towards acceptable social objectives and be based on acceptable notions of the constituent costs and benefits which make up the total social return. To what extent do CBA and the more important alternative methods measure up to these ideals?

As we saw in the previous chapter, CBA is concerned with the maximisation of the aggregate value of goods and services consumed by a specified community. Consumption in this context includes such environmental and other non-marketed goods as can be valued in monetary terms. In principle, a full cost benefit study aims to include anything which affects an individual's welfare, providing it is not insignificant relative to other factors. Individuals are accepted as generally the best judges of their own welfare, except for certain 'merit' goods or bads, such as health or drugs, when the government may consider itself the better judge. The individual's valuation of goods is measured by his market behaviour or by his opinions, though more often by the former. These valuations determine implicitly the relative weight to be attached to such different objectives as improved accessibility, unpolluted air and extra leisure time. Explicit weights are used, however, to represent the value of consumption at different points in time. The objective of maximising the aggregate value of consumption is based on the notion that those who benefit from a project could compensate any losers and that everyone would be better off than in a state of less aggregate consumption value. Such redistribution from gainers to losers may be accomplished at the general level of government taxes and transfers or at the individual project level.

It is important to note that CBA aims to discover whether the net benefits from a project are sufficient for the gainers to be able to compensate the losers and still be better off. It does not attempt to express aggregate consumption in utility units. However, the fact that losers are often not compensated has made distributional analysis of great importance to decision makers. As we saw in chapter 2, the distributional effects of a project can and normally should be demonstrated in a CBA, but I argued that it is generally undesirable to attempt to allow for these distributional effects in a weighted NPV. The truth is, of course, that no evaluation method provides a means by which interpersonal utility can be measured or by which the costs and benefits of a project can be weighted objectively. Nor, for that matter, is there an objective way to choose homogeneous social groups as required by the PBS. In short, it is extremely doubtful that any other evaluation method can do more than CBA to resolve the distributional consequences of a project. More positive arguments are required, however, to demonstrate that the valuations of advantages and disadvantages in CBA are reasonable and indeed better than can be achieved by other methods. The extent to which private values can be measured and can be regarded as a suitable basis for public decisions is crucially important. These issues are discussed at some length in the following section.

In contrast to the emphasis on individual valuation in CBA, planners often refer somewhat obscurely to 'community goals'. Thus Richardson [7] writes: 'He [the planner] may decide that the achievement of the community's goals necessitates deviation from the most efficient pattern of development . . . . Planning should be goal oriented and it is this feature which gives urban planning its positive aspects'. However, it is not clear what community goals are if they are not the sum of individual goals. As Nash et al. [8] point out: 'It is an illusion to think that matrix evaluation methodologies focus on more objectives than do CBA techniques . . . . All one is doing in working in goal objective format is identifying the individual values which one believes should count in project evaluation. This is exactly what an economist does when he measures compensating variations for various effects'. Nor is it clear by what means or by what philosophy, planners who do not use the individual preference framework compare goals and reach judgements. Insofar as PBS, GAM and similar methods fail to base social objectives or measures of value on individual preferences, they must rely on subjective planning judgement. This is judicable only by appeal to authority. Although such judgements can be discussed, in the last resort there is no way in which they can be tested.

Environmental impact statements also suffer greatly from the lack of any systematic conceptual framework. Without an explicit criterion for an environmental cost, there is no rational way to exclude any environmental impacts from an EIS nor any standard way to compare the significance of impacts. Also, as shown in the Appendix, double counting is endemic to an EIS as it tends to describe the project's impact both on the physical environment and on people (usually termed vaguely 'the social environment').

Thus, in conclusion, CBA has a clearly defined social objective, maximising the value of aggregate consumption or the net surplus of a project. This surplus is derived from the preferences shown by individuals towards all, including non-marketed, goods. Other evaluation methods tend to have less clearly defined objectives, and less defined and testable notions of what constitutes a cost or benefit.

3.3 The valuation of preferences

The comparison of costs and benefits implies the use of a common unit of measurement. The choice of monetary units reflects convenience, not materialism. As Beckerman [9] has pointed out, in principle Beethoven's quartets could be used as the unit of measure but they would not be very convenient units. It is not the use of money *per se* which is unreasonable but the relative measures of value which may be unreasonable.

The relative values used in CBA tend to be criticised on two main grounds. These are that individuals do not know what is good for them (a view examined below) and that if they did, their preferences would not be accurately revealed by their behaviour in the market system (see below, pp 64-7).

The nature of individual preferences

The view underlying CBA that individuals know what is good for them and that their preferences are therefore a guide to desirable social change is challenged on two main counts. One is that consumer sovereignty is a myth because preferences are created by the economic system and not freely chosen. The second is that although preferences may be in some sense freely formed, nevertheless individuals are often ignorant of what is best for them.

The sovereignty of the consumer is contested by the argument that monopolists, by restricting the supply of goods, interfere with people's tastes since they are unlikely to want what they have not seen or known. Gintis [10] writes, for instance, that 'capitalism does not provide decent natural environments and hence city folk do not develop capacities to relate to natural environment. Thus decent environment becomes less "preferred" and not a major priority in individual goal-orientations'. A second criticism of consumer sovereignty is that producers create wants through advertising. Thus Mishan [11] argues: 'Not only do producers determine the range of market goods from which consumers must take their choice, they also seek continuously to persuade consumers to choose that which is being produced today and to "unchoose" that which was produced yesterday. To continue to regard the market . . . as primarily a want satisfying mechanism is to close one's eyes to the more important fact, that it has become a want-creating mechanism'.

In practice, restrictions on the range of monetary and non-monetary goods in a capitalist economy depend mainly upon the amount of actual and potential private sector competition and on the importance of the government as a producer of environmental goods. The reader will doubtless have his own view on the extent to which these restrictions, insofar as they occur, also change individual tastes. The power of advertising to mould tastes adversely depends on its ability to persuade a consumer to continue buying a product which he does not really want. It implies that the consumer is unable to judge whether something is beneficial to him. Clearly, as is discussed below, consumers sometimes make mistakes as to what is good for them. However, the view that advertising moulds people's tastes against their better judgement is at best one-sided. Many marketing departments consider it easier to sell goods which the public wants and do considerable research to discover what this is rather than attempt the more difficult task of changing people's tastes. Of course, it is undeniable that consumer tastes are subject to a large number of influences. But this does not mean that consumers do not choose freely in the market place. As Glover [12] has argued, 'determinism (the idea that all human behaviour is governed by causal laws) does not entail that we are always unable to act differently from how we do act'.

Alternatively, it may be held that many individuals hold inferior values because of a lack of education or because they cannot 'see through' the system. As J.S. Mill [13] put it, 'the uncultivated cannot be competent judges of cultivation'. So a planner might argue that he is the best judge of the amount of public open space or the amount of theatre which a community needs. But what happens when the planner's values clash with the consumer's, when for example the consumer wants larger gardens and more football pitches instead of public parks or theatres? Most people would reject the idea that others should dictate what their values should be. There is much to be said therefore for Mishan's conclusion (advertising notwithstanding) that as a maxim of political expediency 'there are ultimate advantages in treating people as if in fact they do know what they want'. [14]

Admitting that an individual's preferences are to be respected, it still does not follow that he always knows the means to achieve his ends. As Mishan [14] has expressed it, 'the gathering pace and power of modern technology act to extend the time gap between the commercial exploitation of new products and processes on the one hand and, on the other, the general recognition of their eventual physical, genetical, and ecological effects'. Individuals make mistakes, sometimes tragically as with the thalidomide drug. Consumer protection is often necessary, especially to delay technical innovations.

In the context of project appraisal it may be possible to allow for consumers' mistakes. In chapter 7, it is shown that many individuals underestimate aircraft noise when they purchase a house and consequently their loss of householder surplus should be included in a CBA. But it is important that evidence substantiate the claim that consumers are suffering as a result of their mistakes, and that this is not just a backdoor route by which planners' opinions are substituted for individual preferences.

The measurement of individual preferences

All evaluation methods, including CBA, use surveys to obtain data on individual attitudes. But CBA differs from other methods in that it relies more on 'revealed preferences', which means that individual preferences are inferred and measured from behaviour in the market place. In principle this provides a more robust basis for measurement of preference than do responses to a set of hypothetical questions. But this is true only if the critics of revealed preference theory can be satisfactorily answered. The critics argue that (a) the logic of the revealed preference hypothesis is inadequate, (b) preferences cannot be valued when markets do not exist and (c) true preferences are not revealed in situations requiring collective responses.

The logic of revealed preference Sen [15] argues that choices are not always 'connected': a choice of one good does not always mean that it is preferred to another and, more generally, preferences cannot be inferred from behaviour. He evidences the story of Buridan's ass who cannot choose between two haystacks and, choosing neither, dies of starvation. The revealed preference theorist might interpret this as a preference for death. Alternatively, he might assume correctly that the donkey made a mistake in taking so long to decide between the haystacks. A greater difficulty for revealed preference theory, according to Sen, would arise if the ass had chosen one or other haystack. The revealed preference theorist would infer that the chosen haystack is at least as preferred as the one not chosen. But all that should be inferred is that the chosen haystack is preferable to starving; there is no 'connection' with the other haystack. The example demonstrates that preferences are revealed only when choices are connected. Sen's conclusion is an important one but it may be regarded more as a warning to revealed preference theorists than as a criticism of them. After all, if Sen can avoid incorrect deductions from the ass's behaviour given its various potential choices, so can the revealed preference theorist. Moreover, attitude surveys (admittedly impossible for donkeys!) further clarify the nature of the consumer's choices as perceived by him.

Absence of markets Methods for the valuation of non-marketed goods were described in the previous chapter and examples arise in each of the following chapters, perhaps most importantly the valuation of aircraft noise in chapter 7. It is possible to cite here only a few of the many studies in which values for environmental factors have been estimated. For example, the Beaver Report [16] costed many aspects of air pollution and Lave and Seskin [17] have estimated the effects of air pollution on health. The Delaware study of Davidson, Adams and Seneca [18] attempted to measure the benefits of improved water quality. More generally Foster [19] has summarised how such environmental factors as visual intrusion, loss of privacy, loss of light and neighbourhood severance can be costed. One method of costing non-marketed environmental effects is to estimate the expense involved in reducing the adverse effects to insignificant levels, but this represents a maximum cost of the environmental impact.

It would, of course, be wrong to imply that quantified measures of non-marketed costs and benefits should be treated other than with caution. Many economic studies measure marginal rather than average community costs and generalisation from particular studies to the general case is dangerous. The value of the leisure time saved by faster transport, for instance, depends on the comfort of the particular form of transport used and the alternative opportunities gained by the saving in travel time. It is rarely the same in different situations, although there are many references in the literature to *the* value of travel time savings. Another problem arises when a market is in disequilibrium because of some unexpected exogenous change. A decision to locate a nuclear reactor near a town may have quite different short and long term effects on local property prices because the cost of moving house slows down both entry to the area by households looking for employment and exit by households fearing serious environmental dangers. But as the discussion of aircraft noise shows, it is possible to allow for the special costs of disequilibrium. Of course, it may sometimes be the case that valuations of individual preferences are so uncertain that they are best treated as intangibles. However, much may be lost by neglecting the revealed preference approach which promotes a framework within which the value of non-marketed goods can be estimated and rationally debated, and little is gained by treating all such goods as intangibles.

Collective decisions There are at least two important situations in which it is difficult to infer attitudes towards collective public decisions from market behaviour. First, individuals do not always have the same attitudes in a collective situation as in an individual situation. When the Channel tunnel was evaluated [20], a high proportion of the estimated benefits was private travel time savings. But if individuals were asked, 'Do you want public money to be spent on Northern Ireland rather than a Channel tunnel?', doubtless many would reply 'yes'. There is no contradiction in this as the 'yes' enables the individual to vote on how other people's resources as well as his own will be used, which is not the case in the purely private choice. Sen [15] gives an example of the same problem. An individual may hold that it is best for everyone to return re-usable cans. However, he may well prefer the situation in which he throws the can away, like everyone else, to one where he alone takes the trouble to return the can. To discover an individual's preferences in such collective situations, Sen concludes that it is necessary to seek his opinions rather than to study his behaviour.

Second, society sometimes provides goods to individuals to promote the donors' objectives as well as the recipients' welfare. Housing subsidies, for instance, may be provided partly to improve social cohesion and reduce crime. This may be described as a social merit good, unlike a private merit good which is provided for the benefit of the recipient. However, there is no market in social (or private) merit goods. Therefore Mishan [21] concludes reasonably that no merit goods should be included in CBA because they cannot be valued scientifically and because their inclusion obscures the meaning of the results. Naturally, to omit social (or private) merit goods from a CBA is not to preclude sensitivity tests for their assumed values nor to exclude them from all mention in the study report.

The assessment of individual attitudes towards collective decisions can be approached in a number of ways. Surveys are by far the most common method but, if the information they collect is to be useful, they must emphasise the resource constraints on government and the trade-offs required in decision making. Second, economic models of the demand and supply of public goods by analysts such as Downs and Breton [22] suggest that it may be possible to infer individual demand for public goods from voting behaviour or participation in pressure groups. Following this approach, Deacon and Shapiro [23] examined two Californian referenda to estimate the demand for conservation of coastal areas and for rapid transport. They concluded that the voting responses were consistent with selfish market behaviour. Currently, this form of analysis is too primitive to be useful for most CBA studies, but more research of this type may indicate the nature of individual preferences in collective situations. Finally, an alternative approach, which is discussed below, argues that decisions on collective goods require a special collective choice procedure either as a substitute for or, perhaps more realistically, in conjunction with CBA.

3.4 Evaluation methods and decision making

Evaluation methods, especially CBA, are considered below in terms of three criteria relevant to decision making.

(a) comprehensiveness,

(b) compatibility with democratic participation and decision procedures, and
(c) the actual costs and benefits of the method in practice.

The comprehensive analysis of alternatives and their effects

In principle, CBA is concerned with all the significant social costs and benefits of alternative decisions. As Lichfield and Whitbread [24] have expressed it, 'Any decision which makes individuals better or worse off than otherwise is legitimately the subject matter of CBA irrespective of the label which may attach to it for purposes of convenience'.

However, supposing that all effects could be traced, questions concerning their significance and the accuracy of their valuation would remain. Some effects would be too insignificant to justify evaluation. Here a CBA criterion may be useful. For example, in an airport study, effects costing less than say $1.0 million might be ignored. Admittedly this principle has to be applied with judgement, for all costs may be disaggregated to less than $1.0 million or consolidated with others to more than $1.0 million. Nevertheless, some such 'rule of thumb' is often useful and can also be applied to the consideration of intangibles.

The accuracy question concerns whether an effect is valued sufficiently accurately to be included in the CBA. Of course, all valuations are inaccurate, and so some form of uncertainty analysis is likely to be required (see section 2.6). Ultimately, however, the decision whether or not to quantify a variable depends upon the acceptable degree of inaccuracy, which is a matter of judgement. Indeed, the decision to include or exclude something may depend upon the best way to present the results. For example, it may be reasonable to put a value on life, but it might be sensible to describe the loss of life as an intangible if its valuation were to lack public credibility.

CBA is sometimes compared (mistakenly) with SA and criticised for inadequate consideration of possible alternatives. If the fault exists, it is contingent to the study rather than inherent in CBA. In any case, the use of systems analysis does not guarantee comprehensive analysis as ultimately most systems are closed and make some assumptions about the outside world. On the other hand, planning-based evaluation methods, partly due to their association with land use planners and engineers, tend to over-emphasise physical infrastructure as a means of solving problems. For instance engineers may attempt to overcome the aviation problem by building new airports rather than by airport management policies (see chapter 6).

Closely related to the study of alternatives is the need to optimise project design. It is generally not sufficient to describe the effects of a particular course of action and to turn the decision over to some decision making authority, as tends to be done in an EIS. Environmental costs and benefits need to be evaluated as part of a continuous optimisation process, in which many alternatives are considered. Only computerised models based on quantitative inputs and outputs such as CBA produces (but which an EIS, for example, tends not to) can provide the comprehensive optimisation of alternatives that is required.

Democratic acceptability

To meet the criterion of democratic acceptability, an evaluation should be clearly presented, capable of being understood by intelligent laymen so that it may be discussed publicly, and compatible with democratic decision procedures. The criterion of clarity implies that along with a recommendation, the chief assumptions, value judgements, distributional effects, sensitivity tests, trade-offs and alternatives be presented. Many CBA reports fall short of this ideal. This may occur because of excessive reliance on the NPV (or IRR) decision criterion, which tends to inhibit the discussion of alternative decision criteria, but this can be avoided easily enough by a broader discussion of the evaluation results. Indeed the Roskill hearings on the proposed third London airport showed that CBA provides a very good framework within which to discuss complex sets of costs and benefits without double counting or obfuscation of the issues. It is extremely doubtful whether other less structured evaluation methods would have produced such constructive debate.

In the previous section, I suggested that collective choice decisions may require some collective choice rule (CCR), such as majority voting, rather than a cost benefit criterion based on an aggregation of individual preferences in individual choice situations. For example, collective choice mechanisms were involved when Californian citizens voted to reduce taxes on real estate or against very strong safety regulations for the nuclear industry and also when the British voted to stay in the EEC. Through voting procedures, citizen preferences were revealed directly whereas CBA often has to discover citizen preferences through indirect means.

The main differences between a CCR and CBA are: (a) most CCR's are based on each individual's ranking of social states, which allows his/her ethical or social views to count, (b) also under most CCR's, each individual's ranking is considered equally important, however indirectly he/she is concerned with the issues in question and regardless of the intensity of his/her feelings and (c) CCR's are solely decision procedures; they do not identify or evaluate costs and benefits or their distribution.

It is clearly an advantage of most CCR's that they enable social and equity considerations to count. [25] A society, like a cathedral, constitutes more than the sum of the parts of which it is made. On the other hand, a CCR can be unfair to individuals; for example, majority voting can be unfair to minorities. Finally, however, CBA and collective choice methods are not incompatible. Many people consider that a cost benefit analysis of some kind is a prerequisite for an informed vote in a collective choice procedure.

The costs and benefits of the evaluation method

Thorough evaluations of complex social issues are expensive of time and professional skills whatever the choice of evaluation method. Possibly CBA, by its emphasis on quantified valuation, is especially expensive but, as I argued in the previous chapter, it is not necessary always to complete an exhaustive CBA. Also the costs of CBA could be reduced, and probably will be, by improved national and international data banks of research findings on cost and benefit valuations to which researchers and consultants could have ready access.

The final attack on CBA is that although CBA may be a fine evaluation method and may indeed not be excessively costly, the benefits of CBA studies are negligible because politicians invariably ignore their results except when it is convenient to embrace them. The truth or otherwise of this charge is an empirical matter, but as far as I know no test of the hypothesis has been made. Were it found to be true that politicians have ignored inconvenient CBA studies, it would still not be clear that CBA should be abandoned. The purpose of CBA, after all, is to show the social costs and benefits of alternative projects, not the political losses and gains. It is defeatist indeed to believe that decision making cannot be improved to the benefit of most members of society.

3.5 Conclusions

Cost benefit analysis has many advantages. It is systematic, based on broadly accepted social principles (that is, on individuals' preferences as revealed in markets and surveys), it can be tested and produces a meaningful result in terms of the aggregate surplus available for consumption. Its major weaknesses are that (a) estimates of environmental costs and benefits must be treated with caution and likewise (b) the demand for certain public or collective goods cannot easily be inferred from household behaviour in situations of private choice; (c) the valuations used in CBA depend upon the existing distribution of income and wealth (if a charter of amenity rights was declared as Mishan [26] recommends, quite different valuations might occur); and (d), a project may have a positive net present value and yet make poor households worse off.

It is a matter for judgement whether CBA provides a satisfactory method for the assessment of most environmental and collective goods. However, no other evaluation method provides a viable alternative. Likewise the problem of distribution arises equally with other evaluation methods. Despite its weaknesses, CBA more nearly meets our criteria for a desirable evaluation procedure than do other planning methods. As Walters [27] writes, 'On the one side there is the super generalist – the planner. His eclectic sweep includes all – even aesthetics and moral welfare. But the planner pays a high price for his omnipresence; there is no analytical discipline nor are there well established propositions of planning . . . . On the other sides there are the particular disciplines such as engineering which offer at least the hard-headed alternative of configurations of hardware and concrete. But the limitations of engineers in dealing with the behavioural and financial aspects of decision-making are well known. It seems therefore that economics can usefully serve as the integrative discipline. In practice one is driven to this conclusion by the great convenience of using the monetary unit of account and by the fact that the economist specialises in the valuation procedure. Just as the accountant has become the integrator of information for business decisions, so the economist is becoming the architect of information for public investment decisions.' Williams [28] summarises the situation more succinctly, 'Even if all Self's strictures on CBA were valid, however, the sad thing is that he has nothing substantive to offer in its place'.

An alternative evaluation strategy towards any given problem would be the employment of a combination of evaluation methods, say a CBA and an EIS. If economists tend to underestimate environmental effects, which are often the most uncertain of the quantified factors and the most important of the unquantified ones, there may sometimes be a case for an EIS as well as a CBA. However, as shown in the Appendix, this combination inevitably produces double counting and confusion, though perhaps not to a serious degree. This approach is also logically inferior to the quantification in monetary terms of all costs and benefits which are quantifiable and to description of those which are not.

In the final resort, CBA is no less and no more than a valuable aid to decision making. Its value lies in its relative superiority over other evaluation methods. But no net present value, however positive, is a sufficient or necessary condition for acceptance of a course of action. Also, often CBA will be used for evaluation, but the decision may be taken by some quite different process of collective choice.

Notes

[1] Throughout this chapter an EIS is understood to be principally a description of the physical impacts of a project or policy, see for example the Airport EIS shown in the Appendix. Also it would probably include some description of the social effects of the physical impacts. As argued in chapter 1, the view that an EIS should embrace all the consequences of a project and all evaluation methods and thus be a comprehensive planning system makes the concept of an EIS as an alternative evaluation method meaningless.

[2] Self P. 'Nonsense on Stilts, the Futility of Roskill', *New Society*, 2 July 1970.
[3] Hills M. 'A Goals Achievement Matrix for Evaluation of Alternative Plans', *Journal of the American Institute of Planners*, January 1968, p.27.
[4] Roskill Chairman, Commission on the Third London Airport, Report, chapters 12 and 13, HMSO 1971.
[5] Lichfield N. and Chapman H. 'Cost Benefit Analysis in Urban Expansion. A Case Study of Ipswich', *Urban Studies*, 1970, p.158.
[6] Richardson H.W. *Urban Economics*, Penguin 1971, pp 183-6.
[7] Richardson H.W. op.cit., p.174.
[8] Nash C. Pearce N. Stanley J. 'Criteria for Evaluating Project Evaluation Techniques', *Journal of American Institute of Planners*, vol.41, March 1975, p.85.
[9] Beckerman W. *In Defence of Economic Growth*, Jonathan Cape, 1974, p.23.
[10] Gintis H. 'Consumer Sovereignty and the Concept of Sovereignty: Explanations of Social Decay', *American Economic Review, Papers and Proceedings*, May 1972, p.276.
[11] Mishan E.J. *The Costs of Economic Growth*, Staples Press, London 1967, p.110.

[12] Glover J. *Responsibility*, Routledge and Keegan Paul 1970, p.199.
[13] Mill J.S. *Principles of Political Economy*, 1848, Penguin 1970, p.318.
[14] Mishan E.J. 'Pollution, Economics and Liberalism', *Current Affairs Bulletin*, 5 April 1971.
[15] Sen A.K. 'Behaviour and the Concept of Preference', *Economica*, vol.XL, May 1973, pp 241-59.
[16] Beaver H. Chairman Report of the Committee on Air Pollution, Cmnd 1322, HMSO 1954.
[17] Lave L. and Seskin E., 'Air Pollution and Human Health', *Science*, vol.CLXIV, August 1970.
[18] Davidson P. Adams F.G. and Seneca J. 'The Social Value of Water Recreation Facilities Resulting from an Improvement in Water Quality, The Delaware Estuary' in Kneese A.V. and Smith S.C. (eds), *Water Research*, John Hopkins Press, Baltimore 1966.
[19] Foster C.D. 'Transport and the Urban Environment' in Rothenburg J.G. and Heggie I.G. (eds) *Transport and the Urban Environment*, MacMillan 1974, pp 161-91.
[20] Coopers and Lybrand Associates Ltd., *The Channel Tunnel: a United Kingdom Transport Cost Benefit Study*, HMSO 1973.
[21] Mishan E.J. 'Flexibility and Consistency in Project Evaluation', *Economica*, vol.41, no.161, 1974, pp 81-95.
[22] Downs A. *An Economic Theory of Democracy*, Harper and Row, 1957, and Breton A. *The Theory of Representative Government*, Aldine Publishing Company, 1974.
[23] Deacon R. and Shapiro P. 'Private Preference for Collective Goods Revealed through Voting on Referenda', *American Economic Review*, December 1975, pp 943-55.
[24] Lichfield N. and Whitbread M. 'The Use of Cost Benefit Analysis for Plan Evaluation: A Rationale', Working Paper, Planning Methodology Research Unit, School of Environmental Studies, University College, London 1972, no.8, p.4.
[25] A dictatorial CCR, whereby one person made the collective decision, would be a case where, except in a world of Philosopher Kings, ethical views would not count.
[26] Mishan E.J. *The Costs of Economic Growth*, Pelican Book, 1967, pp 102-6.
[27] Walters A.A. 'Investment in Airports and the Economist's Role. John F. Kennedy International Airport. An Example and some Comparisons' in Wolfe J.N. (ed.), *Cost Benefit and Cost Effectiveness*, Unwin University Books, 1973, p.141.

[28] Williams A. 'Cost Benefit Analysis: Bastard Science? and/or Insidious Poison in the Body Politic?' in Wolfe J.N. (ed.), op.cit., p.56.

Appendix

Problems with environmental impact statements

There is no standard way to prepare an EIS as the environmental impact of projects differs greatly and there is no analytical discipline to support an EIS. Also the form of the EIS will vary with the use of other evaluation methods in the overall evaluation process. However, the environmental matrix produced for the second Sydney airport EIS illustrates certain problems which appear to be general and liable to arise in any impact statement. [1]

The environmental effects of 16 possible airport sites were summarised in the matrix, figure 3.1, the form of which was developed originally by the US Department of the Interior's Geological Survey. At first sight the matrix provides a clear impression of the environmental effects. Two sites, Wattamolla and Duffys Forest, appear to be extremely bad environmentally and a number of others, including the existing airport, Kingsford-Smith, also seem relatively poor. A closer look at the matrix, however, reveals some problems in interpretation.

(a) The black rectangles do not represent quantified effects and so cannot be added. Strict conclusions that one site is environmentally better than another can be drawn only if one row dominates another, i.e. if it has less black area in each square. It may be noted also that the black areas are qualitative judgements only of adverse effects; no good effects are included.

(b) There is double counting in the matrix: for example, between columns showing the physical impacts on 'earth' and those showing cultural impacts on land uses and aesthetics; between columns showing land uses and those showing recreational effects; and between columns showing sociological effects and a number of effects noted elsewhere in the matrix.

(c) The EIS included many effects which were costed in the CBA carried out at the same time. For example, land costs in the cost benefit study included allowances for the loss of productive land, rehousing and recreational costs all of which were also included in the matrix. In addition, noise costs were estimated in the CBA and shown in the matrix. The possibility that such effects were not costed accurately in the CBA does not justify double counting them.

Inaccuracy is inherent in all estimated costs and anyway the land or noise costs may have been overestimated in the CBA.

(d) Neither the matrix nor the written EIS included all the items presented as intangibles in the CBA. Such items as air safety, airport closure due to poor visibility, and the benefits of airport access roads to non-airport users were treated as intangibles in the CBA, but they were omitted, and would normally be omitted, from the EIS.

It should be emphasised that none of these four problems was due to the particular nature of the project, an airport, or to the nature of the presentation discussed here, the matrix form. The EIS is basically a descriptive method, which does not quantify or evaluate the effects it describes. Double counting is endemic to an EIS because of the lack of a conceptual framework for the analysis. It is easy to double count by first recording the impact on the physical environment and then counting its effects on people or their actions. Problems (c) and (d) above also tend to occur whenever there is a CBA as well as an EIS.

Three other problems in the airport environmental study, which have also occurred in other EIS studies, may be noted. These are the lack of any time dimension for the impacts, the lack of any analysis of the distributional impacts, and the absence of any detailed ecological assessment (as can be seen from the column of queries under the ecological heading). These omissions appear to be due to the primitive state of the art as currently practised, and sometimes to the lack of resources for the EIS, rather than to any inherent inability to deal with them within the framework of an EIS. But they illustrate the heavy resource requirements for an environmental study, especially for an assessment of the ecological effects.

The major problems with the EIS, notably (a)-(d) above, suggest the need for a closer relationship between environmental studies and economics. Economics provides a framework for measuring the costs and benefits of environment effects, for avoiding double counting, and for allowing for inter-temporal effects, all of which are problems in an EIS.

Note

[1] Australian and NSW Governments Joint Committee Planning Sydney Airports – Environmental Study Group Report on the Environment Impact Study 1973.

Category	PHYSICAL																																
Item Group	EARTH																WATER										ATMOSPHERE						
Location / Detailed Aspects	*Land form*	*Reserves raw material*	*Reserves of minerals*	*Productivity of soils*	*Structural stability of soils (slides, slumps)*	*Erosion of soils*	*Salinity of soils*	*Deposition on land (Sedimentation)*	*Dereliction of land*	*Flooding*	*Wetlands*	*Fields of force*	*Radiation background*	*Sorption (Ion exchange complexing)*	*Compaction and settling*	*Stress-strain (Earthquakes)*	*Quality surface water*	*Quantity surface water*	*Quality underground water*	*Quantity underground water*	*Quality estuarine and ocean water*	*Water temperature*	*Siltation waterways*	*Quality of drinking water*	*Quantity of drinking water*	*Eutrophication*	*Air quality*	*Air temperature*	*Air movements*	*Climate*	*Rainfall, snow, ice, frost*	*Fog*	*Low cloud*
Kingsford-Smith			?		n		n	*			*	n	n	n	*	n		*		*	*	n			n			*		*	*		
Towra Point			?		n		n	*			*	n	n	n	*	n		*		*	*	n			n			*		*	*		
Wattamolla			?		n		n	*			*	n	n	n	*	n		*		*	*	n			n			*		*	*		
Long Point			?		n		n	*			n	n	n	n	*	n		*		*	n	n			n			*		*	*		
Bringelly			?		n		n	*			n	n	n	n	*	n		*		*	n	n			n			*		*	*		
Badgery's Creek			?		n		n	?			n	n	n	n	*	n		*		*	n	n			n			*		*	*		
Duffy's Forest			?		n		n	*			n	n	n	n	*	n		*		*	*	n			n			*		*	*		
Horsley/Prospect			?		n		n	*			n	n	n	n	*	n		*		*	n	n			n			*		*	*		
Marsden Park			?		n		n	*			n	n	n	n	*	n		*		*	n	n			n			*		*	*		
St. Marys			?		n		n	*			n	n	n	n	*	n		*		*	n	n			n			*		*	*		
Richmond			?		n		n	*			*	n	n	n	*	n		*		*	n	n			n			*		*	*		
Blue Gum Creek			?		n		n	*			*	n	n	n	*	n		*		*	n	n			n			*		*	*		
Rouse Hill			?				n	*			n	n	n	n	*	n		*		*	n	n			n			*		*	*		
Galston			?		n		n	*			n	n	n	n	*	n		*		*	n	n			n			*		*	*		
Somersby			?		n		n	*			n	n	n	n	*	n		*		*	*	n			n			*		*	*		
Wyong			?		n		n	*			*	n	n	n	*	n		*		*	*	n			n			*		*	*		

n-factor not applicable or absent from all areas considered.

BIOLOGICAL																					CULTURAL																						
FLORA											FAUNA										LAND USE														RECREATION								
Trees	*Shrubs*	*Grass*	*Crops*	*Microflora*	*Aquatic plants*	*Unique or rare species*	*Forests*	*Barriers*	*Corridors*	*Orchards Horticulture*	*Birds*	*Land animals incl. reptiles*	*Fish and shellfish*	*Benthic organisms*	*Insects*	*Microfauna*	*Endangered species*	*Barriers*	*Corridors*	*Fishing/Oyster beds*	*For grazing*	*For agriculture*	*Residential development*	*Commercial development*	*Industrial development*	*Mining, quarrying, extraction*	*Passive recreation*	*Active recreation*	*As a resort area*	*Special Purposes*	*National Park*	*Wilderness*	*Port development*	*Defence establishment*	*Hunting*	*Fishing*	*Boating*	*Swimming*	*Sporting activities*	*Camping*	*Hiking*	*Picknicking*	*General aviation*
								?	?					?		?	*	?	?													*n*			*n*								
								?	?					?		?	*	?	?													*n*			*n*								
								?	?					?		?	*	?	?													*n*			*n*								
								?	?					*n*		?	*	?	?													*n*			*n*								
								?	?					*n*		?	*	?	?													*n*			*n*								
								?	?					*n*		?	*	?	?													*n*			*n*								
								?	?					*n*		?	*	?	?													*n*			*n*								
								?	?					*n*		?	*	?	?													*n*			*n*								
								?	?					*n*		?	*	?	?													*n*			*n*								
								?	?					*n*		?	*	?	?													*n*			*n*								
								?	?					?		?	*	?	?													*n*			*n*								
								?	?					?		?	*	?	?													*n*			*n*								
								?	?					*n*		?	*	?	?													*n*			*n*								
								?	?					*n*		?	*	?	?													*n*			*n*								
								?	?					?		?	*	?	?													*n*			*n*								
								?	?					?		?	*		?													*n*			*n*								

?-factor considered for study program but no details obtained from specialists.

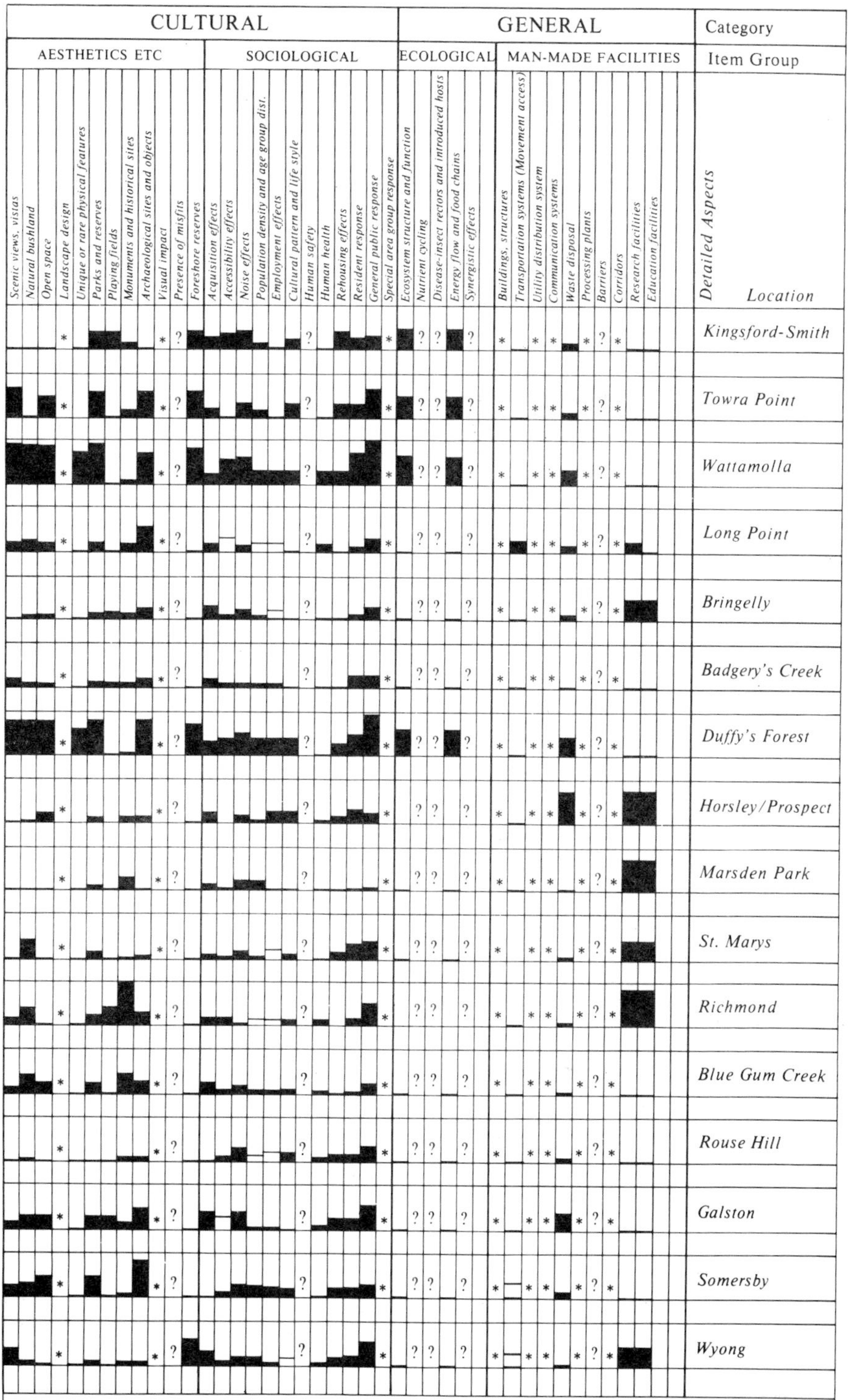

Category	CULTURAL																								GENERAL														
Item Group	AESTHETICS ETC												SOCIOLOGICAL												ECOLOGICAL					MAN-MADE FACILITIES									
Detailed Aspects / Location	*Scenic views, vistas*	*Natural bushland*	*Open space*	*Landscape design*	*Unique or rare physical features*	*Parks and reserves*	*Playing fields*	*Monuments and historical sites*	*Archaeological sites and objects*	*Visual impact*	*Presence of misfits*	*Foreshore reserves*	*Acquisition effects*	*Accessibility effects*	*Noise effects*	*Population density and age group dist.*	*Employment effects*	*Cultural pattern and life style*	*Human safety*	*Human health*	*Rehousing effects*	*Resident response*	*General public response*	*Special area group response*	*Ecosystem structure and function*	*Nutrient cycling*	*Disease-insect rectors and introduced hosts*	*Energy flow and food chains*	*Synergistic effects*	*Buildings, structures*	*Transportation systems (Movement access)*	*Utility distribution system*	*Communication systems*	*Waste disposal*	*Processing plants*	*Barriers*	*Corridors*	*Research facilities*	*Education facilities*
Kingsford-Smith				*						*	?								?					*		?	?		?	*		*	*		*	?	*		
Towra Point				*						*	?								?					*		?	?		?	*		*	*		*	?	*		
Wattamolla				*						*	?								?					*		?	?		?	*		*	*		*	?	*		
Long Point				*						*	?								?					*		?	?		?	*		*	*		*	?	*		
Bringelly				*						*	?								?					*		?	?		?	*		*	*		*	?	*		
Badgery's Creek				*						*	?								?					*		?	?		?	*		*	*		*	?	*		
Duffy's Forest				*						*	?								?					*		?	?		?	*		*	*		*	?	*		
Horsley/Prospect				*						*	?								?					*		?	?		?	*		*	*		*	?	*		
Marsden Park				*						*	?								?					*		?	?		?	*		*	*		*	?	*		
St. Marys				*						*	?								?					*		?	?		?	*		*	*		*	?	*		
Richmond				*						*	?								?					*		?	?		?	*		*	*		*	?	*		
Blue Gum Creek				*						*	?								?					*		?	?		?	*		*	*		*	?	*		
Rouse Hill				*						*	?								?					*		?	?		?	*		*	*		*	?	*		
Galston				*						*	?								?					*		?	?		?	*		*	*		*	?	*		
Somersby				*						*	?								?					*		?	?		?	*		*	*		*	?	*		
Wyong				*						*	?								?					*		?	?		?	*		*	*		*	?	*		

** - factor covered discriptively in report but detail input not sufficient for this numerical assessment.*

4 Cost benefit analysis of a soil conservation project [1]

The Eppalock catchment soil conservation project ran from 1960 to 1975 and some benefits had occurred by 1975 when the cost benefit study was made. The purposes of the study were to provide the government with an assessment of part of the national soil conservation programme, for which the benefits were almost totally unquantified, and to demonstrate the use of CBA to Soil Conservation Authorities. The study was unusual in being partly retrospective but this did not materially change the method of evaluation.

The Eppalock catchment and the conservation project are described in the first section. The public and private project costs, the various benefits of the project, and the intangibles are described in the following sections respectively. The cost benefit results including sensitivity tests and distributional analysis are given in section five. Conclusions are stated briefly in section six.

4.1 The Eppalock catchment and the soil conservation project [2]

The Eppalock catchment

The Eppalock catchment covers an area of 2,073 sq.km. in central Victoria (figure 4.1). It is undulating with some areas rising to 1,000 metres above sea level, but generally slopes fall towards Lake Eppalock at the northern end of the catchment which is about 200 metres above sea level. The catchment has cool, moist winters and hot, mostly dry summers, with an average annual rainfall varying from 1,100 mm in the south to 500 mm in the north. Consequently, the south makes the major contribution to the stream flows in the two rivers, the Campaspe and the Coliban. Most of the soils are acidic throughout their profile and of inherently low nutrient status except for some areas developed from basalt (figure 4.2).

The original forests were cleared in the nineteenth century gold rush and now occupy about one-seventh of the land on the boundary of the catchment. In the north, agriculture has been almost entirely

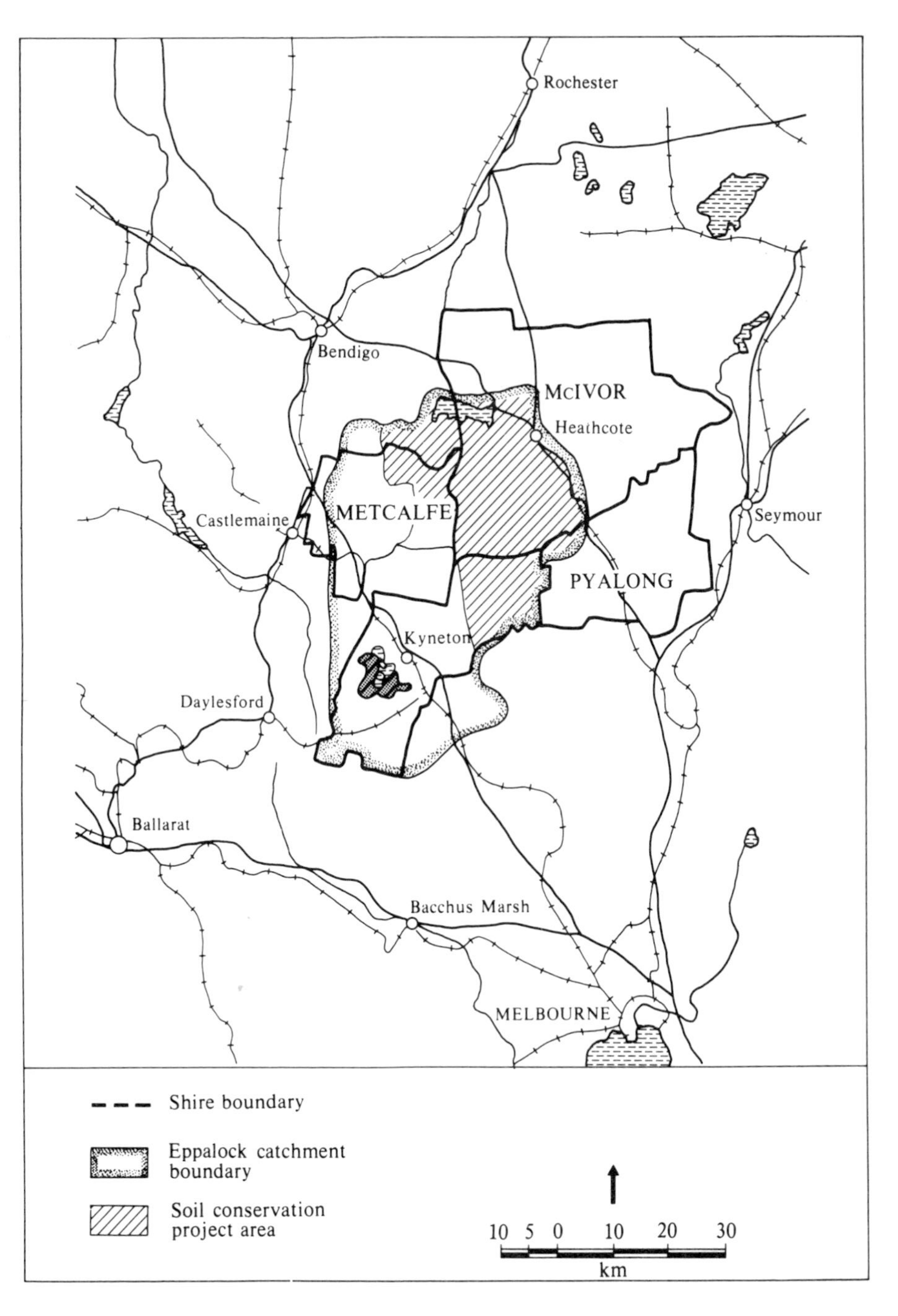

Source: Report 9, Department of Environment, Housing and Community Development, op.cit. [1]

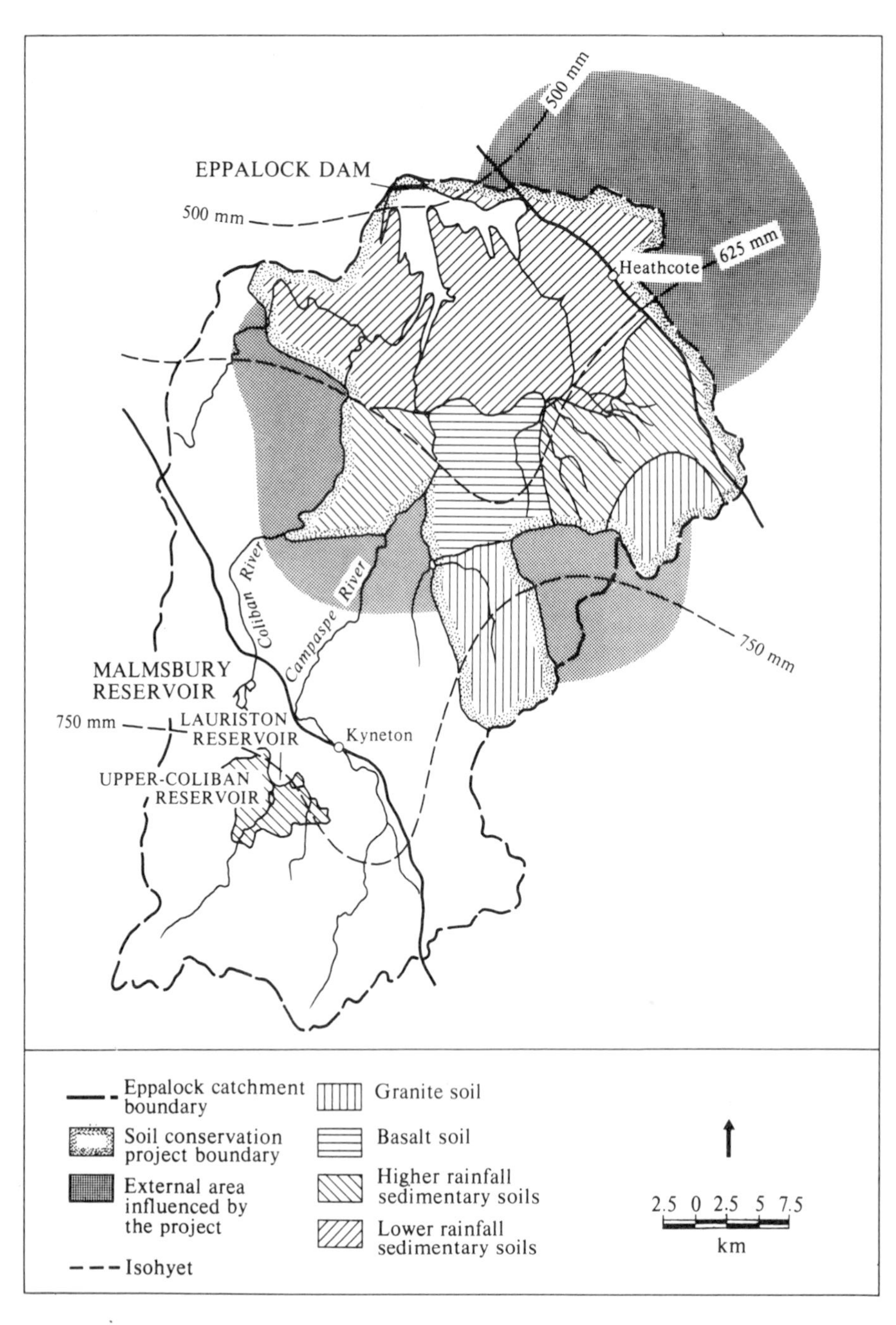

Source: Report 9, Department of Environment, Housing and Community Development, op.cit. [1]

sheep grazing but, in the south, there has also been cattle grazing and cropping. Farm size in 1960 was commonly 250 hectares (ha) to 600 ha and some were less than 160 ha. The average flock was less than 500 sheep.

Persistent intensive land use over the last 100 years, aggravated by rabbits, caused tunnel and sheet erosion resulting in numerous gullies, stony base surfaces on steep slopes and some dryland salting. It also increased the silt loads and irregularity of the flows of the Campaspe river, the flow of which had always been highly variable. Thus in 1959 the Victorian Soil Conservation Authority (SCA) reported that, 'the land in the northern part of the catchment presented an example of extensive land destruction rarely paralleled in other parts of the State'. [2]

The conservation project

The project involved the planning and development of 72,000 ha in the catchment occupied by 373 landholders and had indirect effects on holdings in an estimated 17,000 ha outside the catchment. Some of the capital works (see table 4.1) such as gully control structures, protective fencing and erosion control earthworks, were designed mainly to protect the water storage capacity and water quality in the Eppalock reservoir. Other improvements, including chisel seeding, farm sub-division and improved stock water supplies, related directly to agricultural development. Some continuing maintenance work is also required.

The capital costs of soil erosion control were borne principally by the SCA, which also performed planning and extension work. Other public authorities, for example the Department of Agriculture, made minor contributions to the project. Private landholders paid for most of the works relating directly to agricultural productivity and for all costs involving the purchase and management of extra livestock. [3]

The major project benefits are the increased farm production due to pasture improvement and the preservation of the dam's water supplies. The improved residential value of the catchment and the reduced cost of road maintenance are also benefits which were quantified. Other effects of the project, for example on flood mitigation and on the quality of water in Lake Eppalock, were treated as intangibles.

The cost benefit analysis

The effects of the project, both inside and outside the catchment,

Table 4.1
Works completed in Eppalock project

Description of works	Unit	Quantity
Gully structures		
concrete chutes, drops and weirs	no.	465
groynes and silt traps	no.	896
grassed chutes	no.	248
gabion	cu.m	63
prefabricated fibro-cement chutes	no.	5
rock packing of heads		19
Fencing		
protective	km	275.25
subdivision	km	310
Earthworks		
diversion banks	m	10,126
head batters	no.	1,785
gully plug dams	no.	30
gully battering	m	8,381
tunnel ripping	ha	5.5
Farm water supply		
dam surveyed	no.	53
capacity of dams constructed	Ml	335
pipeline reticulation	m	241
Survey		
contour cultivation	ha	18,571
Tree planting		
trees	no.	119,263
Gully vegetating		
cane grass	sites	29
pampas grass	sites	523
Mulching/sowing		
salt areas, stripped areas	ha	335
Pasture improvement		
chisel seeding	ha	20,891
aerial topdressing	ha	4,184
land clearing	ha	18,861

NOTE: The planned area of the project was 829 sq.km. The number of landholders involved was 373.

Source: *Eppalock Catchment Project*, Victorian Soil Conservation Authority, 1975.

were established by comparison with the hypothetical situation predicted to exist in the absence of the project, which was called the base case. The essential difference between the project case and the base case was considered to be the timing of improvements. Whereas all project improvements were completed by 1975, it was assumed that there would have been some SCA activity in the area in the base case and that direct agricultural improvements would have been completed by 1990 and the soil erosion controls by 2005. [4]

Since differences between the project case and the base case were forecast to be small after 1990, most of the CBA results were calculated for the estimated costs and benefits between 1960 and 1990. [5] All costs and benefits were expressed in 1974-75 domestic prices; historic prices were converted to 1974-75 prices with the use of the consumer price index. A discount rate of 8 per cent per annum, considered to be an inflation free opportunity cost of capital, was used to discount costs and benefits. The consequences of including additional benefits after 1990, of varying discount rates and of adopting alternative values for key variables were also investigated.

4.2 The costs of the conservation project

The public costs

The public costs of the project were the SCA's capital expenditures between 1960 and 1975 and forecast maintenance costs after 1975, expenditures by the Department of Agriculture and by local authorities, and the government's share of the costs of additional fertilizer used by farmers. The additional public costs of the project compared with the base case, modified to represent economic costs as described below, are summarised for selected years in table 4.2. Negative figures indicate that in some years estimated expenditure would be higher in the base case than in the project case.

The SCA budget for the Eppalock project totalled $1.2 million in historic prices between 1960 and 1975. It included most costs of the local Eppalock office and some variable Melbourne head office costs but it was amended in three ways for the CBA. (a) Some $0.2 million in historic prices was added to allow for omitted expenditures, such as vehicle and telephone costs attributable to the project. (b) Unskilled labour was costed at three-quarters of the actual wage to allow for local unemployment and underemployment, including semi-employed small-scale farmers with no alternative part-time work. (c) As previously noted, all costs were converted to 1974-75 prices.

Table 4.2
Additional economic costs of project compared with base case [a] (selected years) $'000, 1974-75 prices [b]

Year	Soil Conservation Authority	Other public bodies	Fertiliser costs	Total
1960-61	157.8	5.8	–	163.6
1969-70	113.8	20.3	17.4	151.5
1975-76	-33.2	–	2.7	-30.5
1989-90	-27.9	–	-2.7	-30.6

[a] All relevant costs outside as well as inside the Eppalock catchment are included.

[b] All monetary figures in this chapter are given in Australian dollars.

Source: Report 9 – Economic Evaluation of Eppalock Soil Conservation Project, Victoria. Soil Conservation Study, Department of Environment, Housing and Community Development (op.cit. [1]). Hereafter, I refer to this study as the EHCD report.

The SCA base case costs, 1960 to 1975, were estimated at $0.3 million in 1974-75 prices after allowing for a shadow price for unskilled labour. The forecast 1976-1990 base case costs were slightly higher than the forecast costs with the project because of the inferior soil conditions in the base case in 1975.

Two other public authorities increased expenditures as a result of the project. The Department of Agriculture held special stocking rate trials between 1966 and 1969 to test the efficiency of pasture improvements. Also, local authorities incurred extra expenditure to conform to the SCA's recommended standards for roads, bridges, etc.

Extra fertiliser usage due to the project resulted in an increased charge on the taxpayer because of a superphosphate subsidy to farmers. Superphosphate usage was estimated to have risen from 10 kgs per ha in 1960 to 45 kgs per ha in 1975 in the project case and from about 9 kgs per ha in 1960 to 45 kgs per ha in 1990 in the base case respectively. The higher fertiliser use with the project was consistent with the higher stocking levels postulated. The superphosphate subsidy after 1975 was forecast to stay constant in nominal terms but to decline in real terms. If the subsidy was wrongly predicted, the distributional effects of the project would be changed. The net present value of the project would of course be affected only if the economic cost of fertiliser was wrongly predicted.

Landholders' land development costs

The main land development costs incurred by landholders were for clearing of stumps, subdivision fences, additional water supply dams, pasture seed and fertiliser. Between 1960 and 1990, these totalled an estimated $4.5 million in 1974-75 prices. For convenience of calculation, the Department used contract rates to estimate development costs, so no allowance was made for the cost of the landholders' own time or labour. (This procedure does not seem quite consistent with the use of a shadow price for labour for estimating the capital costs of the SCA). For the base case it was assumed that similar farm developments would be made, but at a slower rate than in the project case. An indication of the relative cost profiles in the project and base cases is given in table 4.3.

Table 4.3
Landholder land development costs for selected years [a]
$'000 in 1974-75 prices

	With project	Base case	Difference
1960-61	114	72	42
1974-75	195	153	42
1989-90	155	196	-41

[a] Includes the external area affected by the project.

Source: EHCD Report, op.cit. [1]

4.3 The benefits of the SCA programme

Agricultural benefits due to improved pastures

The annual undiscounted agricultural benefits of improved pastures inside and outside the catchment, all due to increased livestock, were estimated with the following formula:

$$B = \sum_{L=1}^{3} \left[(Q_1 - Q_2)(P - C) - A(N_1 - N_2) \right] \qquad (1)$$

where B = net annual agricultural benefit in years 1960-61 to 1989-90

Q_1 = annual output with project

Q_2 = annual output in base case

P = price per unit of output in each year

C = variable costs of producing one unit of output

A = cost of acquiring additional stock

N_1 = annual number of stock purchased with project

N_2 = annual number of stock purchased in base case

L = livestock categories (wethers, mixed sheep flock and cattle).

The following subsections describe the methods for estimating the increase in output from livestock $(Q_1 - Q_2)$, operating profits $(P - C)$, and the capital costs of additional livestock $A(N_1 - N_2)$.

The output from livestock With improved pastures and changing economic conditions, cattle increased from about 10 per cent of total dry sheep equivalents (DSE) in the project area in 1960 to about 25 per cent in 1975. [7] The sheep flocks were divided approximately equally between wether flocks with purchased replacements and self-replacing mixed flocks. The output from this livestock was estimated as a product of the area carrying livestock, the livestock per hectare, and the output per head. However, the area lost to gullying in the base case was estimated to total 0.4 per cent of the grazing area and was relatively insignificant.

Potential stocking rates per hectare were considered to depend on soil type and rainfall conditions (see table 4.4). On average, as a result of the project, about half the estimated potential stocking rate increase had been achieved by 1975. It was also predicted that further productivity gains would allow stocking rates to reach 70 per cent of the potential by 1990. This view was based on the assumption that wool prices after 1976 would rise at least as fast as fertiliser prices so that it would be economically sound for farmers to continue to use fertiliser for pasture improvements.

Information provided by a survey of farmers indicated that approximately half the increase in stocking rates would have occurred without the project. Statistics for shires confirmed this estimate since DSE increases in the catchment between 1960 and 1975 were around 190 per cent compared with an 80 per cent increase in neighbouring shires A slightly higher growth rate in DSE was predicted for the base case than for the project case from 1976 to 1990 (see table 4.4).

Table 4.4
Stocking rates in the catchment

Area	Pasture area (ha) excluding forest	Stocking rate (DSE per ha) 1960	1975	1990	Potential	Without project 1975
		With project				
Sedimentary soils Dry area	25,673	1.3	4.2	5.2	6.9	2.7
Sedimentary soils Moderate rainfall	20,764	1.8	5.3	6.6	8.6	3.6
Sedimentary soils Colibañ sub-catchment	2,151	4.9	8.7	10.1	12.3	6.8
Granite soils	13,332	2.7	7.1	8.8	11.4	4.9
Basalt soils	10,143	1.9	5.8	7.3	9.6	3.9
Weighted average (DSE per ha)		1.9	5.4	6.7		3.8
		1960-75		1975-1990		1960-1990
Average annual increase (DSE per ha)		0.218		0.093		0.109
Total DSE		138,206	390,319	484,361		264,329

Source: EHCD Report, op.cit. [1]

The farmer survey also indicated large increases in stocking rates in some 17,000 hectares adjacent to the catchment, some of which were attributable to the extension work of the SCA project. The increase in production in these areas was assessed as half way between project and base case levels.

As well as increasing stocking rates, pasture improvement was estimated to have increased wool cuts for wethers from 4.1 kgs per head in 1960 to 5.6 kgs in 1974, and wool cuts for mixed sheep flocks from 3.1 to 4.3 kgs per head over the same period.

Operating profits for livestock *Wethers:* Historic wool prices, converted to 1974-75 dollars, were used to estimate 1960 to 1975 revenues. The wool price to 1990 was forecast in constant 1974-5 dollars to recover slowly from the 1974-75 price estimated at $1.23 per kg net on the farm.[8] Operating costs allowed for shearing, crutching, dip drenches, sheep replacement and deaths. It was assumed that wethers would be purchased at one year of age and sold at 5 years of age, and that their average annual depreciation over this period represented the cost of replacement. Annual losses due to death also counted as a cost because of the need to purchase additional replacements. Total operating cost was estimated at $2.26 per head in 1974-75, which was equivalent to $0.53 per kg. of wool.

Mixed sheep flock The mixed flock composition was assumed to be 44 per cent wethers, 31 per cent ewes and 25 per cent weaners. Revenue included wool sales and sheep sales at an annual rate of 20 per cent of the flock. Shearing and crutching costs were as for wethers, but dip drenching and veterinary costs were increased by 50 per cent to allow for the additional health problems of ewes and lambs. The service of rams was an extra operating cost. However, as stocks were assumed to be self-replacing, no replacement costs were required.

Cattle A breeding cow enterprise was chosen to represent cattle farming in the catchment. The calf price in 1974-75 was estimated at $40 per head at the farm. This was based on $47 per head at the sale yard minus the selling costs including freight. In 1974-75 dollars, prices per calf before 1974-75 were significantly higher than at that date. The future calf price was also forecast to recover from the 1975 level to approximately the average level applying between 1960 and 1975.

Total operating costs per head, including veterinary costs, fodder, bull replacement costs and deaths were estimated at $27 per head in 1974-75. No herd replacement costs were allowed as it was assumed that unjoined heifers would be purchased at the same price as that received for cull cows.

Capital costs of additional livestock It was estimated that an average of 8,785 extra DSE's were purchased annually between 1960 and 1975 in the project case compared with the base case. On the other hand, from 1976 to 1990 the increase in livestock in the base case was forecast to exceed that in the project case by 1,289 DSE's annually. Capital costs of livestock up to 1975 were based on historic data and future prices on a projection of the 1960 and 1975 trends.

Summary of livestock benefits Table 4.5 summarises the operating profits for the main livestock groups for selected years.

Table 4.5
Operating profits for livestock $1974-75
(for selected years)

Year	Stock composition DSE's			Gross margin per DSE			Weighted operating profit per DSE
	Wethers %	Mixed %	Cattle %	$	$	$	$
1960-61	45	45	10	2.90	3.20	3.60	5.7
1973-74	35	40	25	7.50	8.50	5.80	8.8
1974-75	35	40	25	4.30	4.30	1.30	3.6
1989-90	35	40	25	5.00	4.50	7.00	5.3

Source: EHCD Report op.cit. [1]

Table 4.6 summarises the additional livestock income and capital costs due to the project for selected years.

Table 4.6
Livestock income and capital costs due to project $1974-75
(for selected years)

Year	Cumulative livestock difference DSE's	Average gross profit margin per DSE $	Additional livestock income $	Livestock cost per DSE $	Additional capital costs $
1961-62	8,785	5.7	50,076	12.5	109,816
1973-74	114,195	8.8	1,004,914	8.3	72,890
1974-75	122,977	3.6	442,716	14.6	128,216
1989-90	113,712	5.3	602,672	6.7	− 8,637

Source: EHCD Report op.cit. [1]

The benefits of extra dam capacity

Eppalock dam was completed in 1962 with a capacity of 312,000 megalitres (ml) and an average annual yield of 100,000 ml. The extent to which its capacity and yield were maintained by the soil conservation project and the value of the extra yield are described below.

Dam capacity and water yield Before the dam was built, engineers estimated that without a soil conservation project siltation would occur at the rate of approximately 600 ml per annum. [9] However, it was assumed for the base case that normal pasture improvements and SCA extension work would have reduced annual siltation linearly from 615 ml in 1960-61 to 339 ml in 1990-91.

On the basis of a survey of parts of the lake in 1968, the Victorian State Rivers and Water Supply Commission (SRWSC) estimated that about 1,250 ml of silt had been deposited in the dam since its opening in 1962, corresponding to some 210 ml per annum. But siltation varies with conditions of rainfall and run off and measurement is complicated by the movement of silt within a reservoir. Accordingly, it was assumed that the siltation rate with the project had fallen linearly from 615 ml in 1960-61 to 246 ml in 1967-68, and was a constant 246 ml per annum after 1967-68 by which time the main areas of sheet erosion had been stabilised.

The relationship between dam capacity and yield is complex because it depends upon the amount and the distribution over time of the inflow, the pattern of demand for water and the way in which the dam is operated, especially the precautions taken to avoid depletion during dry periods. Although the SRWSC have a simulation programme to optimise yield it was impractical to run it for each level of dam capacity. On the basis of SRWSC advice, the study assumed that over the capacity range considered in the evaluation, a 1 per cent decrease in capacity would lead to a 1.5 per cent decrease in yield.

Benefits of water yield Any reduction in the supply of water from the Eppalock dam would reduce the output of dairy farms, which are the marginal consumers of the water, paying the lowest price for it. But unfortunately the price paid by the dairy industry could not be assumed to reflect the national benefit from the water. The industry is organised so that the farmer receives the average of the domestic and the export price of butterfat regardless of where the marginal product is sold. Since the domestic price is twice the export price, the farmer is prepared to pay much more for water than he would if he received, as does the nation as a whole, only the returns from the marginal product which is exported. The EHCD report therefore estimated the net value of butterfat for export in a given year as follows:

$$B = Q(V - C) \qquad (2)$$

where B = the net benefit from a megalitre of water
Q = lbs of butterfat produced per megalitre of water

V = the social value of a lb of butterfat
C = the cost of producing a lb of butterfat

Estimation of Q (104 in 1974-75) and of C (16 cents in 1974-75) is fairly straightforward. But V, which depends upon the relationship between butterfat and butter, was estimated as follows:

$$V = \frac{1}{P}(EP - CB)(1 + TI) \qquad (3)$$

		1974-75 estimates
where P	= the percentage of butterfat per lb of butter	.82
EP	= the export price per lb of butter	28 cents
CB	= the cost of manufacturing and transporting 1 lb of butter	7 cents
TI	= income from trading stock	.20
and V	= the social value of butterfat	31 cents/lb

Calculations of the net benefits of irrigation water were made for each year from 1960 to 1990 and the estimated benefits of a megalitre of water fell from over $20 in the mid 1960s to $15 in 1974-75 to a predicted level of less than $10 in the 1980s. However, the farmer who received about 50 cents per pound of butterfat in 1974-75 obtained a benefit in that year of approximately $33 per megalitre of water. The difference was subsidised mainly by other dairy farmers.

Summary of benefits of extra water Table 4.7 summarises the benefits of extra water for selected years.

Table 4.7
Extra water benefits $1974-75 (selected years)

	Additional yield (ml)	Benefit per ml ($)	Total benefits ($)
1960-61	21	24.0	504
1974-75	1,498	15.0	22,470
1989-90	2,696	7.7	20,759

Source: EHCD Report, op.cit.

Environmental benefits

Between 1960 and 1975, 22,000 ha of land were chisel seeded, 119,000 trees planted, numerous gullies grassed over or otherwise improved and hundreds of dams constructed in the Eppalock catchment. The amenity of the area, both visually and in other ways such as increased birdlife, was substantially improved. Environmental benefits to residents were estimated by comparing the average prices of unimproved and fully improved properties and estimating the extent to which productivity increase could account for the difference. The residual difference in price was taken to be a measure of the additional environmental value of the improved land to landholders. [10]

Although values of improved land in 1974-75 varied from $300 to $750 per ha depending on their soils and location in the catchment, the average value was estimated at $375 per ha. The comparable figure for unimproved land was $150 per ha. Typical improved land carries about 7 DSE's per ha, whereas unimproved land carries about 2 DSE's per ha. On the basis of advice from local valuers, which was consistent with the cost and profit estimates used to calculate the social value of agricultural improvements, $35 per ha was allowed for each DSE carried. Therefore, of the $225/ha difference between improved and unimproved land, about $175 was attributed to increased carrying and $50 to environmental improvements. The value of these environmental improvements was assumed to increase linearly with the project from zero in 1960-61 to $50/ha in 1974-75. In the base case, environmental improvements were assumed to rise from zero in 1960-61 to $30 in 1989-90 and to $50 by 2009-10, by which time expenditures of a non-productive nature such as gully planting might have been completed.

Unlike agricultural benefits, environmental benefits were calculated only within the catchment because of difficulties of quantification for other areas. For similar reasons, no environmental benefits were calculated for visitors.

Benefits of local authorities

Local authorities benefited from the project through reduced maintenance costs for roads, bridges and water supplies. Of these savings, the most important and the only ones quantified were the reduced road maintenance costs. Local authorities estimated that road maintenance expenditures attributable to flood damage had fallen steadily from about $30,000 a year in the early 1960s to $15,000 a year by 1975 as a result of the conservation project. It was assumed that in the base case road maintenance expenditures attributable to flooding would have fallen from $30,000 per annum in the early 1960s to $15,000 per annum by 2009-10.

4.4 The major intangible effects of the conservation project

Flood mitigation

The rate of run off in the catchment was significantly reduced by the extensive chisel seeding and gully regulation, especially after light rains or after heavy rain in dry weather periods. Thus diminished, the flows and silt loads caused less damage to fences and farm roadways in the catchment. However, this was partly offset by the cost of repairs to erosion control banks and additional protective fences which were not fully accounted for in the estimates of landholder costs. Outside the catchment, the major flood mitigation is due to the dam rather than to the soil conservation project. The total benefits of flood mitigation owing to the project would therefore be small, but positive.

Water quality of the Eppalock

The dam water quality was assessed for bacteria levels, colour, turbidity, and chemical composition including salinity. However, paucity of data made the conclusions about the with and without project differences somewhat conjectural.

Bacteria levels in the reservoir measured by E coli vary but at times they are high enough to be a health hazard in the town water supplies so that chlorination may be desirable. Although recreation use is the major cause of the high bacteria levels, increased livestock in the catchment due to the project would also raise bacteria levels.

Colour and turbidity of reservoir water – and consequently swimming conditions and drinking water – would improve as a result of the project since run off from the catchment would be reduced. In this way, the need for a filtration plant might be delayed or its operating costs lowered thanks to the reduction in suspended matter in the water. However, the issue is confused because turbidity also reduces the penetration of sunlight and hence algal growth and in this respect clearer water could actually add to the cost of water treatment for domestic use.

Salinity is a most important factor in water quality since it has widespread effects and cannot be cheaply removed from water. In 1968, salinity levels in the reservoir were measured at 400 parts per million, which is not insignificant, but the effect of the project on salinity is uncertain. The establishment of phalaris would reduce run off and salt discharge from the catchment. However, chisel seeding allows water to soak into the soil rather than run off, and while this is beneficial to pasture and trees, it also means that salts from the soil are dissolved and carried into streams.

Increased stocking rates due to the project would probably promote phosphate and nitrate levels in the reservoir which are already significantly higher than in other storages in Victoria. This could cause high algal growth and affect town supplies adversely.

Weighing up these various contrary influences, the EHCD report concluded that on balance the project had marginally decreased the quality of water in the reservoir.

Secondary benefits

As we saw in chapter 2, the expenditure of project surpluses tends to create a second order of value added, but this should not be accounted a project benefit unless the secondary benefits would be higher than in other projects of comparable size. In the case of the soil conservation project the main local town has a population of only 1,200 whose well-being depends more on the recreational use of the dam than on the conservation project. Wool exporters and dairy manufacturers would benefit from the project but their gain would not be out of the ordinary. The EHCD report concluded that local secondary benefits would not be significant and should not be counted in the CBA.

On the other hand, the EHCD report considered that the project may have had a 'research and development' effect which would improve conservation practice and increase output well beyond the project's area of direct influence. Research value is often credited without justification, and to be significant the spillover research effect must be higher than in the marginal alternative project. Nevertheless, it is probably reasonable to claim some research benefit for the Eppalock project.

Soil and fertility loss

Gully and soil erosion would have caused a considerably higher loss of soil in the base case (estimated by the EHCD report at 305 ml in

1967-68) than in the project case. Also the greater soil movement in the base case would have caused a loss of plant nutrients. The EHCD study concluded that the long run effects of soil and fertility loss were probably not fully reflected in the project evaluation and thus the benefits would be understated.

4.5 The results of the Eppalock study

The central result

Table 4.8 summarises the discounted costs and benefits based on the assumptions and estimates described above, using an 8 per cent discount rate and a 30 year evaluation period. The net present value was estimated at $2.91m and the internal rate of return at 25.4 per cent. On balance the intangible effects were also considered beneficial.

Table 4.8
Summary of central evaluation
($'000 discounted to 1960/61 at 8 per cent)

Category	Costs	Benefits
Eppalock internal area		
SCA expenditure	928.0	
Other public authorities	92.6	61.9
Fertiliser subsidy	66.2	
Landholder expenditure on development	407.1	
Landholder expenditure on livestock	743.6	
Livestock returns [a]		3,956.7
Environmental		670.4
Eppalock external area		
SCA expenditure	5.8	
Fertiliser subsidy	7.9	
Landholder expenditure on development	48.2	
Landholder expenditure on livestock	87.6	
Livestock returns [a]		466.9
Rochester area (irrigation benefits)		
Livestock returns [b]		142.7
Intangibles		
Flood mitigation		Some
Water quality, Eppalock Dam	Slight	
Increased knowledge (research)		Significant
Soil fertility		Significant
TOTAL	2,387.0	5,298.6
Net present value	2.91m	
Internal rate of return	25.4 per cent	

[a] Before tax
[b] Before tax but net of expenditure

Source: EHCD Report, op.cit. [1]

Sensitivity tests

A number of sensitivity tests were made, some of which are described below. None affected the high rate of return on the project.

Discount rate Table 4.9 shows the effect of discount rates of 5 per cent, 10 per cent and 15 per cent per annum.

Table 4.9
Variation of central evaluation results with discount rate

Economic criterion	Discount rate			
	5%	8%	10%	15%
Net present value $m	5.03	2.91	2.04	0.82
Internal rate of return %	25.4	25.4	25.4	25.4

Source: EHCD Report, op.cit. [1]

Period of analysis The net present value of the project was shown to vary positively with the period of analysis (see table 4.10).

Table 4.10
Variation of central evaluation results with period of analysis

Evaluation period	Net present value	Internal rate of return
(Years)	($m in 1960/61 at 8%)	(%)
20	1.79	24.2
30	2.91	25.4
40	3.22	25.5

Source: EHCD Report, op.cit. [1]

Agricultural product prices The method of forecasting agricultural product prices by extrapolating past price trends was, as the report states, a 'relatively simple approach'. To estimate the effects of different prices it would be necessary to predict how farmers adapt their output to changes in relative prices. The sensitivity of the results to errors in forecast prices shown in table 4.11 assumes a pro rata change in the gross revenues of farmers without any compensating adjustments in the composition of their output. This assumption results in an overstatement of the fall in net present value with the fall in price.

Table 4.11
Sensitivity of central evaluation results
to agricultural price forecasts

Price forecast	Net present value	Internal rate of return
	($m in 1960/61 at 8%)	(%)
Central evaluation prices	2.91	25.4
25% increase in prices	3.49	26.1
25% decrease in prices	2.33	24.5

Source: EHCD Report, op.cit. [1]

Stocking levels The sensitivity of the results to errors in estimating the difference between base case and project case stocking levels is shown in table 4.12.

Table 4.12
Sensitivity of central evaluation results
to stocking level estimates

Stocking level	Net present value	Internal rate of return
	($m in 1960/61 at 8%)	(%)
Central evaluation level	2.91	25.4
25% increase in differential	3.81	29.1
25% decrease in differential	2.01	21.3

Source: EHCD Report, op.cit. [1]

Choice of discount year If costs and benefits were discounted to 1975-76 rather than to 1960-61, the net present value would be multiplied by $(1 + .08)^{15} = 3.17$, or rise from $2.91m to $9.22m. The internal rate of return would of course not change.

The choice of year to which costs and benefits are discounted cannot change a positive NPV to a negative one nor can it change the ranking of projects as measured by NPV. However, Layard and Walters [11] have argued that the discount date chosen does affect the unit of measurement and that when there are significant undiscounted intangibles spread over the life of the project, it is appropriate to compare them with the quantified net benefits discounted to the middle of the life of the project.

Distributional effects

Distributional effects are analysed below in terms of (a) landholders (b) government (c) the local region and (d) the nation. To do this, I have modified the quantified costs and benefits shown in table 4.8 to allow for taxation, price effects and local secondary benefits.

Total landholder benefits discounted to 1960-61 were estimated in the EHCD report at $5.24m before tax compared with costs of development and livestock of $1.29. After allowing for tax, farm development costs and payments for extra water, net landholder benefits would be around $2.86m. [12]

Government at all levels paid out $1.10m. It expected to receive back an estimated $1.01 in extra taxes from landholders, $0.07 in payments for extra water and $0.06 in reduced road maintenance expenditures.

The primary local Eppalock benefits, i.e. the after tax surpluses of landholders and local government authorities in and immediately around the Eppalock catchment, totalled an estimated $2.86m. Total local benefits allowing for a typical Australian rural regional multiplier of 1.25, calculated by McColl and Throsby [13], would be $3.57m.

As we saw in section 4.3 gross benefits to Rochester area farmers from the extra irrigation water would be approximately twice the social benefits of the water because of the subsidy to butter exports. Rochester farmers would therefore receive about $286,000 minus $70,000 in payments for water and minus $70,000 for tax. Most of the difference between the revenue received by Rochester farmers and the social benefits of butter production is a loss borne by other butter farmers. [14]

To estimate the national benefits of the project, it is necessary to allow for any downward impact the project may have on wool prices which would reduce the return to other Australian wool producers. The change in price as a function of the amount supplied may be derived from the elasticity formula used in the elementary theory of demand as follows:

$$\eta = \frac{dq}{q} \cdot \frac{p}{dp} \qquad (4)$$

$$\text{and } dp = \frac{dq}{q} \cdot p \cdot \frac{1}{\eta} \qquad (5)$$

where η is the elasticity of demand with respect to price changes
q is the existing amount of wool consumed
dq is extra wool consumed because of the project
p is the price of wool
dp is the change in the price.

For example, in 1974-75, the project generated approximately 0.49m kgs of wool compared with a world output of around 2.6 billion kgs. With wool prices at $1.37 per kg, and a price elasticity of -2,[15] the fall in price would be an estimated $0.00013 per kg. Given an Australian wool output of some 0.8 million kgs in 1974-75, the loss to other Australian wool producers was around $104,000 in that year. Discounted at 8 per cent per annum to 1960-61, this was worth $33,000 in present value terms. Annual calculations were not made, but assuming 1974-75 was an average year for the 1960 to 1990 period, there would be a discounted loss of income to Australian wool producers not involved in the project of approximately $1.0m over the whole period. In other words, the project return can be disaggregated into a $1.91m surplus to the nation and a $1.0m gain (in lower prices) to foreign consumers at the expense of Australian wool growers outside the Eppalock area.

4.6 Conclusions of the study

The SCA project had significant net benefits to society, especially to local landowners. No sensitivity test, intangible effect or distributional result affected this conclusion. The study did not seek to justify individual components of the project, for example works aimed primarily at erosion control. The EHCD report argued that it would be inappropriate to separate the soil conservation practices from the agricultural improvements since the components of the project were integrally related.

Landholder benefits were sufficiently great that it might be questioned whether any public project was necessary. However, a study of the project which assumed a base case with no SCA activity at all also indicated a high social return. [4] The major justification of the project appears to be that the SCA provided technology which the farmers would otherwise have adopted only slowly. Held and Clawson [16] concluded similarly that the major reason for public involvement in soil conservation is the 'amazing lack of knowledge' of farmers about soil erosion. Secondly, only the SCA had the interest and ability to organise a regional programme.

It should be emphasised that the EHCD study was essentially practical and designed to assess the major costs and benefits of a large conservation project. Carried out under tight resource constraints, it was not concerned with the finer points of data precision or analytical finesse. Nevertheless, the study illustrates some important features of CBA. These include the importance of the base case, methods for measuring such benefits as increased water storage and environmental amenity, consideration of intangibles and the estimation of distributional effects. Of special importance, the CBA treated soil conservation as a *means* of achieving multiple objectives, such as improved agricultural productivity, more attractive landscapes and increased water storage, rather than as a benefit in its own right.

Notes

[1] The chapter summarises and comments on the 'Economic Evaluation of the Eppalock Catchment Soil Conservation Project', Report 9, Department of Environment, Housing and Community Development, Australian Government Publishing Service, 1978. This report, referred to in the text as the EHCD Report, was developed from an earlier study by G.P. McGowan and Associates, with which I was associated, 'An Economic Analysis of Soil Conservation in the Eppalock Catchment – Victoria'. Vol.II of 'Soil Conservation Study, Merits of Soil Conservation Programs', unpublished 1976. In deference to the Department's terminology, I have used the word project rather than programme to describe the work in the Eppalock catchment, though from an analytic viewpoint the work could be regarded as a series of projects.

[2] Victorian Soil Conservation Authority, 'Eppalock Catchment Project', 1975.

[3] Ultimately landholders also pay for some of the capital works protecting the dam water supplies as they pay for the extra irrigation water they receive.

[4] The base case assumption adopted by the Department reflected the probable alternative situation. On the other hand, to demonstrate the total net returns to soil conservation, the McGowan study op.cit., assumed no SCA activity in the base case. The two studies, which also differed in other assumptions, both estimated the internal rate of return to be around 25 per cent.

[5] The basic costs and benefits should reflect their estimated or forecast mean values rather than their most likely values, see chapter 2. The EHCD report is not specific on this point, stating simply that 'the Central Evaluation . . . used the most reasonable estimates and assumptions', op.cit., p.13.
[6] The cost of the SCA and other public bodies are from tables 3.1 and 3.2 respectively, EHCD report, op.cit. The fertiliser subsidies (table 3.5 EHCD report) refer only to the catchment area, but the EHCD study multiplied them by 1.12 to allow for the external area in the full calculations.
[7] One cow was assumed to equal 10 DSE's while average cattle capital values were assumed to equal 8 times that of average sheep values. EHCD Report, op.cit.
[8] Based on the average FOB price for greasy wool of 23 micron fibre diameter (60 count). The on-farm price excluded a 12 per cent allowance for selling charges, including commission, freight and insurance.
[9] In submissions to the Victorian Parliamentary Works Committee on Eppalock in 1959, Horsfell of the State Rivers and Water Supply Commission estimated that without a soil conservation project, siltation would occur at the rate of approximately 600 ml per annum, while Thomas SCA estimated that the rate would be 675 ml per annum doubling over 10 years.
[10] To the extent that the unimproved land values reflected the potential for agricultural and environmental improvement, the differences between the unimproved and improved values may understate the combined improvement in productivity and environmental quality, but the significance of this is probably slight. Also it might be questioned why the study did not take the change in land values to represent all the agricultural and environmental benefits instead of computing the agricultural benefits directly and using land values to infer an approximate environmental benefit. However, accuracy and insight are generally increased by measuring benefits directly and where possible by disaggregation of the relevant costs and benefits.
[11] Layard P.R.G. and Walters A.A. 'The Date of Discounting in Cost Benefit Studies', *Journal of Transport Economics and Policy*, vol.X, no.3, September 1976, pp 263-6. The Layard-Walters argument assumes that the decision maker is most concerned with the trade-off between the quantified NPV and the intangibles of the one project. But the decision maker may be more concerned with the trade-off between the NPV and the distributional effects of the project, or between the NPV of two projects. In these latter cases, the Layard-Walters recommendation is, I believe, misleading.

[12] The 1974-75 marginal tax rate was 27 per cent for incomes between $2,000 and $5,000 and 35 per cent for incomes between $5,000 and $10,000.
[13] McColl G.D. and Throsby C.D. 'Multiple Objective Benefit Cost Analysis and Regional Development', *Economic Record*, September 1972, pp 201-19.
[14] As butter was subsidised in the 1960s some of the difference between the revenue received by Rochester farmers and the social benefits of butter production would have been borne by the general taxpayer.
[15] Edwards G.W. 'Optimum Tariff Theory and the Wool Industry', Agricultural Economics Society, Adelaide, February 1971, and Minford P. 'Textile Fibre Substitution and Relative Prices', *Australian Journal of Agricultural Economics*, vol.19, no.3, December 1975, pp 175-96.
[16] Held R.B. and Clawson M., *Soil Conservation in Perspective*, John Hopkins Press, 1965, p.254.

5 Cost benefit analysis of sand mining[1]

Sand mining for rutile, zircon and ilmenite, which can be a highly profitable business, often penetrates areas of great natural beauty. In some situations, the mining causes irreversible change in the landscape and, even when the landscape can be substantially rehabilitated, mining naturally involves major alterations in land use in the short and medium term. In consequence, sand mining has been the cause of severe conflict between business and environmental interests and usually governments have attempted a resolution by means of environmental impact inquiries and/or cost benefit studies.

A full cost benefit study of sand mining, especially one concerned with the national benefits, is a complex task. The assessment of costs includes the opportunity cost of the land, which is its value in alternative uses. The assessment of benefits should take account of the degree of foreign ownership, the relative economic protection for sand mining compared with other business sectors, and the nature of the market in which there are few suppliers. Nevertheless it should be emphasised that the evaluation model described below can be applied generally in situations of land use conflict.

In the first section, the nature of the sand mining industry is briefly described. In the following sections an evaluation model of sand mining and methods for quantifying the inputs to the model are discussed. Because of its importance, the opportunity cost of land affected by sand mining is discussed in a separate section. Conclusions on cost benefit analysis and sand mining are drawn in the final section.

5.1 The sand mining industry

The rutile market

Over three quarters of rutile output is sold to the titanium dioxide pigment industry for use in paints, printing inks, plastics and paper. The remainder is used in welding rod coatings and in titanium metal. Collectively these form a fast growing market so that rutile output and prices have increased significantly since the early 1960s.

Table 5.1
Rutile output and prices
(for selected years)

	World output (tonnes)	Australian price FOB ($ per tonne)	CPI
1963	168,000	67	100
1971	375,000	87	122
1975	330,000	168 (LME price = $200 to $330)	187

Sources: *Minerals Yearbook*, US Department of the Interior. Bureau of Mines Mining Annual Review, 1975, published by *Mining Journal*. Fraser Island Environmental Inquiry, op. cit.

Until recently, Australia produced over 95 per cent of the world output of rutile, although more than half the equity in Australian sand mining businesses is held by non-Australians. [3] Environmental constraints on the exploitation of Australian reserves were a major cause of the fall in world output and the rise in prices in the early 1970s.

The titanian dioxide pigment industry will probably continue to grow faster than national incomes. However, the demand for rutile depends mostly upon its competitiveness in this market in which it presently has a 10 per cent share, compared with the nearly 90 per cent share of natural ilmenite (in 1977, 2 per cent of the market was taken by beneficiated ilmenite which is regarded as synthetic rutile). Paint manufacturers prefer rutile to ilmenite because it provides better covering power. Also, there is environmental pressure on pigment manufacturers to use the chloride process which requires natural or synthetic rutile rather than the sulphate process which depends on ilmenite. But the potentially high demand for natural rutile is subject to severe price competition from both ilmenite and synthetic rutile, and is consequently price elastic. [4]

Australian rutile reserves are sufficient to satisfy a demand for rutile of over 1 million tonnes per annum in the mid-1980s. However, an Australian strategy must account for rival output from South Africa of around 100,000 tonnes p.a. in 1977, which could increase, and for the possibility that other countries, notably Sierra Leone, might exploit rutile reserves.

The zircon market

Zircon has attractive chemical characteristics [5] and many uses in foundry sands and refractories, ceramics, metals, chemicals and abrasives, which have brought about a high growth in world output (75 per cent of which is Australian) and, in recent years, high price increases (see table 5.2).

Table 5.2
Zircon output and prices

	World output (tonnes)	Australian price FOB $
1963	250,000 [a]	26
1971	490,000 [a]	36
1975	520,000	148 (LME price = $170 to $330

[a] Estimate

Sources: *Minerals Yearbook*, US Department of the Interior. Bureau of Mines Mining Annual Review, 1975, published by *Mining Journal*. Fraser Island Environmental Inquiry, op. cit.

Zircon's usefulness is such that demand for it will probably grow at least as fast as national incomes even at the high prices prevailing in the mid 1970s. However, expansion of zircon supplies in Australia, the US and South Africa may cause significant excess supply by 1980. Fortunately for suppliers, the demand for zircon appears price elastic in a number of industries, especially foundries, so that the supply should be sold without a substantial fall in its price. In the Moreton Island study [1], a price elasticity of −2 was considered reasonable, and the market for zircon in 1980 was forecast to clear at $130 per tonne in 1975 prices.

The ilmenite market

World output of ilmenite, virtually all of which is used in the pigment industry, increased from 2.0 million tonnes in 1963 to 3.6 million tonnes in 1973. Australia produced one-fifth of world output and received about $15 per tonne FOB in 1975.

World reserves of ilmenite are sufficient to meet the increasing demands of the pigment industry and any other possible uses for ilmenite without large price increases. Australia suffers the problems of distance from markets and excessive chromite in some ilmenite reserves. On the other hand, the ilmenite is produced at low cost from sands, rather than from rock as it is in many other places, and is often a by-product of rutile and zircon.

5.2 An evaluation model for sand mining

The cost benefit model applied to sand mining may be expressed in rather general terms as follows:

$$NPV = \sum_{i=1}^{n} \frac{(PQ - SC + E_b - E_c)_i}{(1+r)^i} \qquad (1)$$

where NPV = net present value
P = price of mineral sand
Q = quantity sold
SC = social cost of resources used in production
E_b = external benefits
E_c = external costs, including land use costs
r = the discount rate
i = year in the life of the project
n = number of years in life of the project.

The external benefits include social assets created by the mineral sand companies, such as roads and ports. External costs include things like water pollution and destruction of fauna and flora. The classification of land use costs as an externality, E_c, rather than as a resource cost of production, SC, reflects the Australian situation where sand mining frequently occurs in areas providing non-marketed public goods, especially recreational amenities. In many studies, however, this general model is refined (a) to distinguish the national benefits of sand mining from foreign benefits and (b) to enable the stream of surpluses generated by the project to be discounted by the social time preference rate rather than the opportunity cost of capital.

To estimate the national benefits of sand mining, the profits earned on capital owned by non-residents are deducted from the total returns. [6] This makes it necessary to take account of taxation and similar payments to the home government. Therefore if the project were wholly foreign owned, national benefits in any year might be assessed as follows:

$$B_1 = t\,(PQ - C - D - RPQ - L) + RPQ + L + (M - SC) - tok + E_b - E_c \qquad (2)$$

where B_1 = net national benefit per annum from foreign ownership
t = average rate of tax on profits
PQ = value of mineral sands produced
C = total current costs of production per annum (note that these are financial costs and not resource costs)
D = depreciation on capital per annum (again in financial terms)
R = royalties and local government rates as per cent of value of output
L = other payments to state and local governments for leases etc.
M = market costs of inputs of local labour and materials
SC = social costs of inputs of local labour and materials
o = return on capital in alternative local use
k = project capital which would otherwise be employed in the domestic economy
E_b, E_c = external benefits and costs respectively.

Given foreign ownership, the gross national benefit is the sum of the taxes to the host governments, the difference between market and accounting prices for inputs of local labour and materials, and the external benefits to the local community. It is important to note that estimated tax gains depend upon the financial costs of the project (C and D) whereas the surplus on employment of labour and materials depends on their real resource costs (SC) as well as on their market price (M).

The national cost of the project is the cost of foreign equity capital to the local economy (tok) and the external costs to the local community. The cost of this foreign capital (which is its opportunity cost to the local economy) can be expressed as the product of the tax rate, the financial return on capital in alternative local uses, and the proportion of the capital which would be re-employed in the local economy if it were not used in the sand mining project. In some cases, the capital would not otherwise be employed in the local economy, in which case its opportunity cost is zero.

On the other hand, with wholly domestic ownership, national

benefits in any year may be assessed as

$$B_2 = PQ - SC - ED - SOC.F + E_b - E_c \quad (3)$$

where B_2 = the net national benefit per annum from domestic ownership
ED = economic depreciation of capital (note not financial depreciation as in equation 2)
SOC = the social opportunity cost of capital
F = the non-depreciated capital cost of the project in any year.

The other symbols are as before.

Assuming that the project is part foreign and part local ownership,

$$B = (I - W) B_1 + WB_2 \quad (4)$$

where B = total net national benefit per annum
and W = the proportion of the project which is locally owned.

Finally the stream of annual benefits must be converted into a present value of benefits. This may be done as follows:

$$NPV = \sum_{i=1}^{n} \left[\frac{P_i B_i}{(1 + r)^i} + \frac{(1 - P_i)B_i(1 + SOC)^{n-i}}{(1 + r)^n} \right] \quad (5)$$

where B_i = total net national benefit in year i (i = 1 . . . n)
P_i = proportion of benefits consumed in year i
r = the social time preference rate of discount.

Since the appropriate opportunity cost of capital has been taken into account in equations 2 and 3, it is legitimate in this instance to discount the annual surpluses available for domestic consumption, (the B_i in equation 5) by the social time preference rate. As shown in equation 5, the analyst may wish to allow for some of the surplus to be reinvested at the social opportunity cost of capital and to discount this new compound total by the social time preference rate. However, it has been assumed in most sand mining studies that all the surplus will be consumed (i.e. P = 1 in equation 5).

5.3 Quantifying inputs to the evaluation model

Determination of the amount of foreign ownership and the various taxation rates relevant to the project does not raise special analytical problems. The discussion below therefore centres on quantifying the returns to the project, PQ, the social operating costs, SC, and the externalities, E_b and E_c.

Mineral sand prices are normally forecast as a function of the future world demand and supply of mineral sand products. Excess demand will raise prices and excess supply will reduce them. However, demand and supply forecasts are complicated in an oligopolistic industry, such as rutile mining when implementation of a major project can itself affect the forecasts. Firstly, a decision to commit a sand mining project, and therefore to establish a capacity to guarantee mineral sand supplies, may increase the demand for them. This is particularly true of rutile which may be substituted for ilmenite if manufacturers can confidently convert from the sulphate to the chloride process for pigment manufacture. Secondly, in an oligopolistic market, demand for the product depends on marketing effort. And thirdly, committed production plans of one producer or country may discourage production by other producers or countries. These factors are difficult to model but forecasts of rutile and, to a lesser extent, zircon prices should not ignore the possibility that a large project could influence both the demand for the mineral and the amount supplied by competitors.

Forecasts of output from a mineral project are generally based on establishing the amount of mineral by grade of ore and a commercial cut off grade below which exploitation of the ore is unprofitable. Forecasts will naturally be uncertain because the quality of the ore is established by sample drilling and because the economics of exploitation may change. Also from the social viewpoint the commercially determined level of output may not be optimal when tariff protection or government subsidies vary greatly by economic sectors. Some writers argue that protected sectors, such as agriculture and mining compared with manufacturing in Australia, should be encouraged. [8] The contention is that the efficiency of investment and hence the level of national income would be increased if each industry were to operate under a similar scale of taxes and subsidies. Otherwise, industries which are less taxed, or more subsidised and protected, are encouraged even if they are inefficient. Cost benefit analysis could take account of this argument by estimating the additional value added that would accrue to a project if it had equivalent protection to that enjoyed on average by other industries.

For example an export subsidy for sand mining would make lower grade ore commercially viable and increase output and value added.

However although many would agree that less protected industries should be encouraged, there is much disagreement as to the means by which this should be achieved. First there are theoretical objections to the principle of equal protection because no allowance is made for variations in the elasticity of demand. [9] Second, and from a practical viewpoint of more importance, it may be argued that it is preferable to reduce high tariffs rather than compensate for them. [10] Third, owing to the many ways of measuring and allowing for differences in effective protection levels, the introduction of tariff compensation into cost benefit studies of particular projects jeopardises the principle of consistency in project appraisal. Thus it would seem that, although there may be a good case for considering tariff compensation at the industry level, it is not practical to introduce it for project evaluation.

Estimating the social costs of sand mining projects raises fewer special problems of principle than of practice. In principle, the resources used for each stage of the operation, including the rehabilitation of the land would be identified and costed along normal cost benefit lines as described in chapter 2. For example, accounting prices would be estimated to reflect the costs of employing unemployed workers or the value of foreign exchange earnings if the exchange rate were over-valued. In practice, the reticence of mining companies to divulge commercial secrets, (one company refused even to appear at the Fraser Island Inquiry), and the modest funds available for cost benefit studies have encouraged short cut methods of costing projects. One such method is to estimate the companies' average cost to revenue ratios on the basis of their annual accounts and extrapolate these ratios to the project under study. [11] This procedure has the major disadvantages of assuming that a linear relationship exists between costs and revenues and that all projects are similar in terms of costs. It is clearly inferior to a detailed costing of the project.

The main external benefits of sand mining are the residual values of facilities such as ports, roads and structures left after completion of the mining. As a rough guide it is sometimes assumed that the residual value of these facilities would be equivalent to their construction cost. But this represents their maximum value and is relevant only on the assumption that the facilities would be built if the sand mining did not occur. If the facilities would be little used, their residual value would be their estimated value to users which may well be less than their construction cost.

Apart from land use costs, which are discussed below, the major external cost of a sand mining project is its effect on prices and therefore on the revenues received by other national producers. In a simple model, these effects would be determined according to the price elasticity of demand. If this price elasticity were say -1, then an increase in world output of say 5 per cent would cause the prices received by other producers to fall by some 5 per cent. The estimated impact of the project on mineral sand prices would be reduced if allowance was made for the project's impact on the demand for mineral sands and the output of other producers. However, even with these allowances, the effect of the project on the surpluses of other domestic producers may appear to make the project non-viable unless some offsetting benefit is attached to the gains of foreign consumers.

The external cost argument presupposes that the true marginal project can be identified. If any project can be described as marginal, any project considered separately may be non-viable when the 'external costs' are counted against it, although there is a viable industry of substantial size. But in practice little output is fixed for more than a few months ahead; virtually all output is marginal and simply has higher or lower marginal costs. It seems unreasonable therefore to assume that all projects except the one under consideration are fixed. [12] Likewise it would be wrong to prefer an existing sand mining project with high economic and environmental costs to a new project with lower costs. Ideally when such large externalities occur, an industry-wide cost benefit analysis is required to determine simultaneously the optimum level of output for the industry and which projects have the lowest economic and environmental costs. If this is not possible, I believe it is misleading to count the effect the project may have on the prices received by other producers as a cost to it, because this assumes without justification that the project produces the marginal output for the industry.

5.4 The land use costs of sand mining

It is assumed below that the sand mining would take place in undeveloped public land the prime use of which is recreation, and in which there are no established property rights. The cost benefit analyst would estimate therefore the amount individuals would be willing to pay for the use of the land, rather than the amount they would require in compensation for its loss. [13] The value of the land is considered below in terms of (a) the direct benefits to recreational users and (b) other benefits to society.

The benefits of recreation

The benefits of recreational areas to users depend on the number of user-trips and the benefits per trip. These can be represented by the area under the demand curve as in figure 5.1. The more substitutes there are for the beach, the shallower will be the slope of the demand curve and the lower the recreational benefits. If there are no beach maintenance costs, the recreational benefits are given by areas A + B: if there are beach maintenance costs, the net benefits equal area A.

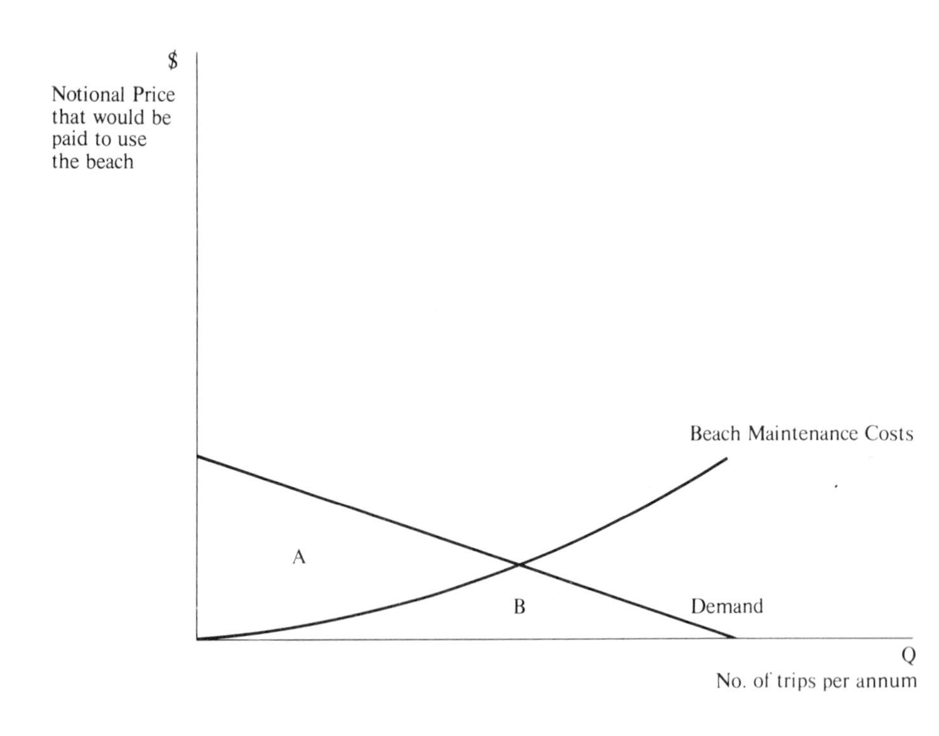

Figure 5.1 Recreational benefits of a beach

Early attempts to quantify recreational benefits tended to proceed broadly as follows. [14] The analyst would estimate a zone of influence around the recreational area, its population and participation rates per head of population, based perhaps on analogous situations elsewhere. He would then attribute a value to the activity depending on its quality, possibly based on some prescribed formula. For example, in 1964, American federal legislation [15] attempted to define uniform values for recreational benefits, which varied from US $0.50 to US $6.0 per day depending on the quality of the benefit. In time, however, dissatisfaction with the crudity of the forecasting method (which made no allowance for substitute recreations for instance) and with the tenuous basis for the benefit valuations, led to the development of alternative forecasting and valuation methods, notably the Hotelling-Clawson (HC) method. [16]

The basic idea underlying the HC method is that the number of recreational trips falls with distance from the place of recreation. If the relationship between trips and distance can be observed, it is possible in principle to estimate the demand curve for the recreational area. The method may best be illustrated by a simple example. Suppose that there are 3 communities with similar types of households located 1, 5 and 10 kms from the beach, that travel costs including time costs are $1 per km, and that each household makes 45, 25 or zero trips to the beach per annum depending on their distance from it. The relationship between travel costs and beach trips is shown in figure 5.2.

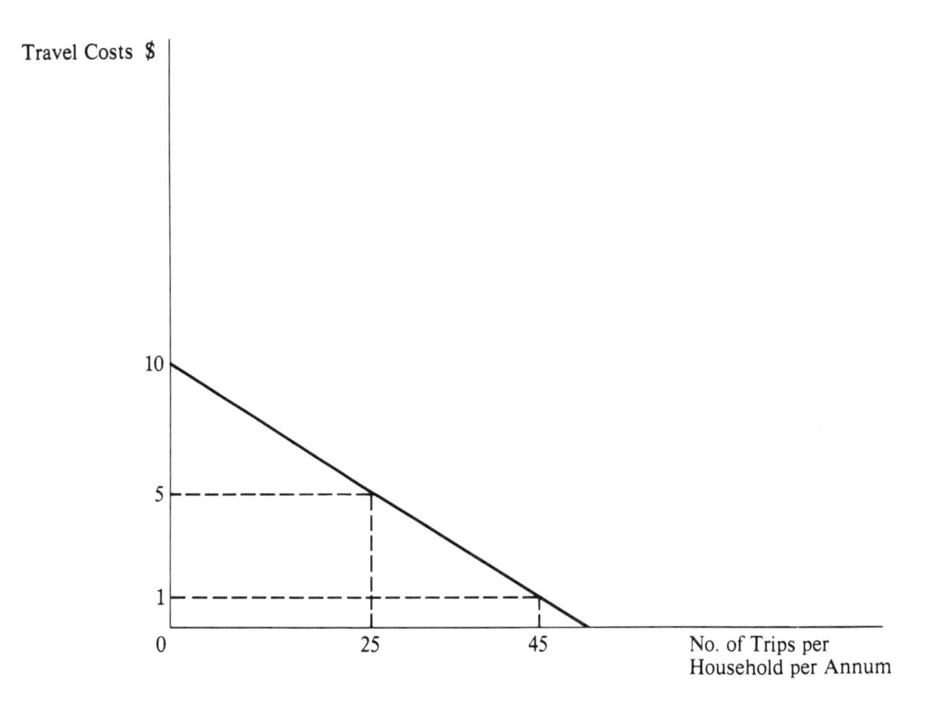

Figure 5.2 Travel costs and beach trips

The demand for trips to the beach can now be estimated in the following way. Since all households in this example are assumed to be similar, we can deduce that if a price of $4 were charged for the use of the beach, those households living 1 km from the beach would now face a total cost, including travel, of $5 per beach trip and would make 25 such trips. At a charge of $9, making a total cost of $10 per beach trip, none would use the beach. Likewise it may be inferred that at a charge of $5, no households living 5 kms from the beach would use it. Figures 5.3 and 5.4 show the demand for the beach of households 1 and 5 kms from it respectively. The areas under the demand curves are the consumer surpluses of households using the beach and represent the estimated amount they would be willing to pay to use the beach.

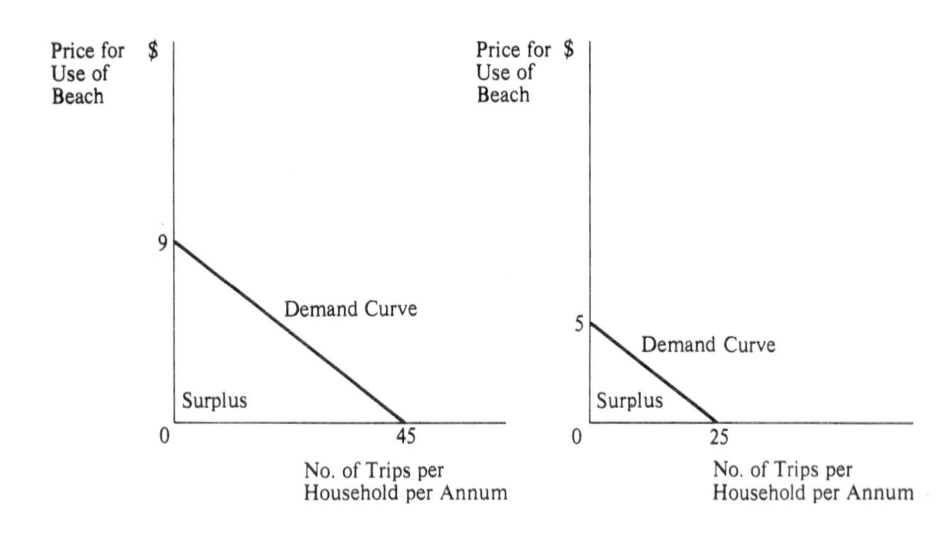

Figure 5.3 Beach demand by households 1 km from the beach

Figure 5.4 Beach demand by households 5 km from the beach

In practice it is of course necessary to refine the HC method quite substantially, especially to allow for populations with different characteristics and for the effect of competitive recreational areas. For example, to make some allowance for household differences, Mansfield [17] estimated a demand function for leisure trips in the English lake district which took account of car ownership as follows:

$$T = a + bW + cC^{-2} \tag{6}$$

where T was trips per head of population, W was cars per household and C was the travel cost. Herfindahl and Kneese [14] also describe how gravity model techniques can be used to model the extent to which demand for an area is affected by competitive recreational areas.

Three further complications in the case of sand mining should be recognised. First, the demand for recreation in the sand mining area must be forecast annually at least for the duration of the life of the sand mining project. Generally the demand for a natural recreational facility grows at a higher rate than income per household because the demand for recreation is income elastic and the supply of natural recreational facilities is inelastic. Allowance also must be made for the increase in population. Second, if sand mining does not preclude recreation, it is necessary to estimate the demand for recreation with the project as well as without it. The social opportunity cost of the land is then the loss of surplus, shown as the hatched area in figure 5.5.

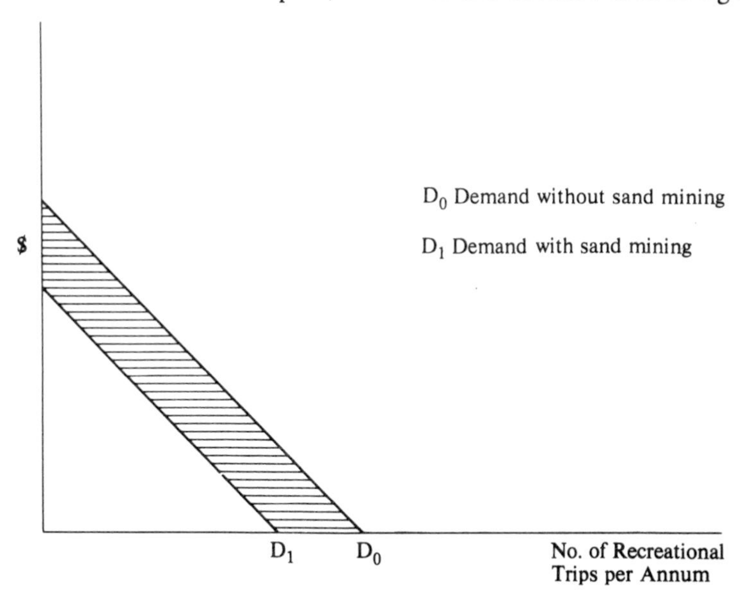

Figure 5.5 Recreational demand with and without sand mining

Third, there may be differences in the recreational value of the land in the post sand mining period. Land rehabilitated after sand mining is generally considered less attractive for recreation than land undisturbed by sand mining, although this will not necessarily be so.

Other benefits of natural areas lost because of sand mining

Indirect benefits Indirect benefits occur when an asset provides services other than those which it is designed to provide, or in the case of natural assets which it normally provides. As we saw in chapter 2, this distinction between the direct and indirect benefits of an asset or project is ultimately arbitrary and is used only for convenience.

It is often claimed that untouched natural areas have scientific value. For example, a major indirect benefit claimed for the ecosystems on Fraser Island was their scientific value. 'There was uncontested expert evidence that Fraser Island is of importance as a natural geomorphological laboratory and a considerable amount of scientific work is still required to 'decide' its geological and geomorphological history' [18] or again 'There was uncontested evidence that many of the lakes on Fraser Island have high value for scientific studies in disciplines such as geomorphology, palynology (palaeontology) and ecology'. [19] Indeed the Fraser Island Report repeated similar scientific claims many times [20] but it never appeared to question the social value of these scientific studies or the extent to which the sand mining operations would interfere with scientific knowledge. While it would be impossible to predict and quantify accurately the benefits of all scientific research, some scepticism about its value is a necessary basis for a rational trade-off of costs and benefits even when these are unquantified.

Another example of Fraser Island's indirect benefits is its inspiration to artists, such as Sidney Nolan and Patrick White. [21] Whether, out of the 163,000 hectares of the island, sand mining of the maximum amount proposed by the mining companies (16,000 hectares) or of some lesser amount, would be compatible with maintaining the Island's awe inspiring character calls for a subjective view. However most people, including many economists, would doubtless agree that artistic inspiration from the Island is a major indirect benefit, albeit unquantified, which should be considered in the decision.

Option benefits 'Option benefits' is a much used but often ill-defined umbrella term. [22] In economics, it refers to the notion that in an uncertain situation, as the future is by definition, individuals may value the option of having a service available for their use. In other words, the present value of a commodity which will be available in the future may be greater than its expected value in use. As the validity of this argument was discussed in chapter 2, only our conclusion is repeated here, that an asset has an option value only when change is irreversible *and* when our knowledge of future costs and benefits arising from its use may substantially improve with time.

In the case of most sand mining operations, there is relatively little uncertainty about the recreational opportunity costs of the areas in question and estimates of these costs are unlikely to change greatly over a few years. Sand mining operations can be rapidly halted. Moreover, after the operations, which normally last 10 to 25 years, sand dunes can be rehabilitated for recreational use even though the original ecosystem cannot be replicated. The option value of most sand mining areas would therefore be negligible. [23]

Interdependent benefits Interdependent benefits arise when individuals do not use a commodity or service even indirectly (as when they read a Patrick White novel), but obtain pleasure from other people using it. Such a pleasure may occur for example when children transmit their enjoyment of the beach to their parents. Alternatively the pleasure may be motivated by philanthropic feelings. Thus individuals contribute to conservation funds to preserve wilderness areas which neither they nor their family or friends may ever see. As noted in chapter 2 however, interdependent benefits are rarely included in CBA because they are difficult to estimate. Also it would be difficult to argue that the interdependent benefits arising from the use of beaches are greater than those arising from say football matches (or university lectures!).

Existence benefits An existence benefit occurs in our terminology when a value is placed on the flora or fauna of an ecosystem, or on the whole ecosystem for its own sake. If the flora and fauna of ecosystems have value to human society – for example recreational, visual or scientific – they would be included in the category of direct or indirect benefits to individuals, though these benefits may not always be quantifiable. Following this distinction, there is no good case for including existence benefits in CBA. Studies which claim existence benefits tend either to count things as benefits which do not matter to individuals or to double count the benefits. As a general principle it is preferable to measure changes in the utility of goods and services available from the environment rather than attach a cost to ecological change per se which may indeed be a change for the better.

5.5 Conclusions

From a national viewpoint, the unregulated operation of the sand mining industry would almost certainly result in abuse of environmental resources and in non-optimal levels of output in many areas and possibly also too little local ownership. *Prima facie* there is a strong case for governmental role in policy making for the sand mining industry, although there may also be a cost in government involvement.

Many of the effects of sand mining can be estimated with the assistance of cost benefit analysis. However, the benefits of recreational or wilderness areas are always difficult to value and are especially so when conflicting assumptions may be made about property rights with respect to such areas. Analytical difficulties also arise from attempts to allow for tariff compensation or for the effect of the output of a project on the surpluses of other producers within the framework of individual project appraisal. These latter difficulties could be handled better within the framework of a national strategy for sand mining. This would be based on, amongst other things, (a) assessment of effective protection levels in sand mining and other industries and development of methods of tariff compensation which would not exacerbate the structural distortion of the economy, (b) estimates of the demand for each mineral sand with particular attention to the oligopolistic nature of the industry and to the critical price elasticities of demand, and (c) evaluation of the national economic and environmental costs of sand mining in different places and at different levels of output. This data combined with an evaluation model for maximising national benefits would enable the analyst to recommend rates and locations of resource exploitation and levels of foreign ownership which should be of considerable use to decision makers.

Notes

[1] Some of the views in this chapter were expressed originally in 'A Review of the Mineral Sands Industry' or in 'Economic Evaluation of Net National Benefits from Sandmining on Moreton Island' by Throsby C.D. and Abelson P.W. See *Moreton Island Environmental Impact Study and Strategic Plan*, A.A. Heath and Partners, 1976, pp 2-148 to 2-177.

[2] Major conflicts have occurred at Tuggerah and around the Myall Lakes in New South Wales and at Cooloolabah, Moreton Island and most notoriously over Fraser Island in Queensland. The major study

of sand mining was the 'Fraser Island Environmental Inquiry', Australian Government Publishing Service, 1976. See also 'Economic Study of Mineral Sand Mining Proposals at North Entrance, N.S.W.', International Engineering Service Consortium Pty Ltd., 1971, and the Moreton Island studies, op.cit.

[3] McKern R.B. *Multinational Enterprise and Natural Resources'*, McGraw Hill, Sydney, 1976. Equity interests in Australian output varied from 100 per cent Australian (Rutile and Zircon Pty Ltd.) to 100 per cent non-Australian (Dillinghams Pty Ltd.). In aggregate over half the ownership of the 23 mineral sand businesses was non-Australian.

[4] Some writers have argued fallaciously that as rutile is only a small proportion of the final price of pigment, the demand for rutile will be price inelastic, e.g. Fitzgibbon A. and Hendricks H. 'An Economic Evaluation of the Proposed Cooloola Sand Mining Project', *Economic Analysis and Policy 1* (2),1970, pp 58-73.

[5] Attractive chemical characteristics include high refractoriness, high density, low thermal expansion, chemical stability and good bonding characteristics. Foley E. 'Users of Beach Mineral Sands', 1976, pp 2-119 to 2-147 in the Moreton Bay Study, op.cit. [1]

[6] Our CBA model attempts to exclude surpluses from mineral sand operations which would accrue to foreigners. Of course, if national benefits are the maximand, any external costs and benefits experienced by foreigners, for example by tourists, should also be given zero weight in the analysis.

[7] I stress the impact that the supply of a project may have on the demand for its output because it has often been assumed in sand mining studies that the marginal project must inevitably reduce mineral sand prices. Of course, without sophisticated econometric studies of the sand mining industry, it would be difficult to quantify accurately the relationships described in the text.

[8] Harris S., 'Tariff compensation: sufficient justification for assistance to Australian agriculture?', *Australian Journal of Agricultural Economics*, vol.19, no.31, December 1975, pp 131-145.

[9] There is a greater loss of social surplus from high tariffs or taxes when demand is price elastic than when it is inelastic. In the perfectly inelastic case, there is no reallocation of resources or investment, but only a redistribution of the surplus from the consumer to the government. Of course, the matter is further complicated if some consumers are foreigners and some are nationals.

[10] Industries Assistance Commission Annual Report, 1974-75, AGPS.

[11] For example, see North Entrance and Moreton Island studies,

op.cit., and Cuthbertson B.A. 'Evidence to Fraser Island Environmental Enquiry', 1975.
[12] Perhaps it should be noted here that both Professor Throsby, my collaborator on the Moreton Island study, and Professor McColl, the economic adviser on the Fraser Island study, have argued privately with me that it is legitimate from a policy viewpoint to consider the project under study as the marginal project of the industry.
[13] The implications for the evaluation of the alternative assumption that individuals should be compensated for the loss of public land are discussed in chapter 2.
[14] This basic process is outlined in Herfindahl O.C. and Kneese A.V., *The Economics of Natural Resources*, Charles E. Merrill Publishing Company, 1974, pp 261-7.
[15] Senate Document 97, 'Policies, Standards and Procedures in the Formulation, Evaluation and Review of Plans for Use and Development of Water and Related Land Resources: Supplement no.1. Evaluation Standards for Primary Outdoor Recreation Benefits', ad hoc Water Resources Council, Washington DC, 4 June 1964.
[16] Clawson M. 'Methods of Measuring Demand for and Value of Outdoor Recreation', *Resources for the Future*, Reprint no.10; 1959.
[17] Mansfield N.W. 'The Estimation of Benefits from Recreation Sites and the Provision of a New Recreation Facility', *Regional Studies*, vol.5, no.2, pp 55-69.
[18] Fraser Island Environmental Inquiry, op.cit., p.10.
[19] Fraser Island Environmental Inquiry, op.cit., p.94.
[20] Fraser Island Environmental Inquiry, op.cit., pp 7, 28 and 60.
[21] Fraser Island Environmental Inquiry, op.cit., p.64. Two of Patrick White's novels were inspired by Fraser Island, *The Eye of the Storm* and a forthcoming one on the story of Eliza Fraser after whom the Island was named.
[22] For example, the Fraser Island Report stated (p.152), 'The procedures described above do not take account of the value of areas preserved to people who benefit from a knowledge that irreplaceable natural areas exist and will continue to exist for the benefit of future generations, even though they may not visit the area themselves. These so called "option values" appear directly relevant to Fraser Island'. However, this does not fit the definition of option values employed by economists who, I believe, originated the concept. Following the terminology of this book, these benefits claimed in the Fraser Island Report would be called 'interdependent benefits'.

[23] It might be argued that there is an option value from the possible scientific benefits of research in sand mining areas, but one must be wary of double counting scientific benefits if they have already been counted as indirect benefits.

6 Cost benefit analysis of airport location

The analysis of airport location needs to be considered in the context of the problems giving rise to the study and of alternative solutions to them. By far the most common problem is air traffic congestion in peak periods, though obsolescent airport facilities or excessive aircraft noise may also be serious problems. Figure 6.1 illustrates some of the major options for dealing with air traffic congestion.

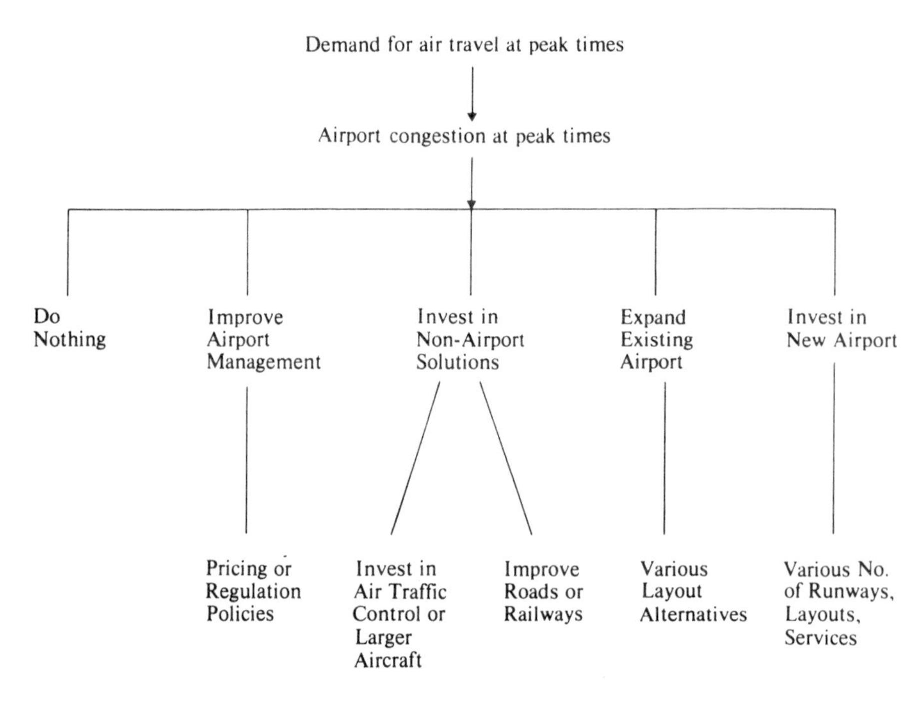

Figure 6.1 Air traffic congestion and some solutions

As figure 6.1 shows, the number of possible solutions to the airport congestion problem is large. Suppose for example that within the 'invest in new airport' strategy there are 10 possible new airport locations, of four possible sizes (1, 2, 3 or 4 runways), with 3 alternative layouts for each site, and a choice of comprehensive or only domestic services. There would then be 10 x 4 x 3 x 2 = 240 options within the 'new airport' strategy as well as options within other possible strategies. The options are further multiplied if a time dimension is added to each. For example a runway may be scheduled to open in any year between say 1985 and 2000.

In this chapter, therefore, the case for a new airport compared with other major alternatives is examined first. Then, assuming that a new airport can be justified, the planning of an airport location study is discussed. Such a study necessarily involves a variety of dimensions, notably: forecasts of air traffic demand, estimates of quantified and unquantified airport location costs, and optimisation of timing in airport development. These issues are considered in turn in sections 3, 4 and 5 respectively. The distribution of costs and benefits is discussed in section 6 and possible uses of the analysis for decision making purposes in section 7. This is followed by a brief summary and conclusion.

6.1 Evaluation of a new airport

In considering the case for a new airport it is convenient to start by evaluating it in comparison with the do-nothing alternative which includes no change in airport management policies and no investment in non-airport solutions. Action in these areas is considered afterwards. It should be noted that although for convenience of expression I refer to 'the case for a new airport', in fact the real need may be only for a new runway plus supporting services which is a much more modest concept. [1]

The major benefits and costs of a new airport are shown in table 6.1. Passenger benefits from use of the new airport arise primarily from reduced delay costs at peak travel hours and improved accessibility, since some passengers will live closer to the new airport than to the existing one. For other passengers the new airport will be less convenient than the existing one, but presumably the gain in reduced delay will more than offset the relatively inconvenient access or they would not use the new airport. Of course, passengers at the existing airport will also benefit from reduced delays.

Airport construction costs should include the full social costs of land. This means that where necessary allowances should be made for losses of householder surplus and for costs incurred in the relocation of facilities like airforce bases. The additional operating cost of the

Table 6.1
Major benefits and costs of a new airport

Benefits	Passenger benefits from use of new airport Passenger benefits at existing airport
Costs	Airport construction costs (including land costs) Extra airport operating costs Extra surface access costs not paid for by passengers
Benefits or costs	Change in flying costs Change in noise costs Urbanisation effects Other items (e.g. effect on general aviation)

new airport will be partly offset however by the fall in operating costs at the existing airport compared with what would have occurred without the new airport. The provision of extra surface access infrastructure or of extra access operations is also a cost debitable to the new airport insofar as these are not paid for by passengers.

A number of consequences of the new airport may turn out to be beneficial or costly. For example, flying distances and associated costs may be reduced or increased as a result of the new airport. Similarly, if population around the new airport is thin, noise costs for the two airports together might be smaller than for the existing airport alone. However, normally total noise costs would increase with a new airport. Various other costs and benefits, notably the effects on residential patterns, would probably be unquantified unless a detailed evaluation of the new airport was made.

Although estimated benefits of a new airport may exceed estimated costs (detailed estimation methods are discussed below) by comparison with 'doing nothing', a new airport can be an expensive way to reduce congestion. The possibility of deferring the airport and instituting peak management policies should therefore be considered.

Figure 6.2 shows two demand curves (D_0 and D_1) for peak air trips and typical cost curves for marginal private and marginal social costs per peak trip. The marginal private costs are those incurred by the air passenger. They include the airport charges levied directly on him or passed on to him by the airlines and any delay which he experiences. The marginal social costs include airport and airline operating costs at peak times, the congestion costs borne by the air passenger and those he imposes on others, and the noise costs inflicted on local residents.

Unless the airport's charges cover all marginal social costs other than the passenger's own congestion costs, marginal social costs exceed marginal private costs as shown in figure 6.2. At some point, shown as A in figure 6.2, it becomes cheaper to bring forward the construction of a new airport than to allow congestion costs to escalate.

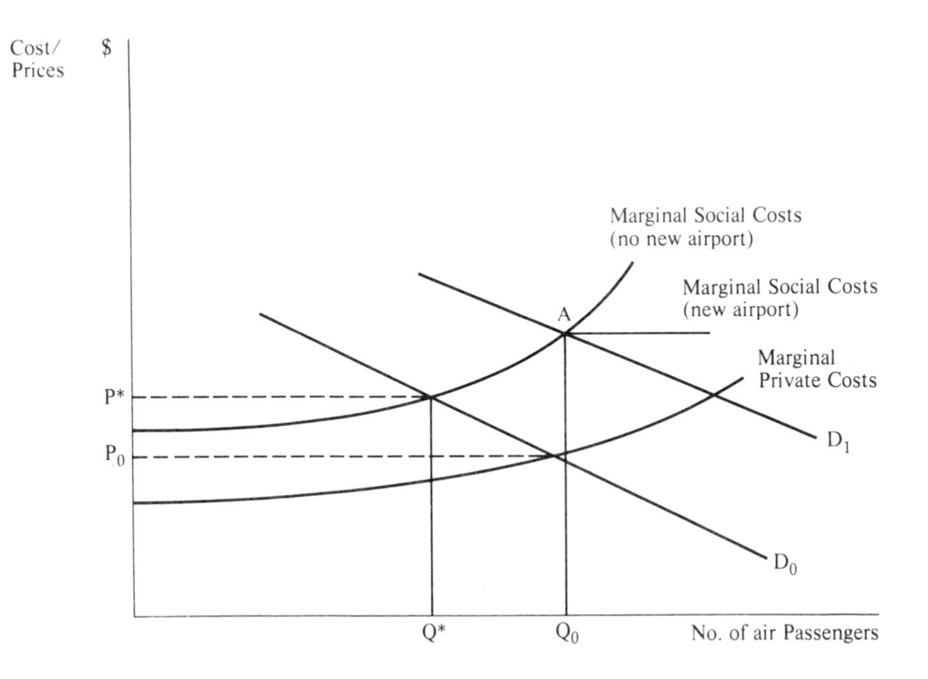

Figure 6.2 Traffic demand and costs in peak conditions

Let us now define the optimum amount of air travel as the amount at which the benefit of the marginal air traveller equals the social cost of his travel. [2] Then given a demand D_0, the optimum amount of travel is given by Q* and the price the marginal traveller would pay, including his own congestion cost, should be P*. [3] If the actual price is P_0, there will be Q_0 trips and we are at the point on the supply curve where the cheapest solution is to build a new airport. This solution has the disadvantages however that the social costs of the marginal trip exceed its benefits. The preferred strategy ensures that passengers pay the full social marginal costs of their trips. If each aircraft, or at least class of aircraft, were charged its social cost, aircraft movements whose marginal cost exceeded their marginal benefit would be eliminated. [4] In terms of figure 6.2, this would mean deferring the airport until demand rose from D_0 to D_1.

Peak charges are of course only one way to manage peak airport traffic. A regulating authority could control the number and composition of peak flights and, with knowledge of the marginal benefits and costs of peak flights, could do so efficiently. However, insofar as the authority's appreciation of the benefits and costs of each flight is imperfect, high benefit or low cost flights would be suppressed and it would be more difficult to achieve equality at the margin between benefits and costs than with pricing policy.

It is important to note that efficient utilisation of existing airports can cast doubt on new airport investment, especially if peak services are substantially under-priced and the rate of growth in aircraft movements is low. (Note that when runway capacity is the critical problem, it is aircraft movements, not air passengers, that matter). The point is that we started by evaluating the new airport under the constraint that peak traffic management was not possible and determined the least cost method of handling the peak, given this constraint. Once the constraint is removed, we not only optimise the method of serving peak traffic but also the level of peak demand through traffic management.

As figure 6.1 shows, two other kinds of investment are also relevant to the airport peak problem. One is aviation-related investment, for example in air traffic control or in larger aircraft. Such investment may save more in congestion costs than it costs to install. This would reduce the marginal social cost of air travel and may be a cheaper solution than a new airport. Secondly, investment in competitive transport modes may reduce the demand for air travel. Insofar as these alternatives are not exploited, when appropriate, the need for a new airport is brought forward.

It is a matter for the analyst's judgement which policy alternatives are outside the terms of reference of the study and should be taken as constraints, and which alternatives should be considered and optimised within the study. If there are constraints it is still necessary to forecast what government policy will be. For the rest of this chapter the need for an airport and also management and investment policies towards peak period traffic are taken as given and the location and timing of the new airport are considered within these constraints.

6.2 Strategy for an airport location study

The problem of airport location can now be expressed, with minor modifications noted below, as the determination of the lowest social cost airport system to meet the forecast air traffic demand. System costs are emphasised because a particular airport location may be cheap by comparison with alternative sites but may conflict with the existing airport. The benefits of air travel would be assumed to be the same for each site except when more accessible sites are forecast to generate extra trips, which would be a benefit accruing from those sites. Urbanisation benefits may also vary between sites. Insofar as benefits do vary, they can be treated as negative costs.

Before a detailed work programme can be drawn up, certain problems have to be resolved. These include

(a) The number of sites to be studied and the amount of time to be spent on examining each site.

(b) The treatment of airport services – which services are to be provided by the new airport?

(c) The treatment of site layout, specifically the number of runways and their configuration.

(d) How far to integrate studies of airport location and timing.

(e) The treatment of uncertainty, especially in the forecasts of air traffic which influence all parts of the study.

(f) The amount of work to be done on the distribution of costs and benefits.

(g) The relationship between the CBA and other studies or procedures, such as environmental impact statements or public participation.

These decisions are interrelated. The number of sites to be studied, for instance, will depend amongst other things on the detail of site design required, the treatment of uncertainty, and requirements for environmental impact statements or public participation. For simplicity, however, each one will be discussed briefly in turn.

The number of sites

It would be prohibitively expensive to consider all possible sites comprehensively. Some procedure for selecting and eliminating sites is necessary. Thus the Roskill Commission on the Third London Airport Study [5] took 4 months to select 56 possible sites and eliminate 52 of them and a further 2 years to examine the short list of 4 sites. Similarly the Sydney study [6] reduced 80 sites to 5 in 6 months, and finally examined 4 of these 5 for a further 18 months. Let us then consider (a) some criteria for selecting an initial set of sites and for proceeding to a short list and (b) some of the strengths and weaknesses of alternative site elimination strategies.

Criteria for the initial list of feasible sites in the Sydney study were that the site would not require the destruction of more than a certain number of homes, would be on land and within 140 kms of the centre of Sydney, and that the terrain around the airport would be sufficiently flat to conform to international flight path regulations. The first criterion was a socio-political constraint, the second and third were estimated to be necessary on economic grounds, the fourth was a safety constraint. Both the Roskill and Sydney studies then drew up a medium list of sites before selecting the short list. The Roskill commission drew up their medium list on the basis of approximate noise, defence and surface access costs and selected their short list by refining these costs and adding land, site preparation and air traffic control costs. The Sydney short listing procedure was more comprehensive, but the study emphasis remained on the detailed analysis of the selected short list. In summary, both studies eliminated sites by a form of reduced cost benefit analysis.

Of course the site selection strategy depends upon the circumstances of the case, but it is instructive to consider a Roskill-type strategy which emphasises very detailed work on a small number of sites. Roskill argued that no site excluded from the short list was likely to be measurably better than the best of the short listed sites. Resources should not be wasted therefore in examining good sites which might run second or third in the race but never come first. Detailed urbanisation studies are especially expensive and public participation is difficult to manage with more than a few sites. However, given the many variables affecting site choice, it is difficult to be sure prior to detailed analysis that a site which is clearly good could never come first (this would occur only if the site was dominated in all aspects by another site). It is of course especially important not to eliminate possible solutions before approaches to major uncertainties, such as the forecast traffic or the expected use of competitive or complementary airports, have been determined.

Airport services

An airport providing comprehensive services to all destinations is expensive as it duplicates the ground facilities of an existing airport and increases the conflicts between air routes and hence air route costs. On the other hand, it reduces the surface access cost of air passengers, who have greater choice between airports. It may be possible to determine an airport's services in advance of the study or perhaps the role of the airport will not materially affect the choice of site. However, if neither condition holds, airport services should be determined as part of the airport location study.

Airport layout

The optimum site layout generally varies between sites since it depends on the nature of the site and surrounding areas as well as on traffic forecasts and other factors. Consequently it is quite possible for one site to be better than another if for instance both have close-space parallel runways, but to be worse if both have wide-space parallel runways. The sites can be compared properly only if the layout for each has been optimised, which, in the case of our example, may mean comparing a close-space parallel runway layout at one site with a wide-space parallel runway layout at another. For similar reasons it may be necessary to compare a 2 runway site (which cannot accommodate 4 runways) with a 4 runway site (which is not a very good 2 runway site). Other examples could of course be given.

The major study choice lies between determining the best layout for each site during the study, costing only these layouts (this was broadly the Roskill approach), and treating each site layout as a separate entity to be fully costed, eliminating only the obviously inferior ones (which was the approach used in Sydney). The latter course is more expensive but often preferable. Similar cost data and decision methods are required to choose between layouts for each site as between sites. A premature choice of layout, especially if the traffic forecasts have not been finalised, may cause an inferior site to be chosen.

Airport location and timing

Airport location and timing are interrelated issues. For example when a site involves especially costly construction, it may be desirable to defer the expenditure and hence the opening date. For similar reasons, it may be wrong to assume a common opening date for all sites. Such an assumption causes an unnecessary cost to be attached to sites which can better be opened at a different time. Although this may not lead to a poor choice of site, the possibility of error is avoided if airport location and timing are determined jointly (see section 6.5).

Uncertainty

The complexity of an airport study normally makes it impractical to estimate the full distribution of the CBA results based on the distribution of possible values for all the independent variables. Therefore the uncertainty analysis will probably concentrate on the effects of the major uncertainties which, in terms of their influence on the CBA results, are likely to be the growth in air traffic, the value of time and the social costs of noise. Urban and regional costs and benefits may also be very uncertain, indeed so much so that they will not always be part of the quantified CBA results.

A practical approach to uncertainty used in the Sydney study is to estimate how airport costs vary with uncertain forecasts to which probabilities can be attached. Thus it is possible to estimate the expected costs, EC, for each site as $EC = P_1C_1 + P_2C_2, \ldots, P_nC_n$, where P_i is the estimated probability of each forecast occurring ($\Sigma P_i = 1$) and C_i is the site cost for each forecast. Sensitivity tests can determine the change in expected costs as values of key parameters vary. (These points are elaborated in sections 6.3 and 6.7).

Final comments on study planning

The study strategy will also be affected by the requirements for distributional analysis (see section 6.6), for environmental analysis (see Appendix to chapter 3) and for public participation. It is noted here merely that public participation may be seen simply as a flow of information between the study team and the public or more fully as a debate on the study methodology and results. Of course it is desirable that the objectives and procedures of public participation should be defined and co-ordinated with the CBA.

Finally it is axiomatic that any large study should be based on (a) a logic diagram specifying the major study relationships, (b) a network specifying the timing of activities, their interdependence and a critical path and (c) a bar chart specifying activities by personnel and by time. [7] This is emphasised because many large studies (not just of airports) are seriously handicapped by inadequate advance planning.

6.3 Air traffic forecasting

Various forecasts will be required depending on the complexity of the study. The list in table 6.2 is intended to indicate some possible forecast requirements rather than to be comprehensive.

Table 6.2
Some possible forecast requirements

Forecast	Some reasons
Number of passengers by origin and destination of flight and by trip purpose (probably business and leisure).	To estimate aircraft movements, time costs in the air and the demand for terminals.
Aircraft sizes.	To convert passenger forecasts into aircraft movements.
Aircraft movements by aircraft type, by time of day, and by origin and destination of flights.	To estimate demand for runway space and runway congestion costs. To design air routes, and estimate flying costs and noise costs.
Number of passengers by origin and destination on the ground and by trip purposes.	To design surface access routes and estimate surface access costs.
Air freight by origin and destination	To estimate additional aircraft movements.

Forecasts of air passengers by origin and destination and by trip purpose are the basis of the forecasting requirements and are discussed below. Forecasts of aircraft size are also discussed briefly. Air freight is normally not very significant as it generates few additional aircraft movements.

It is useful to distinguish three amongst many methods of forecasting air passengers, namely modified trend analysis, category analysis and more complex econometric models. The last of these of course provides the most accurate forecasts but a lack of data and resources may make it impractical to develop them.

By 'modified trend analysis' I mean the separation of the air market into relatively homogeneous travel sectors and the projection of past growth rates for these sectors modified by expected changes in these trends. In Australia, for instance, the obvious sectors are international, interstate and intrastate airline travel which in terms of passenger trips grew at 17, 10 and 5 per cent per annum respectively in the 1960s, and possibly also general aviation movements. Normally aviation growth rates are expected to slow down as markets mature, especially as exponential growth rates of 10 per cent or more per annum would lead to extremely high passenger forecasts. Arguments for slower growth rates include limited leisure time and the energy crisis. In fact these arguments are weak because as yet only a small proportion of the population fly and many air trips last only a few hours, and because fuel cost is a small part of the total cost of air travel. The weakness of such arguments illustrates the dangers of qualitative judgements and the need for quantitative data in forecasting.

Category analysis is a cross-section forecasting method based on the relationship between the number of trips which households or individuals make over a period such as a year (their propensity to fly) and their socio-economic characteristics. The propensity for business trips, for instance, might be related to occupation and income and the propensity for leisure trips to age, household composition and income. However the propensity to fly may change over time, due for example to greater education or to falling real prices of air travel. This change in propensity can be estimated by comparing the number of trips made in the past with the estimated number which would have been made if past propensities to fly were the same as present ones, as shown in figure 6.3. Of course the reasons why the propensity to fly has changed should be considered before predicting that the propensity to fly will continue to change. For example the real price of air travel may not be expected to continue to fall.

The category analysis may be refined by allowing also for the influence of airport accessibility and service frequency on the number of passenger trips. Let us suppose that the expected trips from any zone i are estimated as a function of the household propensities to fly, established by the category analysis. The ratio of actual to expected trips from any zone can then be graphed as shown in figures 6.4 and 6.5.The relationships shown in figures 6.4 and 6.5 can be calibrated on existing traffic data and, with suitable caution, converted into forecasts as follows

$$A_{ij}/E_{ij} = f(C_{ij}, S_j) \quad (1)$$

hence

$$A^*_{ij} = f(C^*_{ij}, S^*_j)\, E^*_{ij} \quad (2)$$

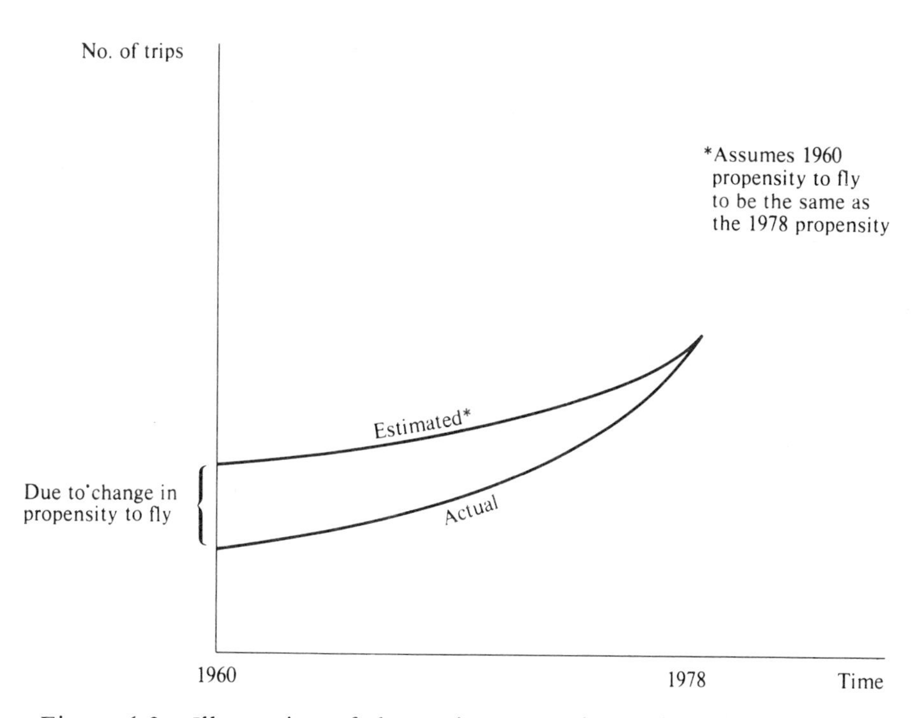

Figure 6.3 Illustration of change in propensity to fly (for leisure or business trips)

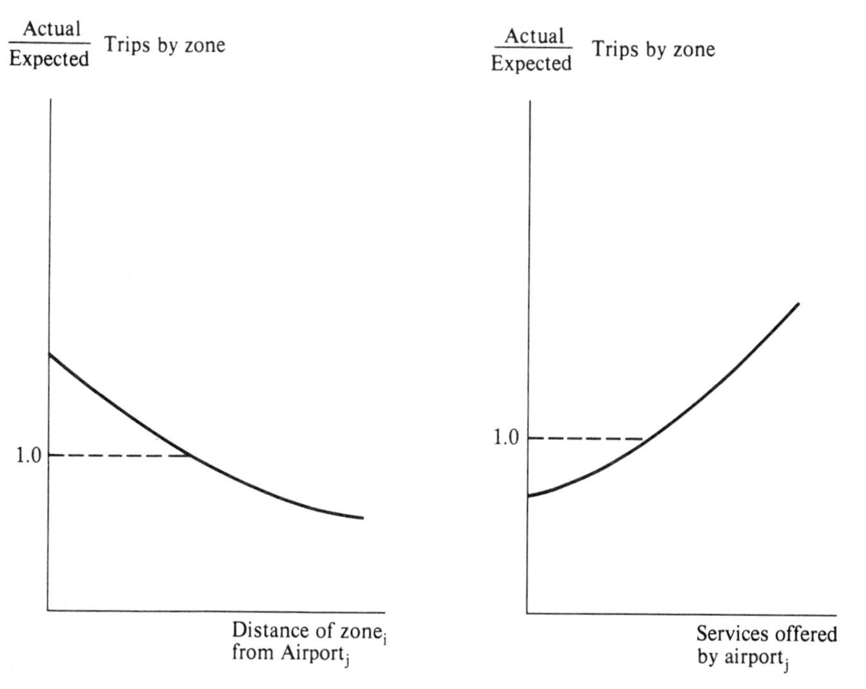

Figure 6.4 Air trips and airport accessibility

Figure 6.5 Air trips and airport services

where A_{ij} = actual trips from zone i to airport j

E_{ij} = expected trips from zone i to airport j

C_{ij} = travel costs from zone i to airport j

S_j = attraction of airport j, measured for example by the number of services it offers

and * denotes forecasts.

Having estimated the total number of passenger flights by category analysis, market shares and flights by time of day may be forecast by projecting trends for them. These forecasts must be modified, however, to conform with the forecast total passenger trips.

More complex econometric modelling might involve cross-section models in which the number of trips by journey purpose in each major passenger market are the dependent variables and the socio-economic characteristics of the population and trip characteristics are independent variables in a one stage model. [8] Alternatively, time series models would relate business travel to such variables as GDP, trade, airfares and speeds, and leisure travel to GDP, the costs of tourism, airfares and speeds and perhaps to a trend variable allowing for changes in taste. In order to avoid conflicts between the results of the cross-section and time series models over say income elasticities, a model combining cross-section and time series data might be developed. [9]

Forecasts of aircraft size would typically be generated by analysis and projection of trends but allowance would be made for expected changes in technology. Because of the uneven nature of developments in aircraft size, as occurred with the introduction of the Boeing 747, sophisticated models of changes in aircraft size are difficult to develop and the analyst will probably rely to some extent on discussions with aircraft manufacturers. Fortunately the positive correlation between the growth of passenger load and the increase in aircraft size narrows the likely range of aircraft movements. It should be noted here that I have assumed high passenger growth rates induce larger aircraft size. But of course larger aircraft may also cause real airfares to fall and so increase passenger trips. Aircraft size should therefore be determined concurrently with passenger trips rather than as a second stage in the forecasting process.

Finally two points should be stressed. First, however sophisticated the forecasting method, uncertainty about the future means that a range of forecasts *ought* to be made. Ideally a distribution of forecasts should be estimated for each site as a function of the probability distribution of each independent variable in the forecasting models and its co-variance with other independent variables. [10] More practical may be the kind of exercise done in Sydney where 5 scenarios representing a range of passenger trips and aircraft movements were developed. Probabilities were attached to each scenario rather than to each independent variable. The least that should be done is to forecast low and high levels of air traffic so that sensitivity tests showing the relationships between the forecasts and the CBA results can be made. Second, if the forecasting method is reasonably sophisticated, the forecasts will be a function of the airport charges, amongst other factors. This does not mean, however, that the benefits of the forecast passengers will necessarily exceed the costs of supplying aviation services to them, since that depends of course on the nature of the pricing policy.

6.4 Quantified and unquantified costs and benefits

Costs and benefits are conveniently considered under five headings, airport construction and operation, aviation, surface access, aircraft noise, and urban and regional planning. Certain relationships between the groups will however be noted below.

It would obviously be impractical to estimate all possible airport effects. In the Sydney study, costs valued at less than $1 million and intangibles which would probably be worth less than $1 million were excluded. This exclusion criterion is not clear-cut because things can always be disaggregated, brick by brick as it were, to less than $1 million or conversely aggregated, time value on time value, to more than $1 million. Nevertheless it provides a useful rule of thumb.

Another problem arises because the life of an airport may be many tens of years and its effect on the environment even longer. The Roskill Commission argued that prediction difficulties made meaningless any evaluation of site difference after some 25 years. Certainly it would normally be difficult to argue that site A is better than site B over 25 years, but that B would be preferable over a longer period such as 50 years.

Airport construction and operation

Construction costs include the costs of land take, site preparation, runways and taxiways, administration services and water and power services. Although the costing should allow for measures to contain soil erosion and water pollution, some residual pollution is likely to occur and would be an intangible cost to each site. Probably the two trickiest problems, on which I comment briefly below, are (a) optimising airport design and (b) estimating the cost of land. Operating costs include the provision of services, such as power, and airport employees. If site opening dates are similar, operating costs may not vary much between sites.

Airport design, which includes such things as the start and finish of runways, aircraft parking areas, terminal locations and so on, should be based on the minimisation of all costs, including noise, aircraft taxing, flying and airport construction costs. It should therefore be determined as late in the study as possible to make use of the most accurate data available. However any delay in finalising airport design complicates work on construction cost estimates, planning of route structures and urban planning.

The general principles for valuing the loss of land including the losses of householder surpluses were discussed in chapter 2 and the value of recreational land was discussed in chapter 5. A few points about problems of agricultural, military and urban land respectively which have arisen in airport studies may however be added.

The market price of agricultural land can be a misleading indicator of its value because it is often greatly affected by taxation and subsidy arrangements. It may be argued that these arrangements reflect government policy and so allowance need not be made for them, but it is more usual to correct for them as Roskill did, on the grounds that the taxes and subsidies represent transfers rather than real resources. Alternatively agricultural land may be valued at the estimated capital value of the stream of expected productive surpluses, possibly with some allowance for the consumption benefits that households enjoy by living on the land.

Potential airport sites are frequently located on military airfields or in areas containing military installations. The cost of relocating military facilities is usually quantifiable, (it is normally assumed that the facilities are necessary) but the environmental implications of relocation and any change for better or worse in defence posture would normally be considered intangibles.

The loss of urban land may also involve intangible costs not included in the fall in local property values and householder surpluses. Certain cultural and historical artifacts, such as Norman churches, have a regional or national value which is extremely difficult to estimate and the Roskill Commission regarded them as intangibles. It may be questioned too whether the estimated loss of property values and surplus adequately reflects the costs of community disruption, especially on land close to the airport site which is not required for airport construction. Sociologists [11] attempted to assess the strength of affiliations in communities around each London site, but could not cost the disruption effects. It is indeed possible that a community may welcome the changes brought about by an airport.

Aviation costs

Aviation costs are used here to include the 'ground-side' costs to airlines and passengers, commercial flying costs, the costs of airspace conflicts, and airport congestion and closure costs.

'Ground-side' costs are the costs of providing and operating airline facilities on the airport, such as maintenance bases, and aircraft taxing costs. The latter, which include both aircraft operation and passenger time costs, can be quite significant. Roskill [12] estimated that they would be about £10 (in 1968 prices) per minute per aircraft in 1980.

To estimate flight-related costs, flight routes are designed for each airport system to minimise flying costs, noise costs and disruption to other aviation activities. Figure 6.6 shows site A as the existing airport and sites B and C as alternative second airports and the lines to the perimeter of the circle represent notional optimised flight paths.

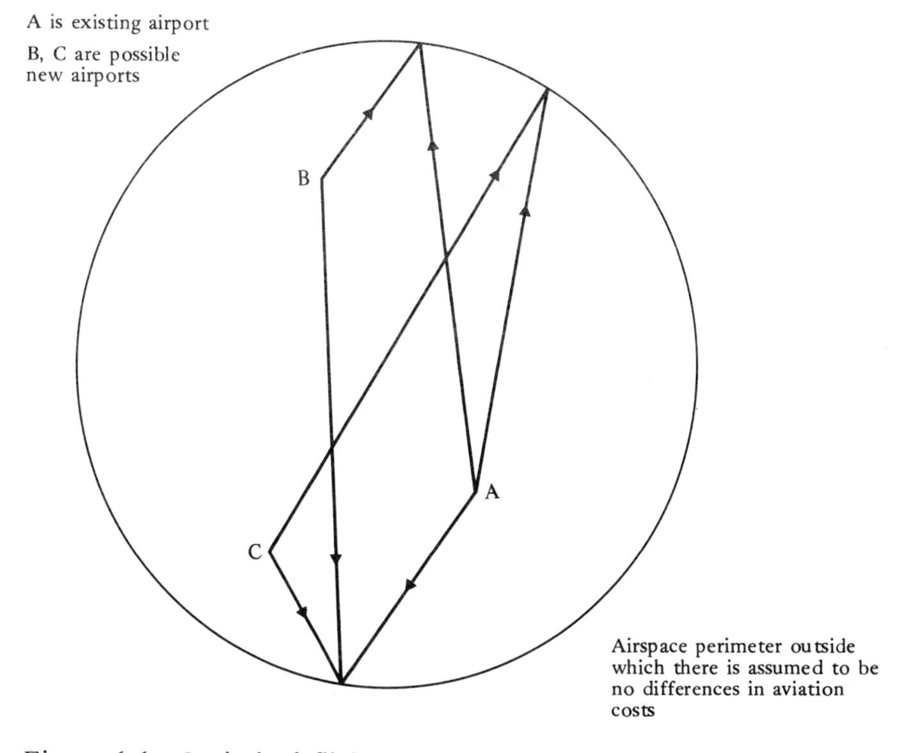

Figure 6.6 Optimised flight paths

Aircraft operation and passenger time costs from sites A and B combined to the perimeter and from A and C combined to the perimeter would be estimated. Costs incurred outside the circle would be assumed to be common to each airport system and ignored. This costing method results in high estimates of commercial flying costs, but the difference between systems would generally be small.

The increased airspace required by the major commercial airports may cause smaller ones to close. [13] Closure costs involve the costs of handling the extra passengers at the major airports, including any additional access costs incurred by passengers. But these costs may be offset by the savings on noise costs at the smaller airports and the value of the closed airport in alternative uses. Airspace conflicts may also cause general aviation and military airfields to be relocated. As well as the relocation cost, consumer surplus in general aviation may fall due to the inferior accessibility of the relocated airfields.

The optimal amount of congestion depends mainly on the trade-off between congestion costs and the costs of providing extra capacity. It is determined as part of the optimisation of the rate of airport development (see section 6.5). Congestion costs are normally estimated as increased aircraft running costs and passenger time costs in the peak hours. In reality congestion may cause some passengers to travel off-peak or even to cancel their flights, but these reactions are difficult to model and to value in the absence of pricing systems which would indicate what individuals were willing to pay for alternative services.

Airport closure may be caused by such elements as snow, high winds or low visibility. If meteorological advice is sufficiently detailed, closure periods and the consequent costs of diverted or delayed aircraft may be estimated. However there will often be some unquantifiable factor, for example airport closure due to poor visibility could not be predicted for some Sydney sites because of insufficient meteorological data. More generally cross wind runways not only reduce airport closures in heavy winds but also increase flight safety in medium winds by offering a choice of runways. Although often considered important, this latter benefit is rarely quantified.

Surface access costs

The main items to be considered are listed by Flowerdew [14] as:

(a) the costs of constructing fixed access links
(b) the variable resource costs of travel to and from each airport
(c) travel time, and
(d) consumer surplus benefits from generated travel.

To estimate these costs it is necessary (i) to distribute the passengers, given their origins and destinations, to the possible airports, (ii) to predict their choice of mode to the airport, (iii) to determine the least cost combination of capital and user costs and (iv) to predict generated traffic.

The first two steps are conveniently done with a gravity model technique which simulates passenger trips between zones and airports by mode of travel. [15] The general formula is

$$T_{ij} = \frac{O_i D_j F_{ij}}{\sum_j (D_j F_{ij})} \qquad (3)$$

where T_{ij} = trips between zone i and airport j
O_i = trips generated in zone i
D_j = trips attracted to airport j
F_{ij} = the behavioural cost of travel between i and j defined as

$$F_{ij} = \exp(-\lambda_p C_{ijp}).\ C_{ijp}^{-n_p} + \exp(-\lambda_r C_{ijr}).\ C_{ijr}^{-n_r}$$

where C_{ijp} is the behavioural cost of travel between i and j using public transport, C_{ijr} is the same using private transport, and the λ's and n's are parameters obtained from analysis of current travel patterns. If the distribution formula results in $\sum_i T_{ij} = D_j$ exceeding the capacity of airport j, a cost may be added to the C_{ij} to ensure that the airport's capacity is not exceeded.

The modal split is given by

$$T_{ijm} = \frac{T_{ij} \exp(-\lambda_m C_{ijm}).\ C_{ijm}^{-n_m}}{F_{ij}} \qquad (4)$$

where the subscript m refers to the mode.

It should be noted that traffic behaviour would be modelled as a function of travellers' behavioural costs, which are their time costs plus their marginal monetary costs (these may include transfer payments such as fuel taxes). On the other hand, access costs in the cost benefit calculus would be measured in terms of resource costs and the losses involved in foregoing preferred leisure time activities.

The prediction of traffic generated by accessibility to the new airport was discussed in section 6.3 and the general method of valuing surpluses from generated consumption was discussed in chapter 2. I argued there that the surplus could generally be valued at approximately half the change in behavioural costs from the without project situation to the with project situation. Using Flowerdew's example 'if 100 more people fly as a result of a saving in access cost of £1 (UK), their average benefit is assumed to be 50 pence'. [17]

Undoubtedly the most important single cost in airport studies is the value of time. Inter-site differences arise especially from differences in the costs of access time to and from airports as well as from differences in flying times and in the times spent at airports. Roskill estimated the costs of lost business time per hour at 150 per cent of business salaries per hour which was meant to represent the value of production lost. However, Carruthers and Hensher [18] found in Australia that the marginal time foregone to make business trips was often leisure time and, allowing for this, estimated that business time savings should be valued at 78 per cent of salary costs. The same writers further estimated that if allowance was made for working during the journey, average business time costs would fall to 63 per cent of salaries. Roskill estimated the costs of lost leisure time per hour at 25 per cent of average salaries per hour, which was the average value of travel time savings found in journey-to-work situations where leisure time would be the time saved. It may be argued that air travellers would attach a relatively high value to time as they are paying a great deal to save it. On the other hand it is arguable that as the surface access journey is part of the holiday, leisure air travellers would not place a high value on savings in access time.

One consequence of using even quite modest values of time is that the operating costs of access to and from the airport may be several magnitudes greater than the capital expenditure on access infrastructure. This may indicate that the access system, which should minimise the sum of capital and user costs, has not been adequately optimised.

The main unquantified aspects of the access system are normally its effects on non-airport users and on the environment. Non-airport users may gain from the provision of extra transport infrastructure and services or lose if the airport traffic creates extra congestion. The environmental effects of roads or fixed links, whether they run through open countryside or provide access to the city centre, can be extremely serious and offset any environmental advantages to be gained by locating an airport a long way away from the population it is to serve.

Aircraft noise costs

The phrase 'aircraft noise costs' is somewhat misleading as it generally includes the costs of all disturbances under the flight path or close to the airport. It includes therefore such things as air pollution, electrical interference with television and fear of aircraft crashes as well as noise itself. Since noise costs are described in detail in the following chapter, only brief mention of them is made here.

Noise costs may be distinguished by the groups of people who bear them, i.e. residents, visitors, tax-payers and businesses. Residents' costs can be measured in terms of reduced property values and loss of householder surplus; visitors also lose some surplus from their visits or pay the costs of going elsewhere; the tax-payer pays for the protection or movement of public facilities such as schools; and business may suffer a loss of profits and surplus due to an unpleasant working environment. It is important also to note that aircraft noise may deter changes in land use that would otherwise occur and that this too has a cost in terms of reduced land values.

Urban and regional costs and benefits

A two-runway airport will probably employ over 10,000 people who, with their families, would make up a population of over 30,000 people. Many others would be required to provide services to the airport employee families or to the airport itself. These requirements are likely to generate substantial population movements with significant effects for housing, economic growth and the environment. Nevertheless airport studies often fail to produce convincing quantitative or even qualitative measures of the resulting costs and benefits partly because planners have failed generally to produce an adequate methodology for evaluating any large scale changes in land use. In the absence of any standard method for evaluating the major effects of airport related urbanisation, one possible economic approach is outlined below.

Two polar planning cases may be envisaged when (a) urban areas are developed from green fields around each site and (b) all urban development is constrained within existing or forecast development areas. To compare green field sites, the net urbanisation benefit per site would be calculated as the difference between the market values of properties housing the airport generated population, which approximate the gross urbanisation benefits, and the public and private costs of supplying the properties, including external costs. This may be expressed as follows:

$$B = Q\,[P - (C_1 + C_2 + C_3)] - C_4 - C_5 \qquad (5)$$

where B = the urbanisation benefit per airport site
Q = the number of households generated by the airport
P = market price per dwelling unit
C_1 = social cost of land required for urbanisation per dwelling unit
C_2 = private non-land costs of development, e.g. building cost per dwelling unit
C_3 = public non-land costs of development, e.g. water and sewerage cost per dwelling unit
C_4 = external costs and benefits to other residents, if not included in C_1
C_5 = external costs and benefits to visitors, if not included in C_1.

Strictly speaking, Q should include the total additional population forecast for each area, but it may be necessary to simplify the analysis by considering only households employed on the airport. In a simple model, one type of house for each household and one residential density level would be assumed, but a model could be developed to handle more than one house type and density level. Property prices reflect the amount households are willing to pay to live in each area and include implicitly their valuation of journey to work costs. The social cost of land is its value in the non-airport situation. Other urbanisation costs would be included in C_2 through C_5, though some costs like the loss of valuable recreational land might not be quantified. The net urban benefit may be positive or negative.

In the alternative polar case, urbanisation around an airport site would not be permitted to change the existing or planned urban structure. Employment locations would vary but residential locations would not. Journey-to-work costs would be the major inter-site differences. If one site involves green field urbanisation and another requires no change to the planned urban structure, the urban benefit of the former should be compared with the value of the marginal urbanisation it displaces. Both would be valued as in equation 5. Although this formulation is somewhat general, it led to a sensible quantification of urbanisation benefits for the Sydney sites a significant advance on the Roskill Commission where urbanisation effects were listed qualitatively and inter-site comparisons were difficult to make. [19]

Generally, as we noted in chapter 2, secondary economic effects of investments are not allowed for in CBA as they result from all projects and can be regarded as transfers between areas. However, it can be argued that secondary benefits will be relatively high in areas of high unemployment. This was indeed argued for the region around Foulness, one of the proposed London sites. Conversely it was argued that an airport at Thurleigh would stretch local resources too far, but this view was not very convincing because resources can nearly always move into an area. Clearly it is a very large task to compare the secondary effects of alternative sites and such effects are likely to be unquantified, though hopefully not ignored.

6.5 The rate of airport development

The major cost of bringing forward airport construction is the opportunity cost of the capital involved. If construction costs from land take to airport opening total say $1,000 million, then, with an opportunity cost of capital of 10 per cent, there is a $100 million benefit from deferring the airport by 1 year. On the other hand, the new airport would reduce existing airport congestion and surface access costs. Flying, noise and urbanisation costs may rise or fall depending on the circumstances. The problem therefore is to find the rate of development which minimises total social costs for the given traffic forecasts. Conceptually the problem is easy enough to understand and for a few cases the solution can be calculated manually. If many sites and site layouts are being considered, the dynamic programming problem, as it is called, may be most conveniently solved with the use of a computer. [20]

To allow for a range of forecasts, Roskill argued that a runway should be timed to open when the expected costs of opening it are less than those of not doing so. Abstracting from all costs except the main ones – construction and congestion costs – the Commission's procedure can be illustrated as follows. [21] 'Let $F(D,t)$ represent the probability of demand for air travel in the year t being less than or equal to D and $f(D,t) = dF(D,t)/dD$. Let $c(D,t)$ be the cost of congestion in year t and k be the cost of bringing forward the construction 1 year.

Then the problem is to select t such that

$$\int_{D^*(t-1)}^{\infty} f(D,t-1)c(D,t-1)dD < K \leqslant \int_{D^*(t)}^{\infty} f(D,t)c(D,t)dD \quad (6)$$

when D*(t) represents the level of demand which can be catered for in year t without producing congestion costs.

To solve this inequality, it is necessary to estimate K, the cost of bringing forward construction 1 year, D*(t), the available capacity without congestion, f(D,t) the likely demand for air travel, and c(D,t) the congestion cost'. As congestion costs rise fast after a certain level of congestion, assuming no traffic management, the expected cost approach is likely to bring airport timing forward compared to the date that would be chosen if the timing was based on the most likely or mean traffic forecast.

The Roskill method is conceptually attractive but it was based on some unrealistic assumptions. First, the assumption that there would be no traffic management at Heathrow has turned out to be false. Second, the Commission ignored the possibility that at a cost the construction process can be slowed down or expedited according to the growth in traffic. Roskill therefore probably over-estimated the costs of delaying airport construction. It may also be noted that although Roskill attempted to optimise the opening of the airport for a range of forecasts, it evaluated airport sites on the basis that they would open at the 'optimum' date *and* that the most likely traffic forecasts would actually occur. No allowance was made in the evaluation of site location for possible variations in traffic forecasts.

An alternative approach was adopted in the Sydney study in which the rate of airport development was optimised for each of the five traffic scenarios separately. The expected cost (EC) for each airport site was then calculated as $EC = P_1C + P_2C_2, \ldots, + P_5C_5$ where the P_i were the probabilities attached to the occurrence of each scenario and the C_i were the costs of the site under each scenario. The Sydney method does not of course resolve the problem of optimum timing for a range of forecasts. It also has the significant disadvantage that it assumes that the optimum timing for each scenario can be determined as if the rate of growth predicted by the scenario would certainly occur, although the very point of the scenario approach is to build uncertainty into the evaluation. In defence of the Sydney approach it may be argued that the elasticity of the construction programme does make it possible for the opening of a new runway to coincide with the need for it. Also if a new airport is not required for many years as is the case in Sydney, it may be necessary to evaluate alternative locations allowing for considerable variations in the forecast traffic, but airport construction may start when the rate of traffic growth is more certain.

6.6 The distribution of costs and benefits

To distribute costs and benefits to social groups it is necessary to determine (a) which groups matter (b) how costs may be passed on from one social group to another and (c) what data, if any, will be required in addition to that collected for the CBA.

Groups of obvious importance in an airport study would be the government, the airport authority, airlines, air passengers and residents around airports. More contentious is the possible sub-division of these groups. Governments can be divided into central and local, airlines into foreign or national, air passengers into foreign or national and into business or leisure, residential areas around airports into those which gain and those which lose from the presence of an airport, and so on. But groups may also need to be consolidated. For instance, to determine how each airport affects households by income groups, it would be necessary to consider jointly the effects of the proposed airport on air passengers and on residents around airports. As was noted in chapter 2, the selection of groups which matter is ultimately a subjective process.

Costs may be passed on in many ways. For example, airport construction costs may be met initially by an airport authority and be passed on to airlines or to passengers, or be paid for by tax-payers. The issues may be clarified by an example of an incidence matrix as shown in table 6.3. This shows how costs might be distributed initially to selected social groups, with the x's marking positions in the matrix likely to be filled. The distributed costs would include transfer payments such as fuel taxes, and in principle at least secondary benefits, which are not normally included in the CBA, as well as all the costs in the CBA. The bottom row of the matrix indicates that models would be required to convert the initial incidence effects into final incidence effects on households according to their incomes. [22] Sometimes a sequence of models would be required, as when the airport authority charges airlines, the airlines charge businesses, and businesses either charge higher prices to consumers or pass on lower profits to shareholders. Needless to say, estimates of the way in which costs are passed from one social group to another are subject to large margins of error. Consequently, the analyst may decide to identify

Table 6.3
An example of an incidence matrix
Total discounted costs $m

Cost areas	Social groups										
	Government		Airport authority	Airlines			Businesses			Air passengers by area	Residents by area
	Central	Local		Foreign	Local public	Local private	Foreign	Local public	Local private		
Construction											
Land take		X	X								X
Other capital		X	X								
Operating		X	X								
Aviation											
Groundside	X	X		X	X	X	X	X	X	X	
Airspace	X	X		X	X	X	X	X	X	X	
Congestion/closure	X	X		X	X	X	X	X	X	X	
Surface access											
Capital	X	X									
Operating	X	X					X	X	X	X	
Generated traffic	X	X					X	X	X	X	
Aircraft noise	X	X						X	X		X
Urban and regional											
Housing/environmental											X
Other secondary economic effects							X	X	X		X
Final incidence models relating incidence to households	Taxpayer models		Airport model	Foreign trade model	Public enterprise model	Shareholder consumer model	Foreign trade model	Public enterprise model	Shareholder consumer model	Income models	

only the initial effects. If so, he should make it clear that he has described only part of the distribution story.

6.7 The decision process

If the analysis has proceeded broadly as described above the decision maker might be faced with summary data along the lines shown in table 6.4. Discounted costs minus benefits would be available for each site layout by scenario. Expected net costs would be estimated for the forecast mean values of the independent variables and for plausible variations in the values of the more important variables. The distributional and intangible effects of each site layout would be described and possibly expected net costs would be estimated with the use of distribution weights.

Table 6.4
Information for decision making
($ million discounted)

Site layout	Net costs	Expected net costs			Unquantified factors	Incidence analysis
	Scenario 1 ⟶ m	Mean values of independent variables	Sensitivity tests on variable values 1 ⟶ n	Distribution weights 1 ⟶ P		
1 ↓ k						

k = number of site layouts
m = number of scenarios
n = number of sensitivity tests
p = number of runs with different distributional weights

Note. Disaggregate data on the costs and benefits of each case would also be available.

The choice of sensitivity tests and distribution weights would vary with the situation and the decision makers' preferences. Sensitivity tests might be made on the following uncertain parameters: time values because they have a major influence on total costs, noise costs and urbanisation benefits because they are difficult to quantify and politically sensitive, land take costs because they are irreversible, and scenario probabilities which are fundamental to the analysis. Following the argument in chapter 2, I do not believe that distribution weights can be chosen sufficiently objectively to justify using them as an integral part of the CBA. However it may be useful to show what distribution weights would be required to change the ranking of sites judged by the expected net cost criterion. [23]

The normal CBA approach would be to select the site, or site layout, with the lowest expected net cost for the estimated mean values of the independent variables providing that there were no very adverse unquantified factors or distributional effects associated with the site. But if there is little difference between the expected net costs of the better sites, the cost benefit analyst may not be able to eliminate all sites. Broadly speaking the analyst may eliminate sites with either a strong or a weak criterion. With a strong criterion site A would be eliminated only if it were worse than site B on all significant tests, including distributional tests, i.e. if it were dominated. Note that it would not be sufficient for site A to be worse than site B on some tests and worse than site C on others, because A might still be the preferred site overall. With a weaker criterion, site A would be eliminated if it had a higher expected net cost than site B both for the mean values of the independent variables and for the majority of sensitivity tests and if its distributional effects were no better than those of site B. Clearly, however, once sites are eliminated on the basis of 'most' tests, the decision depends on the value judgements of the decision maker. The cost benefit analyst may be able to simulate political value judgements, but it may be more judicious at this stage to present the results to the decision makers rather than risk usurping their role.

6.8 Summary and conclusion

It is important to assess the need for a new airport in terms of the problem or problems to be solved (the most common being the lack of runway capacity in peak periods) and the major alternative solutions. These include expanding the existing airport, investing in non-airport solutions, and improving airport management. After discussing the costs and benefits of a new airport, it was shown that the timing and even the need for a new airport could be affected by these alternatives, especially by efficient peak traffic management.

The main part of the chapter was concerned with methods of forecasting air traffic and of estimating the net costs of meeting this forecast traffic at alternative airport sites. The quantified and unquantified costs and benefits were considered in 5 groups – airport construction, aviation, surface access, aircraft noise, and urban and regional planning. We also saw that the rate of development of airports and airport location are interrelated problems, that distributional analysis requires data and models not necessarily collected or developed in the CBA, and that the decision process should allow, amongst other factors, for uncertainty in the forecasts and in key parameter values.

The utility of CBA was not discussed in this chapter and it must be admitted that there are those who argue that even if CBA was a logically valid evaluation process, it would not be useful as the answers would be ignored by politicians. Thus in London, the politicians initially chose Roskill's least favoured site, Foulness, and in Sydney, they chose a site, Galston, which was not even on the recommended short list of sites. Both decisions have, however, now been reversed. Moreover it would be difficult to prove that the CBA was irrelevant, because it is arguable that politicians like to know the costs of their decisions and that they originally chose Foulness and Galston respectively because in their view the estimated cost penalties were a reasonable price to pay for the environmental and political gains. [24] In the final resort, however, political acceptance is only one criterion for the adoption of an evaluation method which should stand or fall primarily on its scientific merits. In this respect, it is not easy to see how such a complex problem as an airport location study could be handled in an organised way except by cost benefit analysis.

Notes

[1] This is no mere academic point. Too often administrators jump from the need for new runways to grandiose plans for 4 runway airports, as happened in the setting up of the Roskill Commission, and the result can be disastrous.

[2] This is of course only one possible definition of the optimum amount of air travel. It could be argued, for example, that the marginal benefit of air travel should exceed the marginal costs by some proportion as some households may bear costs, e.g. noise costs, which are not compensated.

[3] Walters A.A. estimated that application of this type of pricing principle would have increased landing fees at Kennedy airport from US $25 to US $300 for peak flights in 1973. 'Investment in Airports and the Economist's Role. John F. Kennedy Airport. An example and some Comparisons', in *Cost Benefit Analysis and Cost Effectiveness* by Wolfe J.N. (ed.), Unwin University Books 1973, pp 140-54.

[4] It is sometimes suggested that an airport authority should auction off peak time slots. However, this has the disadvantage that aircraft imposing high social costs on other aircraft or on local residents would not be penalised.
[5] Roskill, Commission on the Third London Airport, Report, HMSO, 1971.
[6] The selection of the 5 short listed second airport sites for Sydney is described in Sydney Area Project Team Handover Papers by R. Travers Morgan and Partners, published by the Department of Transport, Canberra. The final assessment of 4 of the 5 sites is being made at the time of writing.
[7] A network will of course contain implicitly the logic of the study but it is generally desirable to examine the logic explicitly and independently of any time dimension.
[8] Quandt R.E. and Baumol W.J. 'The Demand for Abstract Transport Modes. Theory and Measurement', *Journal of Regional Science*, vol.6, 1966, pp 13-26.
[9] Sydney Area Project Team Handover Paper no.10. 'Air Travel Demand Forecasting', R. Travers Morgan and Partners, 1974. Published by Department of Transport, Canberra 1977.
[10] Reutlinger S. 'Techniques for Project Appraisal under Uncertainty', IBRD Report no.EC-164, 1968.
[11] Roskill, Papers and Proceedings, vol.VIII, part 2, section 4, 'Disruption of Community Life: A Comparative Study of Foulness, Nuthampstead, Thurleigh and Cublington', HMSO, 1970.
[12] Roskill, op.cit., Papers and Proceedings, vol.VII, p.139.
[13] For example Roskill estimated that both Cublington and Foulness would close Luton. Roskill, op.cit., Papers and Proceedings, vol.VII, p.242.
[14] Flowerdew A.D.J. 'The Case of the Third London Airport' in Layard R. (ed.), *Cost Benefit Analysis*, Penguin, 1972.
[15] Roskill, op.cit., Papers and Proceedings, vol.VII, pp 271-2.
[16] The literature sometimes refers to 'perceived marginal monetary costs' on the grounds that motorists do not perceive the actual marginal monetary costs. Some of this so-called lack of perception may however be due to travellers holding values of time other than those attributed to them.
[17] Flowerdew A.D.J. op.cit. pp 443-4.
[18] Carruthers R.C. and Hensher D.A. 'Resource Value of Business Air Travel Time' in Heggie I.G. (ed.) *Modal Choice and the Value of Time*, Clarendon Press, Oxford 1976, pp 164-85.
[19] Roskill op.cit., Papers and Proceedings, vol.VIII, part 1, 'Airport City Urbanisation Studies for the Third London Airport', HMSO 1970.

[20] Lack G.N.T. 'The Search for a Second Sydney Airport: a Dynamic Programming Model', Proceedings Second National Conference of the Australian Society for Operations Research, 1975, pp 99-126.
[21] Abelson P.W. and Flowerdew A.D.J. 'Roskill's Successful Recommendation', *Journal of the Royal Statistical Society*, series A, general vol.135, part 4, 1972, pp 467-502.
[22] The bottom row of the matrix also indicates that 'income models' are required. Note that bold assumptions about the likely growth in household incomes and their distribution over the life of the airport are required if the effect of the airport on households according to their income group is to be estimated.
[23] See for example, Nwaneri V.C. 'Equity in Cost Benefit Analysis. A Case Study of the Third London Airport', *Journal of Transport Economics and Policy,* vol.IV, no.3, 1970, pp 235-54.
[24] The then British Prime Minister, Mr Heath, presented the Foulness decision as a symbol for environmental protection. Buchanan (Roskill Report, op.cit. p.160) summarised this view in his eloquent if demagogic dissent from Roskill, 'The choice of Cublington would be a grievous blow to conservation policies. It is not merely that there would be a direct setback in the area influenced by the site, even more serious would be the general sense of disillusionment that would come to every person and organisation labouring in the conservation movement, and come just at a point in time when the urgency of the subject comes daily more apparent . . . . A decision which conceded the importance of the choice (of Foulness) would be an event of great significance for the future of Britain'. As Flowerdew [14] remarked, on this basis the greater the cost penalty attached to Foulness, the more important it would have been to choose it!

7 Aircraft noise and use of cost benefit analysis

In the economic analysis of any form of environmental pollution and of policies to reduce it, there are four essential steps. These are (a) the development of a measure of the pollution, (b) estimation of its cost, (c) calculation of the cost of reducing it and (d) determination of the preferred policies, as based on minimisation of the sum of pollution and abatement costs and other factors, such as equity, which might affect the choice of policy. Accordingly, this general procedure is followed in our analysis of aircraft noise. [1] In the first and second sections, measures of exposure to aircraft noise and the costs of aircraft noise are discussed respectively. The third section contains a brief description of the main methods for reducing aircraft noise and their costs, and a discussion of the use of cost benefit analysis to develop a set of policies with regard to aircraft noise.

7.1 Measures of exposure to aircraft noise

Aircraft noise under flight paths close to airports exceeds most industrial noise both in intensity and unpleasantness. On take-off, a jet aircraft causes around 120 dBA at ground level close to an airport and around 100 dBA 2 kilometres from it [2], which is equivalent to the noise level in an exceptionally noisy factory. [3] On approach, engine power is lower but so is the flight path and jet aircraft cause 90 dBA at ground level some 7 kilometres from the airport. This is equivalent to the noise from a heavy diesel lorry or an unsilenced road drill at a distance of some 7 metres. By comparison, normal conversation at a distance of 1 metre generates a sound pressure level of 65 dBA. Moreover, although dBA allow for the fact that some people tend to hear some frequencies more than others, they do not allow for the subjective response to different types of noise. The Australian Standards Association [4] recommends that for comparative purposes 5 dBA should be added to allow for unpleasant noises, such as the impulsive noise of a pneumatic drill or the whine of a jet aircraft.

In order to assess the effect of aircraft noise on households, we require a measure of noise exposure which corresponds with people's reactions to noise. This measure should take account of the frequency and time of day of aircraft flights as well as their noisiness. Ideally it would reflect all effects of aircraft noise, including interference with sleep and television, and even the effect of noise on the ability to hear. Also it would possess cardinal qualities, so that for each unit change in the measure of exposure there would be a unit change in the amount of annoyance felt. This is a tall order and, as we shall see, noise exposure measures tend to fall short of this ideal.

Most models of noise exposure are of the following general kind,

$$\text{Index of exposure} = (\overline{\text{PN}}\text{dB}) + K \log N - a \qquad (1)$$

where $(\overline{\text{PN}}\text{dB})$ is the average peak noisiness of aircraft, N is the number of aircraft, and K and a are constants. For example, in the Noise Exposure Forecast model used in the US and in Australia, the total noise exposure (NEF) is defined at a point as:

$$\text{NEF} = 10 \log_{10} \left(\sum_i \sum_j \text{anti log} \frac{\text{NEF}_{ij}}{10}\right) \qquad (2)$$

in which

$$\text{NEF}_{ij} = \text{EPNL}_{ij} + 10 \log \left(\frac{\text{Nd}_{ij}}{20} + \frac{\text{Nn}_{ij}}{1.2}\right) - 75 \qquad (3)$$

In this formula, NEF_{ij} is the noise exposure forecast value of aircraft class i along flight path j and EPNL_{ij} is the effective perceived noise level of aircraft class i on flight path j. Nd_{ij} and Nn_{ij} are the numbers of movements of the ith aircraft type on the jth flight path by day and night (2200 hours to 0700 hours) respectively. The number 75 is a normalising constant to distinguish the NEF value from the effective perceived noise level. [5]

The NEF model is considered relatively sophisticated because of the EPNL measure and the night-weighing factor. The EPNL is a psycho-acoustically derived measure which attempts to allow for sounds of a differing spectral content within a single measure scaled to subjective response. The night-time factor means that one night-time operation contributes as much to the NEF as nearly 17 similar day-time operations. An important implication of the model is that there are economies of scale in noise annoyance, such that a doubling of operations on one flight path on one day increases the NEF score by only 3 points. Figure 7.1 shows estimated NEF's for Sydney in 1972-73.

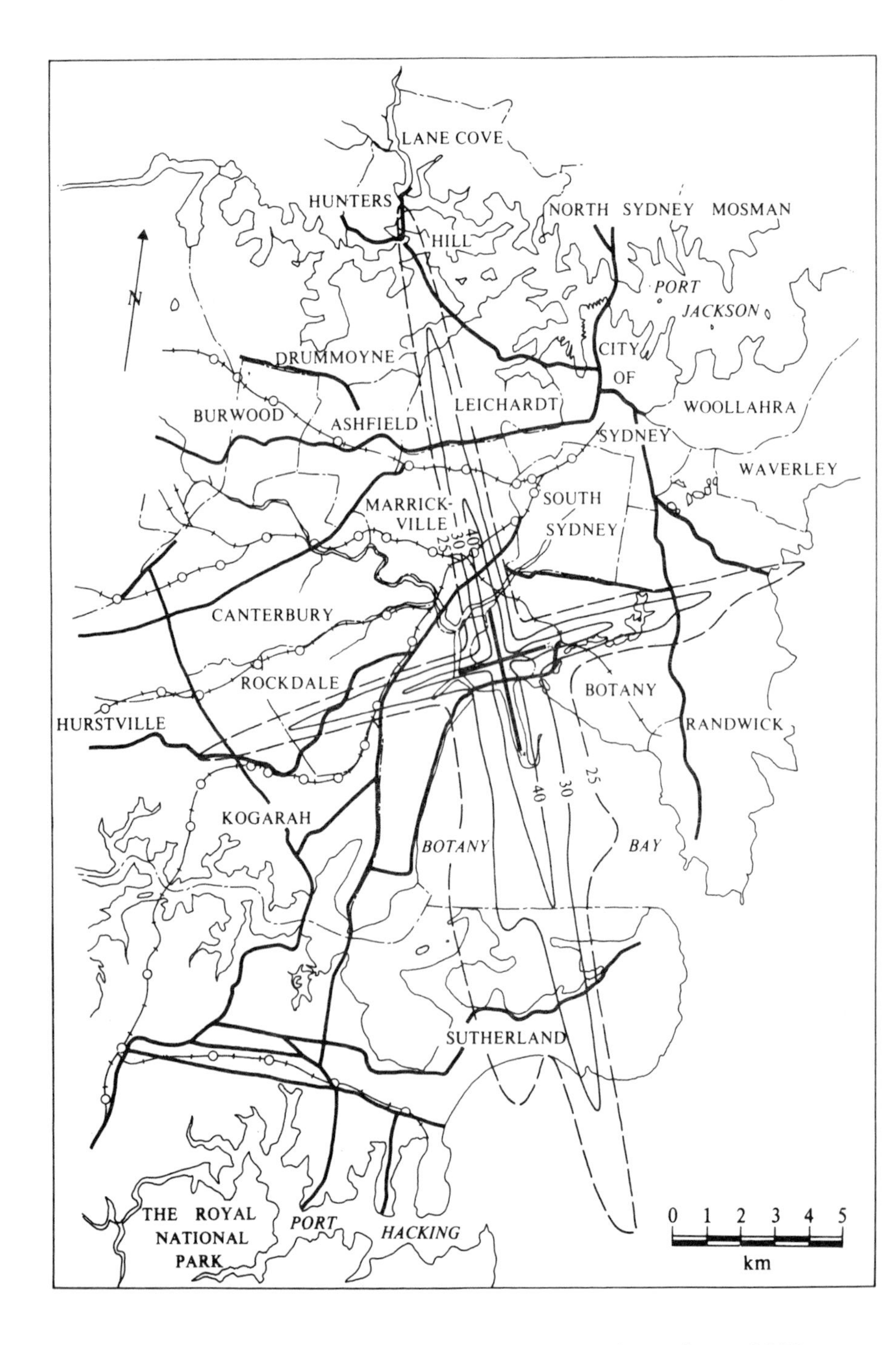

Figure 7.1 Estimated Noise Exposure Forecast in Sydney, 1973

The NEF model was tested by Tracor in 7 cities in the US [6] and by R. Travers Morgan in Sydney. [7] The Tracor study found that 30 per cent of people are highly annoyed and 57 per cent are moderately or more annoyed at aircraft noise at the 30 NEF level. It also showed that the proportion of households with a given degree of annoyance rises as the NEF increases (see figure 7.2). Likewise, the Travers Morgan survey showed that the average annoyance expressed for each of 12 activities disturbed by aircraft rose significantly with the NEF measure.

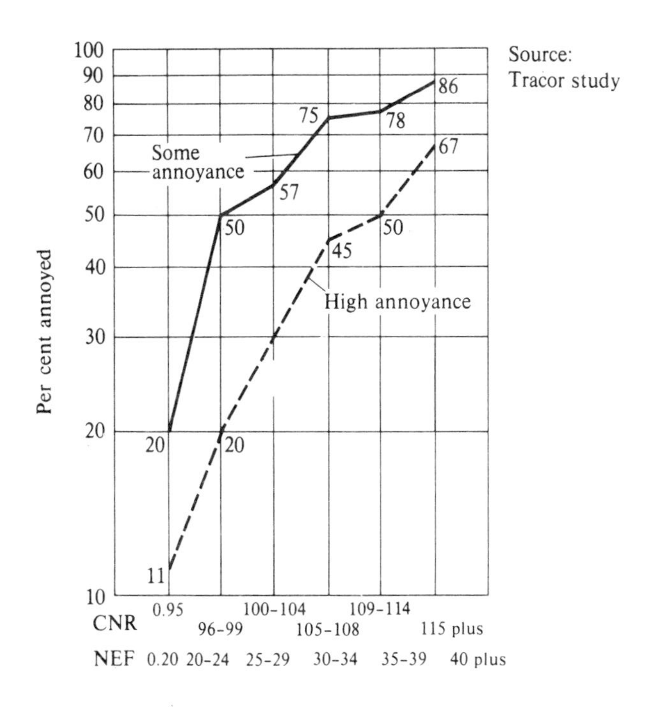

Figure 7.2 Reported annoyance by noise level

The relationship between individual expressions of noise annoyance (as measured by a Likert scale [8]) and the NEF score was however found by Tracor and by Travers Morgan to be weak ($r^2 = 0.16$ and $r^2 = 0.11$ respectively), which implies that the NEF explained relatively little of the variance in individual annoyance. Likewise the correlation between noise annoyance and the noise and number index in the UK was low ($r^2 = 0.13$). [9] Moreover, as shown in the following chapter, there appears to be a non-linear relationship between house price depreciation and NEF's. There are various reasons for the poor correlation between individual noise annoyance and noise exposure models. First, individual variance is inevitable as some people who dislike aircraft noise are deterred from moving away from it by the cost of moving, while others may move into the area without appreciating the extent of the noise. When Tracor included such psychological variables as fear of aircraft, susceptibility to noise and attitudes towards air transport as well as the NEF score as explanatory variables of annoyance, the R^2 increased to 0.62. Secondly, noise exposure models are necessarily simplifications of the real world. The NEF model appears less reliable at low traffic volumes when the peak noise variable dominates the NEF score; and it probably results in an under-estimate of noise annoyance close to an airport because it does not allow for reverse thrust on landing or for ground running (this may account partly for the non-linear relationship between house price depreciation and NEF). Also the night weighting factor represents an expert guess rather than a proven fact.

We may conclude then that the NEF measure is a poor predictor of individual attitudes and of the effects of marginal changes in noise levels. But this does not mean that it is a poor index of average community attitudes. Both Tracor and Travers Morgan showed that the number moderately and severely annoyed by aircraft noise is related to the NEF index. And Galloway [10] has shown that most other noise exposure models are based on equation 1 and are similar to the NEF measure. Thus it seems reasonable to accept the conclusion of the Kennedy Airport Study [11] that 'the NEF is now a generally accepted rational method for describing the degrees of community annoyance associated with noise exposure in the vicinity of existing airports'.

7.2 The costs of aircraft noise

The main part of the analysis in this section is devoted to the noise costs of households living under flight paths as these are normally considered to be the most important costs. The costs of businesses, tax-payers and visitors to noisy areas are also briefly described.

Noise costs of residents around airports

The effect of inflicting noise on households in quiet areas is illustrated in figure 7.3. [12] The basis of the figure is the assumption that there is a given stock of homogeneous houses in an area with a certain level of quiet. The D_q curve represents the number of buyers of this quiet stock at different prices over a period such as a year. The D_n curve represents the demand when noise is imposed on the area. The S_q and S_n curves represent the houses offered for sale in quiet and noisy conditions respectively over the same period. Of course the demand and supply curves may not be parallel. For instance, if aircraft noise was imposed on a peaceful rural community the S_n curve might be very elastic although the S_q curve was quite inelastic. With the infliction of noise, property prices in this example would fall from P_q to P_n and the number of movers would rise from Q_q to Q_n.

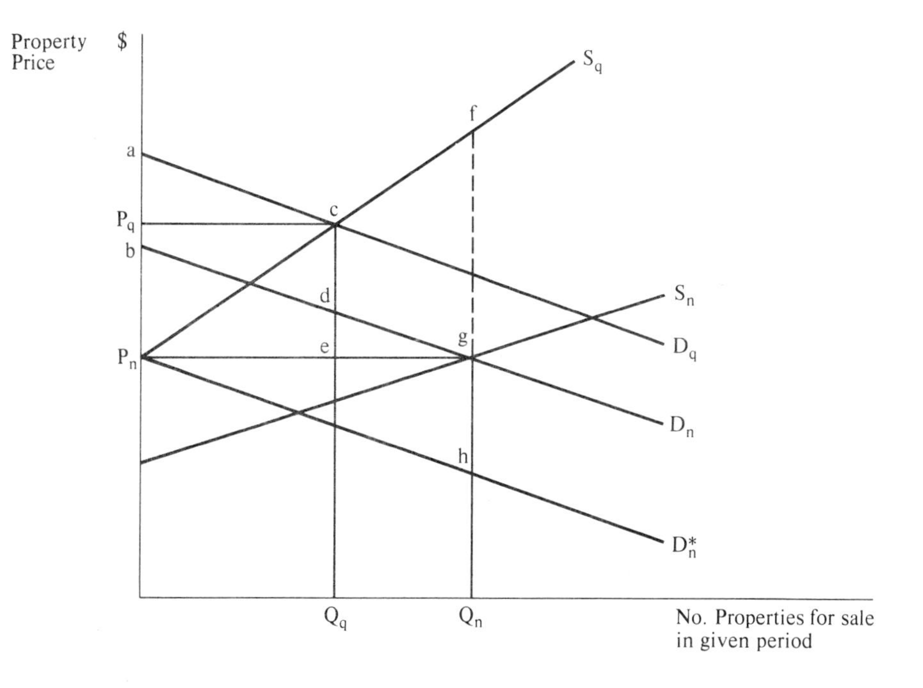

Figure 7.3 The effect of noise on property prices, surplus and turnover rates

Four household groups, each with different noise costs, can be identified in figure 7.3:

(a) Households who would move anyway, Q_q, suffer a depreciation in their property values (D). They each lose $(P_q - P_n)$; and their total loss is given by the area $P_q ceP_n$. [13]

(b) Households who move because of noise, $Q_n - Q_q$, suffer a loss of householder surplus (S) as well as D. Their loss is given by area cegf. It should be noted that the s_q curve allows for movement costs. The marginal mover is prepared to move for the slightest incentive. With surplus defined thus, it is unnecessary to allow for movement costs as well as loss of surplus.

(c) Households who stay suffer a loss of surplus represented by the difference between the S_q and S_n curves to the right of the line fg.

(d) Households who move into the area incur no loss if they are informed buyers because lower property values compensate them for the aircraft noise. Indeed they would obtain a surplus equal to the area bgp_n. But this is offset by the loss of surplus to householders who would have moved into the area if it was quiet. This loss is represented by area acP_q.

A survey in Sydney [7] showed however that inmovers into noisy areas substantially underestimated the effect of aircraft noise. Eighty per cent of inmoving households declared that they had underestimated the amount of noise and 24 per cent actually claimed to regret moving into the area because of the noise. Thus the true demand curve (one based on an accurate perception of the extent of the noise) might be described by the curve D_n^*. In this case, in-movers suffer a loss equal to area $P_n gh$.

The analysis becomes more complex when additional time periods are considered. The demand for noisy houses in the second period, given by curve D_{n2} in figure 7.4, is assumed to fall below D_{n1} on the grounds that households relatively indifferent to noise would move into the noisy area in the first period. On the other hand, the supply of noisy houses in the second period, given by the curve S_{n2}, is assumed to be lower than in the first period (hence S_{n2} is drawn above S_{n1}) as those households most anxious to sell would do so in the earlier period. The intersection of the D_q and S_q curves represents a notional long run equilibrium situation for the same stock of houses if quiet were to prevail. For simplicity the figure excludes the effects of dynamic influences like population and income growth.

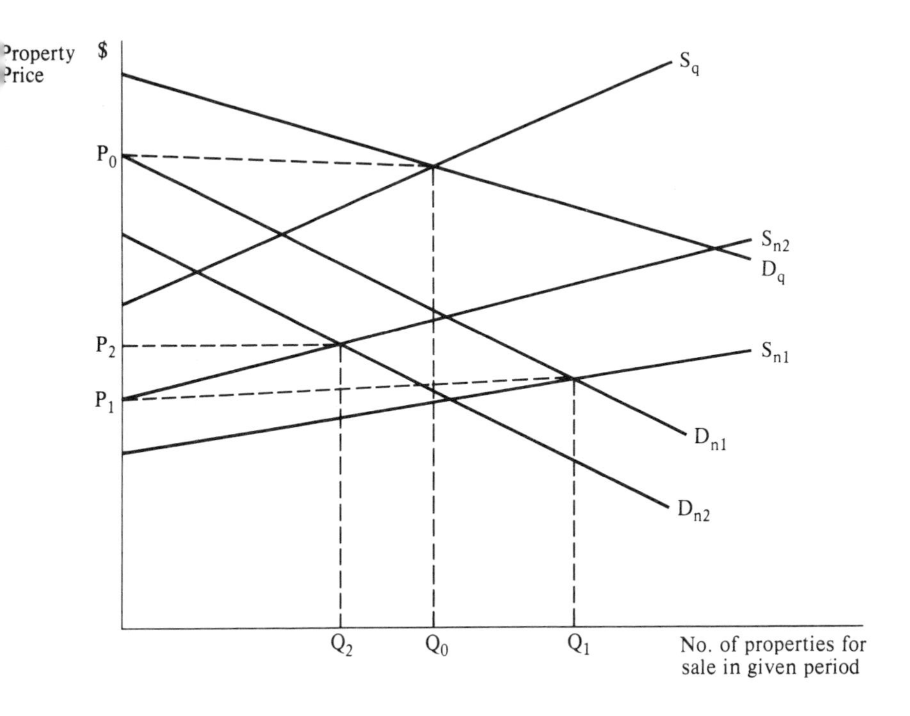

Figure 7.4 Possible effects of noise illustrated with respect to two time periods

An important inference from figure 7.4 is that the depreciation of property price, the difference between P_o and P_1 or P_2, and the loss of surplus, the difference between the S_q and S_n curves, due to noise are not unique values but vary over time. This is borne out by studies quoted by Walters [14] in which estimated depreciation rates vary from 0.7 to 2.25 per cent of house price per NEF unit. Many factors, including household preferences, income levels, moving costs and the availability of quiet houses, affect property price depreciation due to noise. Thus higher incomes as well as differences in attitudes towards noise probably explain the higher rate of property depreciation around Gatwick than around Heathrow airport.

It may also be observed that in the hypothetical example shown in figure 7.4, movement rates in the second noisy period are lower than in the quiet equilibrium situation. This is theoretically one of many possible outcomes, but in practice it is not very likely. According to Walters [15], the little research into household turnover that had been done suggested that annual turnover rates are likely to rise by 20 to 30 per cent and that in total some 8 per cent of all households are likely to move because of noise. Detailed research in Sydney [16] has now shown that over the 12 years from 1959 to 1970, turnover rates were 25 per cent higher in what became by 1970 the 25 to 29 NEF area and 50 per cent higher in the 30 to 40 NEF area than in quiet areas. Approximately 10 per cent of all households in the 25 to 29 NEF area moved out on account of the noise and 22 per cent left the 30 to 40 NEF area because of noise. By 1971 and 1972, by which time it might be argued that adjustments to noise had been completed, turnover rates were no higher in the noisy than in the quiet areas. Of course turnover rates due to noise will, like house price depreciation and surplus, vary with the circumstances.

In order to complete the noise cost model described above, it is necessary therefore to predict the number of households who would move because of aircraft noise. In the London airport study [17] this dynamic process was modelled on the assumption that households would move either naturally or when their noise annoyance (N) exceeded the costs of moving (D + S). The value of D was assumed to depend upon house price and was expected to rise over time. The value of S was estimated to have a distribution from 0 to around 100 per cent of house price, with a mean of 52 per cent of house price. To establish N, the Roskill research team assumed that the median N would equal D and adopted a distribution of N based on the distribution of noise annoyance found in the first London noise survey. [9] The median assumption was justified by the argument that equilibrium in the housing market requires as many households to want a noisy house at the reduced price as would want a quiet house at the higher price. The value of N was also expected to rise over time.

The Roskill model was an ingenious attempt to simulate the dynamic process of household reaction to noise, but it can be criticised on a number of grounds. First, it made no allowance for uninformed in-movers. Second, it was based on the rather gross assumption that house price depreciation and loss of householder surplus would be the same at each site. Third, and most important, the assumption that median N would equal D was based on equilibrium analysis and cannot easily be justified in periods of adjustment to noise. Put in terms of figure 7.3, there is no reason why the difference between P_q and P_n would be identical to the loss of surplus shown by the difference between the lines S_q and S_n. The median assumption implies that existing residents and in-movers would have similar attitudes to noise which is unlikely at least in the adjustment period. Even if they were to have similar attitudes, this may arise because in-movers underestimate noise costs, in which case D does not adequately reflect these costs. These are not just theoretical arguments. A householder surplus survey in Sydney [18] showed that surplus is much lower in areas affected by aircraft noise. Taking two areas similar except with respect to aircraft noise and excluding retired households and those with infinite surplus, Travers Morgan estimated that mean surplus in the quiet urban area, where the mean house price was about $30,000, averaged around $8,100 (Australian) compared with $7,200 in the 26 to 30 NEF area, $5,700 in the 31 to 35 NEF area and $3,800 in the 36 to 40 NEF area. This substantial loss of surplus due to noise indicates that N is often significantly greater than D. [19]

Once it is recognised that households who remain in noise affected areas may lose S as well as D and also that at the margin, as shown in figure 7.3, the difference in noise costs of movers and stayers is negligible, the advantages of a complex dynamic noise cost model based on detailed predictions of the number of movers and stayers seem slight. It should generally be possible to construct satisfactory simplified models of noise costs in which households who would move anyway lose D. Most other households, not only those forced by noise to move, would lose D + S, where S could vary from around zero to quite high amounts. In time as households adjust to the increase in noise, the loss of S would fall, and in long run equilibrium households would lose only D.

The benefits of reducing noise can be estimated conversely in terms of higher property values and surpluses. Estimation of the benefits may appear to be complicated because property values and surpluses reflect expectations of future noise as well as appreciations of current noise. Consequently, if noise abatement occurs when it is expected, property values and surpluses may not rise. But if the abatement does not occur when expected, property value and surpluses would fall. Thus the benefits of noise abatement can be estimated as the difference in property values and surpluses with and without noise abatement.

Other noise costs

Three other noise costs, to businesses, to taxpayers and to visitors to the area, were described in some detail by the Roskill Commission and are discussed only briefly here. Business costs due to aircraft noise would be based on the depreciation of property value due to the fall in expected profits, which might occur because of loss of custom or higher production costs, perhaps due to insulation costs. If the noise was intolerable and no business possible, depreciation of non-moveable assets would be 100 per cent. Since no study of business property depreciation due to noise had been made, the Commission assumed that it would be similar to private property depreciation.

Taxpayers bear costs when public facilities such as schools or hospitals have to be relocated or insulated. Strictly, the change in the quality of the facility as a result of its relocation or insulation should also be considered but this would rarely be given a quantified value. If neither relocation nor insulation occurs, local residents suffer and property prices and householder surplus would fall.

The main noise cost to visitors is their diminished enjoyment of recreational facilities in the noisy area. In principle, this can be measured by the lower price visitors would be willing to pay for these facilities. Note that if lower prices were actually paid, this may be reflected in business depreciation and should not be counted twice. If visitors switch to similar recreations in other areas, they suffer an increase in travel costs. Alternatively they may switch to other recreational occupations. Clearly the data required to measure all losses of visitors' surplus is expensive to collect so that estimates of the loss will be very tentative. Moreover the difficulties of even identifying all such losses of surplus means that they are likely to be underestimated.

There is, finally, another set of aircraft noise costs which tends to be overlooked; that is costs which arise when land use changes or when new uses are inhibited by aircraft noise. Suppose for example that it is proposed to convert rural land valued at $2,000 per block to urban land valued at $10,000 if it were quiet and $4,000 if it were noisy. The noise cost would be the difference between the quiet and the noisy urban value. Alternatively, if noisy urban land was worth less than noisy rural land, the aircraft noise would inhibit the conversion of land from rural to urban use. In this case the noise cost would be the difference in value between quiet urban land and noisy rural land. Thirdly it may be added that land use zoning controls which prevent certain activities in noisy areas also have a cost, this being the difference between the potential value of quiet land and the actual value of permitted land use.

Concluding comments on noise costs

The costs of aircraft noise in a populated area are clearly high. Thus the Kennedy airport study [20] concluded that 'in a NEF 30 area the sound of a jet plane is intrusive, it intrudes upon sleep, it prevents conversation, and it interrupts many kinds of relaxing activity . . . it is difficult not to acknowledge that this level of noise exposure is an adverse factor in even the most conservative definition of a healthy residential environment.'

In order to take such effects into account in the London airport location study, the Roskill Commission developed their dynamic noise cost model outlined above. Thus the Commission estimated that the residential noise costs around one of the inland sites, Nuthampstead, where an estimated 95,000 households would live within the 35 NNI area, would amount to £72.2 million in 1968 prices discounted to 1982. [21] Other noise costs were estimated to add a further 50 per cent to this figure. Noise costs around London's Heathrow airport, where there are some 700,000 householders within the 35 NNI area (equivalent to approximately 25 NEF), would of course be many times higher.

It may often be desirable however to analyse noise costs in more detail in order to estimate the effects of changes in policy, for example, changes in flight paths or in the number of aircraft flights. This can be done in principle by estimating how a change in policy would affect the NEF's around the airport and consequently how the noise costs of households would be reduced. The general approach can be expressed as follows:

$$N = F \times H \times P \times C \qquad (4)$$

where N = the change in noise cost as a result of the policy change
F = the change in NEF's as a result of the policy change
H = the number of households affected
P = average property value
C = average noise cost per household per NEF, including loss of surplus, expressed as a percentage of property value.

An example may clarify the formula. If there were 100 daytime aircraft movements over one flight path, an extra movement would increase each NEF score by .043. Suppose also that there were 30,000 households under the flight path, with an average property value of $40,000, and an average noise cost per NEF, including loss of surplus, equal to 1.5 per cent of the property value. The total capitalised noise cost for an extra daily aircraft movement in perpetuity could be estimated as follows:

$$N = .043 \times \frac{1.5}{100} \times 30{,}000 \times \$40{,}000 = \$774{,}000$$

If $774,000 is divided by 365, we obtain the capitalised noise cost of $2,120 for an extra aircraft movement one day a year in perpetuity. Given a discount rate of 10 per cent per annum, this would represent a noise cost of $212 per aircraft movement.

Equation 4 is a general model which enables us to assess the costs or benefits of any policy change and provides the basis for levying charges on noisy aircraft. Like any model, it is a simplification of the real world and limited by the accuracy of the data. In this respect it must be remembered that the NEF is a crude measure of annoyance and a poor measure of the effects of marginal changes in aircraft operations and that the noise cost model requires information on depreciation and loss of surplus which may be difficult to obtain and which varies from time to time and from place to place.

7.3 Evaluation of policies to reduce aircraft noise costs

As shown in figure 7.5, there are numerous possible policies to reduce aircraft noise. The problem is how to select and implement them in a rational and consistent manner.

Many regulations to reduce noise at source have been introduced. For example, the International Civil Airlines Organisation has developed regulations which specify maximum noise levels for new aircraft according to their weight. [22] Partly due to them, the second generation of turbofan engines is much quieter than older engines. For example, the 747 carries twice as many passengers as the 707 or DC 8, but it is over 5 EPNdB quieter on both take-off and landings. [23] Many airports impose controls on operations including the night curfew, use of preferred runways and flight paths and weight restrictions on aircraft loads. Land uses, too, are often zoned in order to obtain noise compatible activities close to an airport.

Notwithstanding the use of these regulations, the technical capacity exists to build quieter aircraft [24] or to 'retrofit' existing aircraft with quieter engines. [25] Alternatively, airport managements could discriminate against noisy aircraft or introduce greater controls on

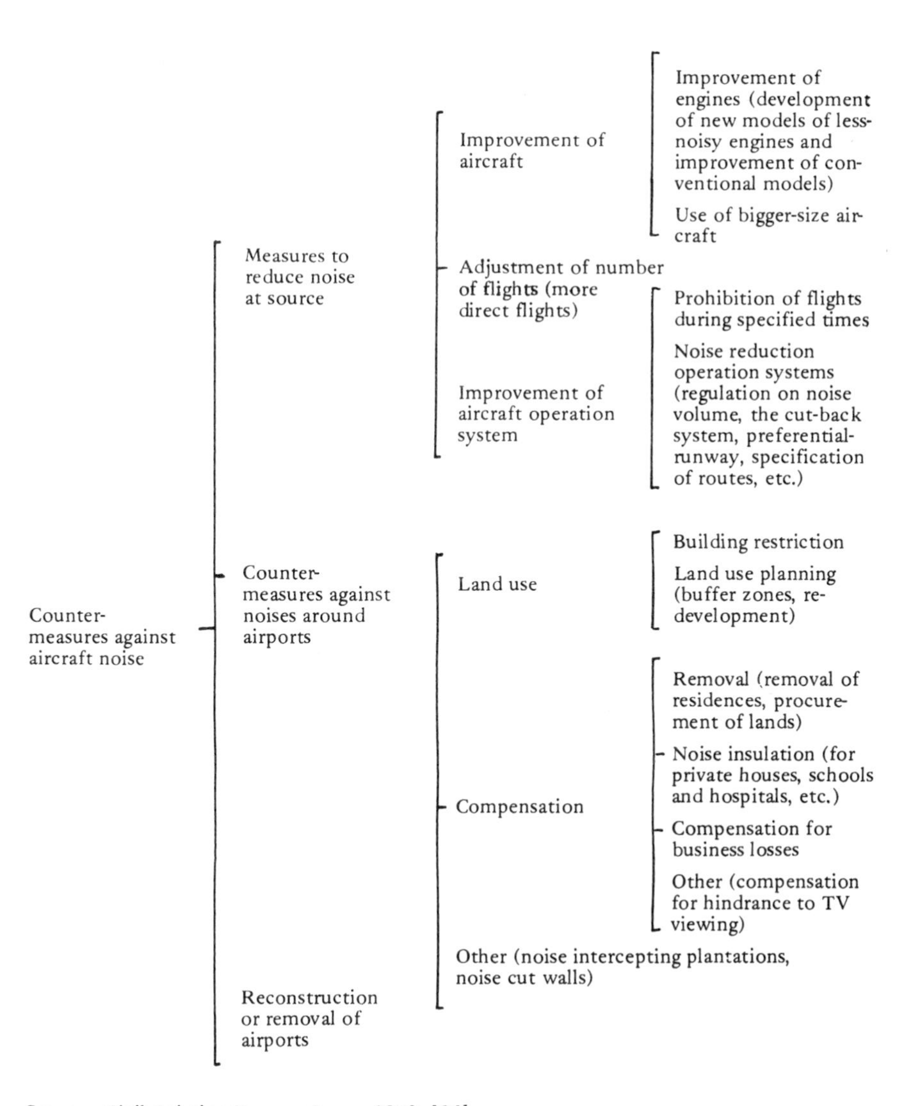

Source: Civil Aviation Bureau, Japan, 1973. [26]

Figure 7.5 Possible policies towards aircraft noise

noisy operations. However, such policies inevitably have a cost in terms of more expensive investment in aircraft or higher operating costs and passengers are also likely to lose some consumer surplus if the number and times of flights are further restricted. Likewise, land use restrictions may involve a reduction in business profits or householder surpluses.

The basic evaluation principle is that each policy instrument for noise abatement should be adopted so long as its marginal cost is less than its marginal benefit. (This is synonymous with the objective that the sum of pollution and pollution abatement costs be minimised). Thus suppose that the marginal costs and benefits of reducing night flights are as shown in figure 7.6. The assumptions underlying this figure are (a) that there is little cost to a small reduction in night flights but that marginal costs rise as more night flights are suppressed (this is the normal economic assumption that the value of something rises as it becomes scarce), and (b) that the benefits of reductions in night flights rise as the reductions increase (this is consistent with the NEF formula in which noise annoyance is a function of the log. of the number of flights). Given the situation as in figure 7.6, the solution is to reduce the number of night flights by OA.

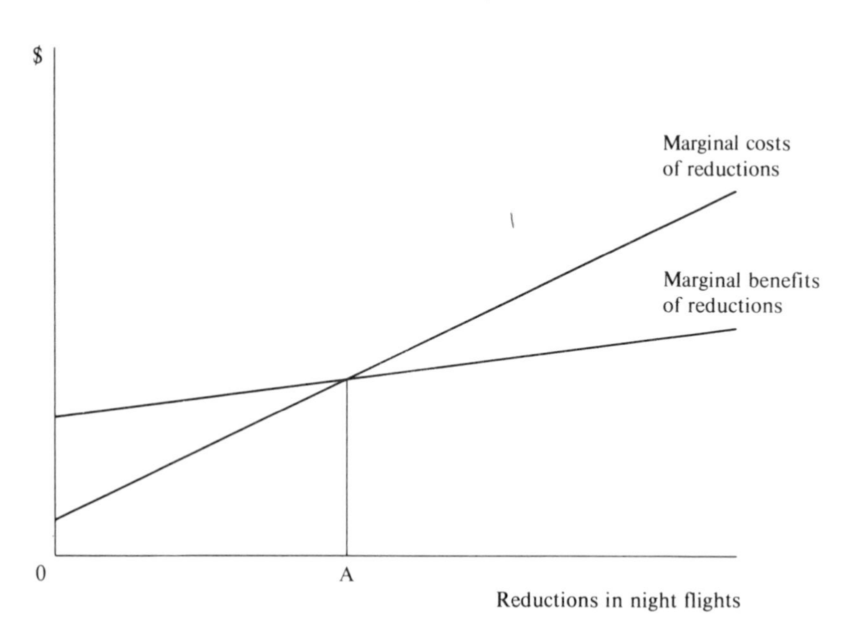

Figure 7.6 Marginal costs and benefits of reductions in night flights

In practice the evaluation procedure is complicated by the interdependence of policies which obliges the analyst to consider them simultaneously. For example, restrictions on aircraft loads would reduce the marginal costs of night flights and so increase the socially optimum number of night flights. But the evaluation principle is not affected by this complication.

Equity issues do however raise several questions of principle. First, whose costs matter? For example, the households around the airport will be mainly nationals, whereas many of the airline manufacturers, airlines and air passengers will be foreign; of course some costs imposed on foreigners may be passed back to the local community. Second, should estimates of noise costs be based on what households are willing to pay for quiet, because if so, noise reduction policies would be more 'beneficial' in affluent areas. Third, should noise costs be estimated on the assumption that households ought to have property rights to peace and quiet, as Mishan suggests? [27] Such estimates would be based on 'compensation' rather than 'willingness to pay' values (see chapter 2). And fourth, should a premium be added to the estimated noise costs to allow for the fact that in practice households often receive no compensation for noise costs?

As usual it is easier to pose such political questions than to answer them. For example, politicians are likely to discount foreign interests, but the aviation industry is supremely international and overt discrimination against foreigners invites retaliation. Concerning the second question, preferential treatment for the rich is avoided if the noise costs of rich and poor households are assumed to be equal. However, this implies acceptance of the assumption that society does not wish to protect relatively highly valued areas, which may be unwarranted. Thirdly it may be observed that Mishan's argument about property rights has currently little legal support. Under existing UK law, for instance, households are compensated for noise resulting from new runway developments on the basis of estimated property depreciation, which is a willingness to pay value. [28] Concerning the fourth question, it may indeed be the case that many households, through notions of justice or of self-interest, would wish to see premiums attached to uncompensated losses, but it is difficult to see how weights for these losses could be adduced scientifically. In general, as discussed in chapter 2, we recommend that the analyst should identify the costs and benefits of major social groups, but the weights, if any, would be determined, often implicitly, by those responsible for the decisions.

It has been assumed above that policies to reduce aircraft noise costs would be introduced by means of regulations, but these have a number of drawbacks. In an international industry like aviation, any one country is limited in the amount of regulations it can impose on foreign manufacturers and operators. But in any case regulations are often crude, inflexible instruments of policy. As Walters [29] points out, for example, 'the use of maximum noise levels as the method of regulation encourages the design of engines so that they fall just below the certified maximum noise emission. It may be possible to reduce noise considerably below these levels at small cost'.

An alternative approach favoured by many economists is to charge the aviation industry for the noise costs they impose on the community, for instance by including a noise cost component in the landing fee. The charge should be made on each aircraft movement and should reflect the marginal social cost of each movement. [30] Noise pricing would discourage marginal flights with low net benefits and would encourage the adoption of quieter aircraft and operating procedures. Pricing noise would be an efficient (low cost) policy because the desired noise reductions would be made by those who could do so most cheaply. Thus Walters [31] argues that 'the great attraction of the "price" compared with the "authorities" (regulation) approach is that it leaves airlines, airport owners and the travelling public free to make their own choices . . . and to get the prices right seems the most significant policy measure which can be undertaken'.

In conclusion to this section, it is apparent that no one policy such as quieter aircraft or land use zoning is likely to resolve the problem of aircraft noise. If regulations are used, a combination of policies is required. In this case, ideally the marginal benefit from each policy should equal its marginal cost (ignoring here distributional issues). Although this ideal will not be attainable, it should be possible to achieve a strategic combination of policies which takes a broad account of their net benefits. Alternatively, the imposition of noise charges would ensure a similar result in terms of noise levels, but almost certainly at lower cost to the aviation industry, which would be free to minimise cost in an optimal fashion, and probably also with savings in the number of officials implementing the noise abatement programme.

7.4 Summary

The NEF model provides a reasonable measure of community annoyance associated with aircraft noise around fairly busy airports. Its main practical limitation is that it is not a precise measure of the effects on households of marginal changes in noise levels – trying to obtain such a measure would be a useful research task. It also appears that the NEF unit may not be cardinally related to annoyance, but allowance can be made for this in estimates of noise costs. There are a number of other shortcomings of the NEF model, such as its failure to allow for ground running and the arbitrary night weighting factor, which could also be refined with more research.

The cost of aircraft noise to local residents can be estimated by reference to house price depreciation and losses of householder surplus. These latter losses may occur even if householders do not move as a result of noise. Although depreciation, losses of surplus and household movements vary with the circumstances, sufficient evidence on these consequences of aircraft noise now exist to enable the analyst to predict the likely order of magnitude of aircraft noise costs to residents. Conversely, the benefits of noise abatement policies can be assessed by the difference in house prices and householder surpluses between the with and without policy situations. In addition, the noise costs of businesses, tax-payers and visitors to the area should be taken into account.

A rational programme to reduce aircraft noise costs would be based on the principle that each policy instrument should be implemented up to the point where its marginal cost equals its marginal benefit. This is equivalent to minimising the sum of noise and noise abatement costs. The principle may be modified however to allow for distributional consequences. Inevitably, the considerable difficulties in estimating the marginal benefit of noise abatement, especially when the interaction between policies is considered, place a severe constraint on the analyst. Indeed, a major reason for preferring charges to regulations is that aircraft manufacturers and operators are better placed than public officials to estimate their own marginal costs. But whether regulations or pricing policies are adopted, it appears that the aircraft noise costs around many airports are high and that the development of a package of policies towards aircraft noise, based on quantified objectives for future noise levels and a timetable for meeting these, would be desirable. Indeed a similar case can be made for quantified plans to reduce most forms of environmental pollution.

Notes

[1] The phrase 'aircraft noise' is used here to denote all forms of disturbance from aircraft flying overhead, including air pollution and electrical interference with television as well as noise disturbance.

[2] Serendipity Inc. 'A Study of the Magnitude of Transportation Noise Circulation and Potential Abatement', vol.II, 1970, Aircraft and Aircraft Systems Noise, Report no. OST-NA-71–1, for Department

of Transportation, USA.
[3] Taylor R. *Noise*, Pelican 1970.
[4] Standards Association of Australia, Noise Assessment in Residential Areas, Report no.1055, 1973.
[5] Galloway D.J. and Bishop D.E. 'Noise Exposure Forecasts: Evolution, Evaluation, Extensions and Land Use Interpretations,' National Technical Information Services, USA 1970.
[6] Tracor Inc. 'Community Reaction to Aircraft Noise', vols I and II, NASA Contract, NASW 1549, 1971.
[7] R. Travers Morgan and Partners, 'Report on the Aircraft Disturbance Survey', Handover Paper no.1, Department of Transport, Canberra, May 1974.
[8] The Likert system used by Tracor and Travers Morgan involved respondents answering 15 and 12 questions respectively about aircraft disturbance and describing themselves as very annoyed, moderately annoyed, little annoyed or not at all annoyed. These answers were scored with 3, 2, 1 and 0 points and summed to obtain a total annoyance score.
[9] Noise, Final Report, CMND 2056, London, HMSO, 1963.
[10] Galloway W.J. 'Noise Exposure Forecast as Indicators of Community Response', SAE/DOT Conference on Aircraft and the Environment, 1971.
[11] National Academy of Sciences, 'Jamaica Bay and Kennedy Airport, A Multidisciplinary Environmental Study', 1971, p.94.
[12] Figure 7.3 and its analysis are adapted from I.G. Heggie's illuminating analysis of noise costs in *Transport Engineering Economics*, McGraw Hill, 1972, pp 105-8.
[13] Households who would move in a quiet or a noisy situation are sometimes called 'natural movers'. It is of course possible that some households would move in a quiet situation but not in a noisy one, either because they like noise or because the fall in property value due to noise constrains their movement.
[14] Walters A.A. *Noise and Prices*, Clarendon Press, Oxford, 1974, pp 97-105.
[15] Walters A.A. op.cit., pp 107-113.
[16] R. Travers Morgan and Partners, Handover Paper no.12, 'Householder's Surplus Survey', June 1974, Department of Transport, Canberra.
[17] Roskill, Papers and Proceedings, volume VII, parts 1 and 2, HMSO, London 1970, and Roskill, Report of the Commission on the Third London Airport, HMSO 1971.
[18] R. Travers Morgan and Partners, Handover Paper no.12, 'Householder's Surplus Survey', June 1974, Department of Transport, Canberra.

[19] One implication of the conclusion that N is often greater than D, is that the Roskill model (which assumes median N equals D) would produce an underestimate of the number of movers. Thus the Roskill forecasts of turnover rates around the proposed third London airports were less than half those actually found in Sydney. It is difficult to explain this by the difference in circumstances; if anything, the rural character of the areas around the London sites would have led one to predict a higher turnover in the English situation.
[20] National Academy of Sciences, op.cit., p.95.
[21] Roskill Report, op.cit., pp 268-73. It may be inferred from our criticism of the Roskill model or more particularly its assumptions that the estimated noise costs in the London study probably understated the real costs.
[22] Convention of International Civil Aviation, Aircraft Noise, Annex 16, 1971.
[23] Unlike the dBA measure of noise, EPNdB allow for the subjective response to frequencies. Thus to allow for jet whine, the EPNdB measure is normally some 10 points higher than the dBA.
[24] FAA Report no.70-11, 'Economic Impact of Implementing Acoustically Treated Nacelles and Direct Configurations Applicable to Low By-Pass Turbofan Engines', 1970.
[25] NASA, Conference on Progress of NASA Research relating to Noise Attenuation of Large Subsonic Jet Aircraft, 1968.
[26] Civil Aviation Bureau, Ministry of Transport Japan, Report on Counter Measures against Civil Aircraft Noise in Japan, 1973.
[27] Mishan E.J. *The Cost of Economic Growth*, Pelican, 1967, pp 102-6.
[28] HMSO, Development and Compensation, Putting People First, CMND 5124, London 1972.
[29] Walters A.A. op.cit., p.119.
[30] Strictly the correct solution is that the charge should be equivalent to the marginal social cost of each aircraft movement at the socially optimal number of movements. See Turvey R. 'On Divergencies between Social and Private Cost', *Economica*, August 1963, pp 309-13.
[31] Walters A.A. op.cit., p.118.

8 Property prices and the values of amenities[1]

This chapter describes the estimated prices of various amenities implicit in the variation in property prices in two municipalities of Sydney. Of particular interest are the negative prices for aircraft noise, road traffic and railway noise and the positive prices for a good view, a spacious street, good access to shops and a high quality neighbourhood. [2] To put the empirical work in perspective, the meanings and use of implicit amenity prices must be discussed. Like other prices, implicit prices are the response at the margin to supply as well as to demand factors and they do not necessarily reflect average household willingness to pay prices. However, I argue that implicit prices do provide a basis from which approximate willingness to pay prices can be generated and used in cost benefit studies.

In the first section, I discuss house price models and the data base from which amenity prices were estimated. The implicit amenity prices are reported in the second section and the application of these results in cost benefit studies is discussed in the third.

8.1 Description of the study

House price models

The implicit price approach to valuing goods (sometimes called the hedonic price approach) which underlies this chapter, has been succinctly summarised by Rosen [3] in the following terms.

> The hedonic hypothesis (assumes) that goods are valued for their utility-bearing attributes or characterstics. Hedonic prices are defined as the implicit prices of attributes and are revealed to economic agents from observed prices of differentiated products and the specific amounts of characteristics associated with them. They constitute the empirical magnitudes explained by the model. Econometrically, implicit prices are estimated by the first step regression analysis (product price regressed on characteristics) in the construction of hedonic price indexes.

In general the utility of a house, or what households are prepared to pay for a house, depends on the size of the land, the size and quality of the house, accessibility to work and recreation, and environmental factors including the quality of the neighbourhood. Of course each of these major utility-bearing elements can be broken down into smaller utility-bearing attributes, the quality of the house for instance depending upon the central heating, the modernisation of the kitchen, the garage and so on. It may be noted, however, that if changes in land use are contemplated, the land may have investment as well as consumption value. In order to estimate amenity values, it was considered desirable therefore to exclude from the study properties which had undergone, or were likely to undergo, significant land use changes.

Under certain extremely restrictive, perfect market conditions – similar household preferences and incomes in different cities, costless household movement between cities and a free competitive market in the supply of land and housing – the prices households would be willing to pay for the utility-bearing characteristics of a house would be similar in different cities. In practice, needless to say, such conditions do not prevail, and both house prices and hedonic attribute prices vary between cities. Likewise household preferences vary, household movement is costly, and housing is not supplied in a perfectly competitive market even within a city. Moreover, from an econometric point of view it is not easy to measure all the differences in the utility-bearing characteristics of properties in different parts of a city. For example, differences between localities in accessibility, in the quality of the view and in the supply of public sector goods are often difficult to model on a city wide basis. Consequently, our study of the implicit prices of amenities was based on differential house prices within two large neighbourhoods. Limiting the area of study in this way increases the precision of the study and hence confidence in the results. But it has the limitation that implicit amenity prices in other areas may differ from those estimated in this study as the demand and supply conditions, which determine prices, vary from area to area.

Turning to the detailed specification of the house price model, four regression models were used in our study. The first one, the ordinary linear regression, can be expressed as follows,

$$P_i = a + \sum_{j=1}^{n} b_j x_{ij} \tag{1}$$

where the P_i are house prices and the x_{ij} are the set of j attributes for the ith house. In the linear model, property attributes have absolute dollar values regardless of the other characteristics of the property; for example, a single garage would be worth the same amount in a $20,000 or $30,000 house.

In the second model, some of the independent variables are expressed in log. or exponential rather than in linear form. Dummy variables are of course unchanged. Taking the log of an independent variable implies diminishing marginal costs or benefits; for example a sixth room in a house would be worth less than the fifth room. The exponential implies increasing costs or benefits; thus $P_i = f(e^{NEF_i})$ implies that house prices fall by increasing amounts for each increment in NEF (Noise Exposure Forecast, see chapter 7). This model can therefore be expressed as follows,

$$P_i = a + \sum_{k=1}^{n^1} b_k x_{ik} + \sum_{l=n^1+1}^{n^{11}} c_l e^{x_{il}} + \sum_{m=n^{11}+1}^{n} d_m \ln.x_{im} \quad (2)$$

where $n^1 < n^{11} < n$.

In the third model, the log of house price is a function of linear variables. In this model, housing attributes are valued at a given percentage of house price; thus a single garage would be x per cent of house price, for all levels of house prices:

$$\ln.P_i = a + \sum_{j=1}^{n} b_j x_{ij} \quad (3)$$

In the fourth model, the log of house price is a function of log variables as well as linear ones. The double log. relationship shows the percentage increase in house price for a one per cent change in the independent variable:

$$\ln.P_i = a + \sum_{r=1}^{n^{11}} b_r x_{ir} + \sum_{m=n^{11}+1}^{n} c_m \ln.x_{im}. \quad (4)$$

The results reported below draw on all four regression models.

Data collection and the nature of the independent variables

The two Sydney municipalities of Marrickville and Rockdale were chosen as the study areas as they are close to the airport and lie partly under the N-S and E-W flight paths respectively (see figure 7.1). Marrickville is an inner city municipality whereas Rockdale is suburban, but both municipalities rank amongst the poorest six out of the forty in Sydney, with an average income of less than $5,000 per household per annum in 1971. [4]

The study included all houses sold in the two municipalities between January 1972 and September 1973, excepting a few with highly unusual features, e.g. very extensive modifications or subdivision into flats. Purpose built flats were excluded because of special difficulty of predicting their prices without internal examination of the property. The sample finally included 592 house sales in Marrickville and 822 house sales in Rockdale. The data collected for each house and the main data sources are shown in figure 8.1.

By way of introducing the independent variables, it may be noted that they were measured in three ways. First, some variables were measured on an objective cardinal scale, for instance the *number of rooms* was described by such a scale. Second, some variables were measured on a subjective scale, also intended however to be cardinal. For instance *road traffic* levels were measured on a three-point scale of noisy, normal and quiet and *views* were measured similarly on a three-point scale of good, average and poor. [5] Thirdly, the existence or non-existence of some attributes could be objectively described by dummy variables. For example dummy variables were used to represent a car port, a single garage, a double garage or no garage.

The second of these methods of measurement, which involved subjective judgements, was probably the most contentious. The main requirements were that the field researchers would simulate the house buyer's perception of the traffic noise or view, etc. and that their attributions were consistent. Tests were made to ensure consistency, but accurate simulation of buyer's perceptions cannot be guaranteed, especially as it is the perception of the marginal purchaser not of the average person which determines the hedonic price. The important conclusion is drawn that if an attribute based on a subjective scale is not a statistically significant determinant of house price, this may be due to imperfect scaling rather than to the inherent insignificance of the attribute. Despite this potential problem, most of the subjectively measured attributes were significant for either Marrickville or Rockdale houses.

The main independent variables used in the regression equations, other than those already mentioned, are described briefly below.

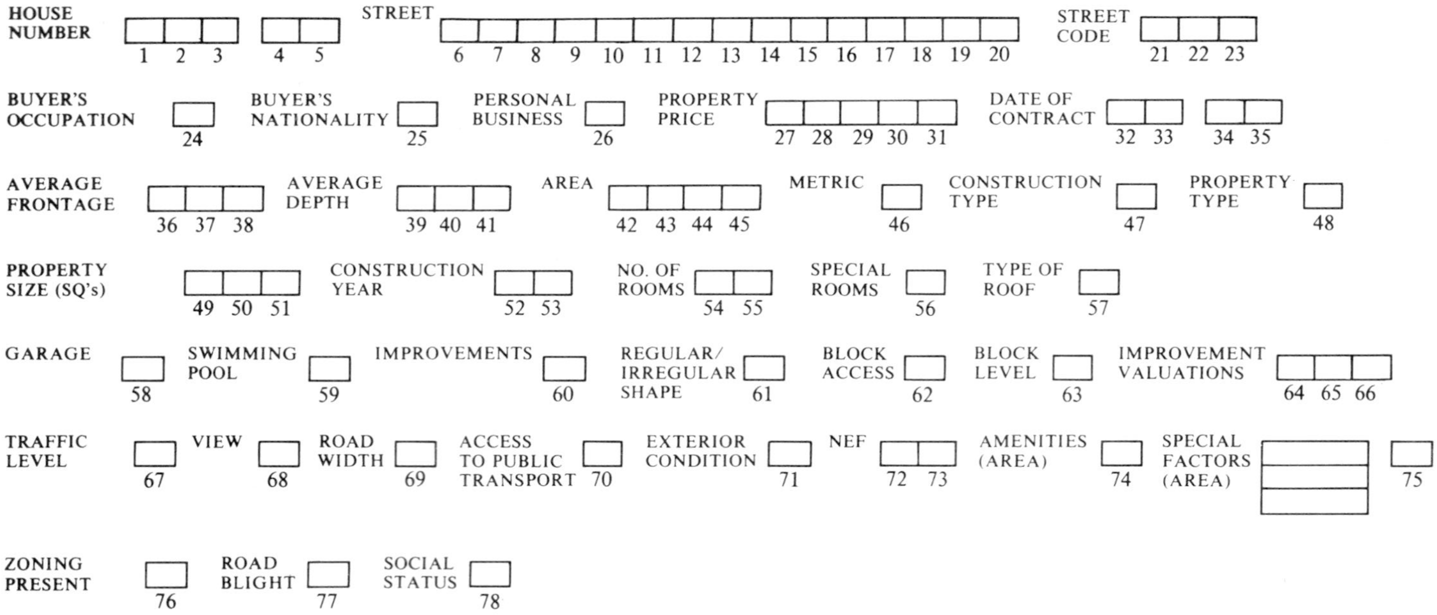

HOUSE NUMBER 1 2 3 4 5 STREET 6 7 8 9 10 11 12 13 14 15 16 17 18 19 20 STREET CODE 21 22 23

BUYER'S OCCUPATION 24 BUYER'S NATIONALITY 25 PERSONAL BUSINESS 26 PROPERTY PRICE 27 28 29 30 31 DATE OF CONTRACT 32 33 34 35

AVERAGE FRONTAGE 36 37 38 AVERAGE DEPTH 39 40 41 AREA 42 43 44 45 METRIC 46 CONSTRUCTION TYPE 47 PROPERTY TYPE 48

PROPERTY SIZE (SQ's) 49 50 51 CONSTRUCTION YEAR 52 53 NO. OF ROOMS 54 55 SPECIAL ROOMS 56 TYPE OF ROOF 57

GARAGE 58 SWIMMING POOL 59 IMPROVEMENTS 60 REGULAR/ IRREGULAR SHAPE 61 BLOCK ACCESS 62 BLOCK LEVEL 63 IMPROVEMENT VALUATIONS 64 65 66

TRAFFIC LEVEL 67 VIEW 68 ROAD WIDTH 69 ACCESS TO PUBLIC TRANSPORT 70 EXTERIOR CONDITION 71 NEF 72 73 AMENITIES (AREA) 74 SPECIAL FACTORS (AREA) 75

ZONING PRESENT 76 ROAD BLIGHT 77 SOCIAL STATUS 78

Sources: Valuer General, Field Inspection, Zoning Maps.

Figure 8.1 The data collection form

The *'date of contract'* for the sale was important because of the high rate of property price inflation in 1972-73. The data was transformed into a monthly scale, with January 1972 = 1, February 1972 = 2, etc. so that the variable came to represent the monthly inflation rate.

The *frontage and depth* of the land, which were measured in feet, have obvious significance.

Construction type meant a brick or non-brick building.

Property types, classed as detached and semi-detached and as one or two storeys, were represented by dummy variables. They were intended to reflect the quality of the building, but they are partly correlated with the size of the land or number of rooms so that some regressions were run without them.

The *construction year* was estimated and converted in the regression analysis to the estimated age of the house, for which a negative coefficient was of course expected.

The *type of roof* included tile, slate and other roofs.

Significant *improvements* were represented by a dummy variable. Typically these would show up in modernised windows or extensions at the back of the house, and would doubtless be correlated with renovation of the inside of the house.

Block access other than normal included either rear access, which is generally regarded as an advantage for parking, or a corner position, which would be noisy.

A dummy variable for *block level* indicated a house on the top side of a sloping street or one built well above street level.

Road width was measured on a three-point scale of wide, normal and narrow, reflecting the spaciousness of the environment, which we would expect to be an attractive attribute, having of course allowed separately for the amount of road traffic.

The quality of *public transport service* was represented by a dummy variable, distinguishing households living within half a mile of a public transport service from others. It turned out however that virtually all households in Marrickville and most in Rockdale lived close to public transport which was not therefore a significant discriminating factor in house prices.

The *exterior condition* of each house was measured on a four-point scale – very good, good, average and poor. [6]

NEF stands for *Noise Exposure Forecast* which, as discussed in the last chapter, is a measure of aircraft noise nuisance to households. Relationships between house prices and various forms of the NEF variable were tested. These forms included NEF −25, which gives all NEF scores of 25 or less a value of zero and assumes a linear relationship between house prices and NEF scores of greater than 25, NEF -30, which is calculated in similar manner, and $e^{\frac{NEF-25}{10}}$ and $e^{\frac{NEF-30}{10}}$, which suggest that for a given increment in NEF house prices fall more at higher levels of NEF.

Area amenities meant primarily access to shops, which was measured on a three-point scale in Marrickville and a four-point scale in Rockdale.

Present zoning reflects the allowable land use in a sub-area of a municipality. Each council had some five codes allowing different residential densities and commercial uses.

Road blight means here the cost to a house of a plan to widen the road at some future time.

Social status, measured on a three-point scale of high, average and low, reflected the quality of the neighbouring houses in the street and their effect upon house prices.

One other variable, not shown in figure 8.1, *proximity to the sea* (within half a mile of it) was added for Rockdale but was not relevant to Marrickville.

Despite the large number of variables included some important ones were perforce excluded or were included crudely. Characteristics of the interiors of the houses, for example, were excluded. Nor was any allowance made for such attributes as privacy, the amount of sun in winter, or air pollution, though the last of these would be strongly correlated with road traffic. The public transport variable was also rather crude. It may be noted that distance to work was not included as an independent variable since it was considered a relatively unimportant determinant of property price differences within the municipality – partly because of the uniform quality of public transport and partly because of the availability of local jobs. But distance to work would surely be an important determinant of property price differences between municipalities.

Brief description of properties

Marrickville house prices in 1972-73 ranged from $14,000 to $35,000 and averaged$21,000. [7] Some three-fifths of the 592 sample houses were detached dwellings and two-fifths were terraced or semi-detached properties, but in style and quality the houses were a fairly homogeneous group. Over 90 per cent were brick and most were considered to be in good condition. Over three-quarters were judged to have been built before 1914. And fully three-quarters of the houses were considered to have an average inner city view. However, significant differences between houses were noted for both road traffic, over one-third of properties experiencing heavy traffic conditions, and aircraft noise with some two-fifths of the properties standing within the 25 NEF. Furthermore 10 per cent of the houses stood on roads scheduled for significant widening.

House prices in Rockdale varied from $13,000 to over $45,000 in 1972-73, with the average in our survey being $24,000. Although more than 90 per cent of the 822 sample houses were detached, in other respects they displayed more heterogeneous characteristics than Marrickville houses. Only about two-thirds of the houses were of brick construction. Some one-third of the houses were built before 1914 and the rest during the intervening years up to the present day. The views, with some houses overlooking the Pacific Ocean, also vary greatly in quality. About one-sixth of the houses experience heavy road traffic and one-third stand within the 25 NEF.

It is generally thought that the attributes of houses are interrelated. Houses with good views and peaceful surroundings tend to be kept in good condition. The quality of the neighbouring houses tends to be in keeping with the qualities of the environment, and so on. In practice, however, it turned out that multi-collinearity between the variables was lower than might have been expected. Some examples of correlations are given in tables 8.1 and 8.2, which show that multi-collinearity is slightly higher in Marrickville than in Rockdale. In particular, 'social status' tends to be correlated with the other positive amenities of a house, and houses suffering from aircraft noise often experience high road traffic levels. However, most of the correlations between the independent variables are low and the regression co-efficients are not significantly affected by the inclusion of other variables in the equations.

8.2 Results of the house prices study

General results

The major results for Marrickville and Rockdale are reported in tables 8.3 and 8.4 respectively. Regressions with the log of the house price as well as those with ordinary house price as the dependent variable, are included for both municipalities. Likewise some regressions in which certain independent variables, such as age and frontage, are expressed in log rather than linear form are included. Also reported are regression results for equations in which such variables as road

Table 8.1
Some correlations between variables: Marrickville

	Road traffic	View	External condition	NEF	Road blight	Social status
Road traffic	1.0	.152	.077	–.298	–.087	.325
View		1.0	.156	–.135	–.077	.271
External condition			1.0	–.102	–.046	.198
NEF				1.0	–.082	–.331
Road blight					1.0	–.123
Social status						1.0

Table 8.2
Some correlations between variables: Rockdale

	Road traffic	View	External condition	NEF	Road blight	Social status
Road traffic	1.0	.315	.076	.011	–.000	.126
View		1.0	.004	.034	–.001	.080
External condition			1.0	–.036	–.021	.159
NEF				1.0	–.056	.064
Road blight					1.0	–.009
Social status						1.0

traffic, social status and property types are omitted in order to examine the effects of removing such multicollinearity as exists between variables. For Rockdale, where there is greater dispersion of house prices than in Marrickville, regressions were also run separately for low and high price houses to investigate whether household incomes affect implicit amenity prices.

When most of the independent variables were included in the Marrickville regressions, equations 5 to 9, the R^2 varied from 0.66 to 0.68. This compares reasonably with the amount of explanation obtained in the studies reported by Ball [8] especially given the relatively large number of observations in our study and the exclusion of internal house characteristics other than the number of rooms from our study. A slightly higher R^2 was normally obtained with ordinary house price rather than the log of house price as the dependent variable. but the residuals were more biased in the former case, being higher for the higher priced houses. On these grounds it could be argued that the model is better specified with the log of house price as the dependent variable. However all the coefficients reported for each Marrickville equation are significant at the 95 per cent level and possess the expected signs.

The R^2 for the equations including all properties in Rockdale was normally slightly lower than in Marrickville, being around 0.62, due probably to the larger sample in Rockdale as well as to the wider price and quality range. It may be noted that a marginally higher level of explanation was obtained with the log of house price rather than with ordinary house price as the dependent variable (equation 12 compared with equation 11). As can be seen from table 8.4, nearly all coefficients were significant at the 95 per cent level and all possessed the expected signs.

To round off this summary, the major determinants of house price differentials within municipalities, as shown in table 8.5, were house quality and size, land size and inflation. Environmental factors and neighbourhood effects explained a smaller proportion of house price differences. The significance of the individual variables in equation 5 and 11 is shown in table 8.6. Of course 'significance' is relative to the context, which is the explanation of intra-municipality house price differentials. A low score for any factor, for example accessibility, in table 8.5 or 8.6 does not mean that it is always unimportant with respect to house prices. Moreover, as described in the following section, the estimated hedonic prices of amenities were far from negligible.

Table 8.3
Marrickville: Summary of regression results [a]

Equation	5	6	7	8	9	10
R^2	.68	.66	.68	.66	.66	.62
House price	Ordinary	Log.	Ordinary	Log	Ordinary	Ordinary
Constant	5,365	9.3	4,998	9.1	7,860	8,450
Monthly inflation	253(21)	.012(.001)	253(21)	.012(.001)	256(22)	265(23)
Frontage (ft)	35(12)	.002(.0006)	34(13)		52(13)	88(11)
Log. frontage (ft)				.074(.017)		
Depth (ft)	9(4)	.0004(.0002)	9(4)		13(5)	13(5)
Age (years)	−14(5)	−.0009(.0003)	−14(5)			−16(6)
Log. age (years)				−.062(.017)		
Not brick	−2,525(431)	−.121(.020)	−2,532(431)	−.127(.021)	−3,179(421)	−2,155(42)
No. rooms	1,137(102)	.050(.005)	1,140(102)		1,073(103)	1,359(10)
Log no. rooms				.291(.031)		
Road traffic	−713(202)	−.028(.010)	−716(202)	−.025(.010)		−700(227)
Road blight	−1,923(323)	−.093(.016)	−1,914(323)	−.083(.016)	−2,052(335)	−1,709(34)
Road width	459(150)	.029(.007)	458(150)	.030(.007)	432(149)	440(162)
External conditions	515(133)	.020(.006)	519(133)	.018(.006)		426(143)
Area amenities	305(138)	NS	307(138)	NS		273(149)
Improvements	1,258(401)	.054(.019)	1,275(401)	.051(.019)	1,427(415)	1,366(43)
$e^{\frac{NEF-25}{10}}$	−382(114)					−330(126)
NEF−25	NS	−.004(.001)	−74(23)	−.004(.001)	−120(22)	
Zoning C_1 (higher density)	−559(223)	−.020(.010)	−569(223)	NS	−726(229)	−562(241)
Rear access	955(277)	.045(.013)	953(277)	.045(.013)	924(288)	1,075(29)
Corner access	−1,048(399)	−.040(.019)	−1,048(398)	−.040(.019)	−999(412)	−1,132(42)
Property – detached one storey double front	1,699(318)	.057(.015)	1,696(319)	.056(.015)	1,747(330)	
Property – detached two storeys	3,866(773)	.168(.038)	3,884(775)	.170(.037)	3,491(803)	

Table 8.3 (cont.)

Property – semi-detached 1 storey	−6,573(761)	−.287(.038)	−6,597(762)	−.290(.038)	−6,412(792)	
Property – semi-detached 2 storeys	NS	.040(.020)	NS	.046(.020)	NS	
Single garage	1,019(260)	.045(.013)	1,010(260)	.045(.012)	1,111(269)	1,316(270)
Car port	−1,083(424)	−.064(.020)	−1,086(425)	NS	−1,171(442)	−1,366(433)
Roof – galvanised iron	−630(298)	−.042(.015)	−626(298)	NS	NS	NS
Roof – slate	921(310)	.052(.015)	912(310)	NS	NS	NS
Social status						867(277)

[a] A blank means that the variable was excluded from the run. 'NS' means that it was included but was not significant at the 95 per cent level.

The figures in brackets are the standard errors.

Table 8.4
Rockdale: Summary of regression results [a]

Equation	11	12	13	14	15
R^2	.61	.62	.37	.37	.46
House price	Ordinary	Log.	Ordinary	Log.	Log
Houses in regression	All	All	$P > \$25,000$	$P > \$25,000$	$P < \$25,000$
Constant	13,254	9.6	19,591	9.9	9.8
Monthly inflation	330(26)	.013(.001)	166(41)	.005(.001)	.009(.001)
Frontage (ft)	72(12)	.003(.0005)	34(17)	.002(.0006)	.002(.0006)
Depth (ft)	11(4)	.0003(.0001)	23(6)	.001(.0002)	
Not brick	−3,000(297)	−.134(.012)			−.100(.012)
Age (years)	−129(10)	−.005(.0004)	−108(12)	−.003(.0004)	−.002(.0005)
No. rooms	252(48)	.008(.002)	163(49)	.005(.002)	
Above road	1,390(606)	.055(.025)	3,042(1122)	.104(.037)	
View	440(220)	.017(.009)	887(425)	.035(.014)	
Road width	416(222)	.018(.009)			
External condition	392(134)	.015(.005)	427(211)	.014(.007)	.013(.006)
Road blight	−3,241(1566)				
Area amenities	352(145)	.016(.006)	396(222)	.014(.007)	.016(.006)
Close to railway					−.121(.011)
Close to sea	502(263)				
Social status	936(379)	.043(.015)			
Improvements	812(292)	.033(.012)			
$e^{\frac{NEF-30}{10}}$			−916(575)		
NEF−25				−.0022(.0016)	
Roof galvanised iron	−1,728(400)	−.092(.017)			−.084(.015)
Roof slate					−.083(.027)
Roof other (not tile)	3,522(755)	.152(.031)			
Single garage	1,504(328)	.073(.014)		.036(.024)	.049(.012)
Double garage	2,751(619)	.099(.026)	1,791(676)	.056(.022)	
Car port	−3,510(713)	−.145(.029)	−1,815(902)	−.060(.030)	−.054(.017)
Property – detached one storey, double front					.037(.013)
Property – detached 2 storeys	9,075(1446)	.265(.059)	6,994(1376)	.180(.046)	.081(.021)
Property – semi-detached 1 storey	−11,663(1566)	−.374(.064)	−14,694(3540)	−.485(.118)	

[a] In these runs all variables were included throughout, and blanks indicate a lack of any significant result.

The figures in brackets are the standard errors.

Table 8.5
Proportion of house price variations explained by groups of variables

	Marrickville	Rockdale
	%	%
House quality and size	43	45
Land size	10	7
Inflation	8	6
Environmental factors	6	3
Neighbourhood effects [a]	1	1
Accessibility	neg.	neg.
Total	68	62

[a] Includes residential zoning, local amenities and social status.

Table 8.6
Variables in order of entry

Marrickville (equation 5)	R^2	Rockdale (equation 11)	R^2
No. rooms	.28	Construction year	.24
Frontage	.37	Construction type	.35
Month of contract (inflation)	.45	Frontage	.41
Construction type	.49	Month of contract (inflation)	.47
Property – semi-detached terrace 1 storey	.53	Single garage	.50
Property – detached single storey double front	.56	No. rooms	.51
Road blight	.58	Property – semi-detached 1 storey	.52
$e^{\frac{NEF-25}{10}}$	.60	Property – detached 2 storeys	.55
External condition	.61	Roof galvanised iron	.56
Property – detached 2 storey	.62	Roof other	.57
Single garage	.63	Improvements	.57
Construction year	.64	External condition	.58
Depth	.65	Block level	.58
Improvements	.65	Depth	.59
Road width	.66	Area amenities	.59
Road traffic	.66	Double garage	.59
Car port	.67	Car port	.60
Corner and rear access	.67	Social status	.60
Corner access only	.67	Road width	.61
Residential zone C_2	.68	Road blight	.61
Area amenities	.68	View	.61
Roof slate	.68	Closeness to sea	.61
Roof galvanised iron	.68		

Implicit prices for amenity attributes

Aircraft noise As shown in all the equations in table 8.3, aircraft noise is a significant determinant of house prices in Marrickville. The values of the coefficients for different forms of the aircraft noise variable can be summarised as follows.

Form of variable	Coefficient	Order of entry in step-wise regressions	Approx. price difference between quiet and very noisy houses
$x = e^{\frac{NEF-25}{10}}$	-382	1	$1,340
x = NEF-25	- 74	2	$1,100
x = NEF-30	-125	3	$1,250

These Marrickville results suggest that the relationship between house prices and the NEF measure of aircraft noise is better represented by a non-linear than by a linear function. The variable $e^{\frac{NEF-25}{10}}$ always entered the stepwise regressions before other forms of the noise variable and the co-efficient for the NEF-30 variables was higher than for the NEF-25 variable. It may be inferred however that there is some house price depreciation due to noise outside the 25 NEF. Within the 25 NEF, the price of aircraft noise was estimated at 0.4 per cent of house price per NEF, which implies a total price difference of some 6.0 per cent between a quiet and a noisy house. [9] This was rather less than the difference found in the studies reported by Walters [10], most of which suggested that house prices fell by 1.0 per cent or more per NEF over 25. One reason for this difference may be the larger number of variables included in our study. For instance, when traffic noise and exterior condition are dropped, as in equation 9, the NEF coefficient rises by 60 per cent. It may be argued, however, that if aircraft noise causes a reduction in home maintenance and hence in property values, this fall in value may reasonably be ascribed to aircraft noise. A second possible reason for our relatively low depreciation due to aircraft noise, is that Marrickville residents, who have chosen an inner city lifestyle and who have low incomes, have a relatively low preference for peace and quiet.

Some support for the hypothesis that the relationship between house prices and NEF is non-linear was also found in analysing the higher priced houses in Rockdale (see equation 13), where the variable $e^{\frac{NEF-30}{10}}$ was significant at about the 90 per cent level. The equation implied that noisy houses experienced about $3,250 or 10 per cent price depreciation compared with quiet houses. No significant relationship could be established, however, between NEF and house prices for the sample of all houses, or of lower priced houses, in Rockdale. This probably reflects the inadequacy of the NEF model as a measure of the annoyance caused by aircraft noise when the number of aircraft movements is low, and the failure of households to appreciate the severity of aircraft noise when they buy houses (see chapter 7).

Road traffic and road widening. The price difference between a house on a quiet road compared with one on a noisy road in Marrickville was estimated at $1,400 or 5.6 per cent of house price. In addition to this, houses on corners sold for $1,000 or about 4 per cent less than other houses, and some of this depreciation would doubtless be attributable to traffic noise. However no statistical relationship between road traffic and house prices was established in Rockdale.

The price of a house on a road scheduled for widening in Marrickville was estimated to fall by $1,923 or by 9.3 per cent of the average house price. The comparable figures for Rockdale were $3,241 and 13.5 per cent of house price.

Views, block levels, spacious roads and other environmental amenities. The values of a good view, of a house built above road level and of a house on a spacious road are most evident in equations 11 and 12 for all houses in Rockdale. A good view in Rockdale was valued at about $440 compared with an average view which was in turn worth $440 more than a poor view. In addition, a house built above road level was estimated to be worth $1,450 or 5.5 per cent more than a house at road level or below it, and a house on a wide road was estimated to be worth $832 or 3.6 per cent more than a house on a narrow road. And in addition to all this, a house in a good neighbourhood ('social status') was estimated to be worth about $1,900 or 8.6 per cent more than a house in a poor neighbourhood and a house close to the sea was worth a further $550. A house which combined all these environmental qualities would sell at an estimated premium of some $5,500 more than a house with none of these qualities, which amounted to nearly 25 per cent of the value of the average house in Rockdale in 1972-73.

There is also clear evidence from the Rockdale equations 11 to 15 that the demand for a good view and for a house built above the road level is income-elastic. A good view compared with a poor one was estimated to be worth 7.0 per cent of the price for high priced houses compared with 3.5 per cent of the price for all houses and was not significant for lower priced houses. A house built above the road was estimated to be worth about 10.0 per cent of the price for high priced houses compared with 5.5 per cent of the price for all houses, and was also not significant for lower priced houses.

Unlike Rockdale houses, most houses in Marrickville are built on flat terrain and have a rather uniform inner-city view, so that not very surprisingly, no statistical relationship between block level or views and house prices was established. However, houses on wide spacious roads in Marrickville were estimated to be worth about $900 or 6 per cent more than houses on narrow roads. Indeed, this differential is percentage-wise significantly larger than that estimated for Rockdale, which may be seen as a slight compensating factor for the lack of views in Marrickville. The quality of a good neighbourhood compared with a poor one was estimated to be worth $1,000 or about 9 per cent of house price in Marrickville, which was similar to the valuation for a good neighbourhood in Rockdale.

Other related amenities. Unlike the attributes discussed above, garages are not amenities in the sense that amenities are normally external to the property, but as roads have figured prominently in our discussion, the value of garages is perhaps of interest. Single garages in Marrickville were valued at approximately $1,000 or 4.5 per cent of house price. In addition, rear access to a house was worth an estimated $1,000, some of which value was probably attributable to its utility as a parking space or as leading to parking facilities in the back garden. Single garages in Rockdale were valued at $1,500 and double garages at $2,250. As a percentage of house price this would be 7.3 per cent and 10 per cent respectively. However, car ports at the front of houses actually reduced house values by nearly $1,000 in Marrickville and by an estimated $3,500 in Rockdale.

Good access to shops and commercial entertainment was estimated to be worth $600 per house in Marrickville or about 3 per cent of house price, and about $1,000 in Rockdale or about 5 per cent of house price. Good access to shops was also worth about 5 per cent of the value of both high and low priced houses in Rockdale, when these were examined separately (equations 14 and 15).

Finally it may be noted that being close to the railway reduced the price of low priced houses in Rockdale by an estimated 12 per cent, (equation 15). The proximity to rail variable was meant to reflect the advantage of access to public transport, but apparently this was outweighed by the disamenity, chiefly noise, of living close to a railway.

8.3 Implicit amenity prices and willingness to pay values

In order to determine whether estimated implicit amenity prices reflect willingness to pay values, it is convenient to ask two main questions. First, do the estimated prices reflect equilibrium prices determined by willing buyers and sellers? And second, to what extent do equilibrium prices reflect willingness to pay values? Four reasons are given below for considering that estimated implicit prices are not always equilibrium prices. But in each case, reasonable allowance can probably be made.

(a) In our house price model, household attitudes towards certain amenities or disamenities are represented by scales. Estimated implicit prices derived from this model reflect buyer preferences only if the scales accurately represent household attitudes. Since the scales are often quite simple, they can do only rough justice to the complexity of individual preferences, but nevertheless, the orders of magnitude obtained with the use of such scales are probably reasonable representations of preferences.

(b) Markets may be imperfect because of buyer ignorance. In this case, survey information may indicate the approximate amount by which house price depreciation due to the disamenity is an understatement of the household's true preferences.

(c) Hedonic prices may not capture the indirect or dynamic secondary effects of amenities or disamenities. Heavy road traffic, for instance, may reduce property values directly and indirectly as neighbourhood values fall and house maintenance expenditures are reduced. To determine these effects, it would be necessary to examine the interrelationship between the 'independent' variables in the house price model.

(d) Fourthly, the property market takes time to adjust to major land use changes. In these disequilibrium situations, some households will be living where they do not wish and will incur losses of householder surplus and possibly movement costs. Neither of these is reflected in implicit (or explicit) prices, but both are part of the cost of inflicting new disamenities on households and should be taken into account when necessary.

Let us assume now that hedonic prices are equilibrium prices paid by informed, willing buyers and consider to what extent they can be taken as general willingness-to-pay prices. Our starting point is Rosen's comment concerning hedonic prices: 'here as elsewhere, price differences generally are equalising only on the margin and not on the average. Hence estimated hedonic price-characteristics functions typically identify neither demand nor supply'. [11] Freeman argues similarly that the 'observed relationship between property values and air quality is not a demand curve for clean air, but rather represents an opportunity locus or a sort of supply curve for households'. [12] But both writers argue that hedonic prices provide a basis for estimating the demand for amenities.

Figure 8.3a, taken from Freeman, depicts the annual rent V(Q) as a function of air quality (Q). Figure 8.3b, also from Freeman, shows the change in property values with the change in air quality as a function of air quality R(Q) and the demand for air quality $D_i(Q)$ and $D_j(Q)$. The R(Q) function is the marginal purchase price of air quality and 'can be interpreted as the locus of the equilibrium marginal willingness to pay amounts of all households'. [13] If all households have the same preferences, the slope of the demand curve will be the same as the marginal price curve. More likely, preferences will differ as shown in figure 8.3b. Given this situation, how can the real demand for amenities be estimated?

Rosen and Freeman have described similar two-step procedures for estimating demand curves for amenities. Following here the Freeman version, the first step is to estimate amenity prices as in this chapter. Secondly, 'it is hypothesised that the air quality chosen by the ith household in the jth city depends upon the marginal purchase price of Q in that city, R(Q), and household socio-economic characteristics such as income, age, etc.

Specifically, for the ith individual living in the jth city,

$$Q_i = f[R^j(Q_i), Y_i, age_i \ldots].$$

This equation can be estimated from the pooled data for all cities.

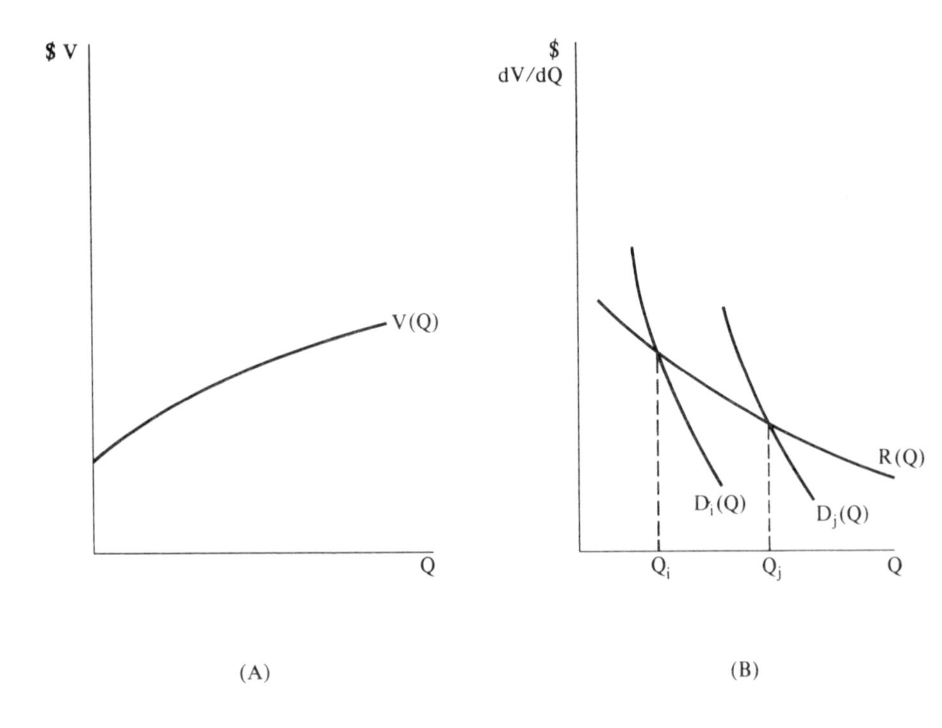

Figure 8.3 The rent function and household demand curves for air quality

The inclusion of the marginal purchase price function amounts to an experimental shifting of the supply curve or opportunity locus, to obtain price variation, while controlling for income, age, etc. The coefficient on the variable, $R^j(Q_i)$, is either the slope or the elasticity of the demand curve for clean air, depending on whether the equation was estimated in the logs or linear form. If the changes in Q are small enough so that the marginal utility of income can be assumed to be approximately constant, then the estimated demand function can be used to calculate the benefits of air quality improvement'. [14] Freeman goes on to show that given such a demand function, for a marginal change in amenity level affecting all households, the sum of the individual households' marginal willingness to pay is a precise measure of the aggregate marginal benefit. However for non-marginal amenity improvements (or deterioration) multiplying the marginal willingness to pay times the change in amenity summed over all households will result in an upper bound (or a lower bound) of the true benefits (or costs).

To summarise, hedonic prices may not represent willingness to pay amenity values because markets are imperfect or in disequilibrium or because preferences vary and average values do not equal marginal values. One result of this is that hedonic prices may vary between areas. Most of these difficulties can be resolved and relevant willingness to pay prices estimated with plausible assumptions about market imperfections and disequilibrium effects, and with survey data about consumer preferences. Alternatively, if the hedonic prices represent equilibrium situations, willingness to pay prices may be calculated with the aid of a Freeman-type two-step econometric model to estimate the demand curve for amenities, the first step of which is obtaining amenity prices along the lines shown in this chapter.

8.4 Summary

The chapter described a study of house price transactions for over 1,400 properties in two municipalities in Sydney, analysed in terms of some thirty independent variables. Plausible hedonic amenity prices were estimated, for example, for aircraft noise, road traffic, road widening, railway noise, the quality of view, block level, the spaciousness of the roads, proximity to the sea, access to shops, and the quality of the neighbourhood. Moreover, these hedonic prices were generally statistically significant at the 95 per cent level though the two municipalities are amongst the poorest in Sydney, and therefore contain many households who might be expected to place a relatively low valuation on amenities.

Hedonic amenity prices represent average household willingness to pay values for amenities only if markets are assumed to be perfect and in equilibrium and if household preferences are similar. However, reasonable approximations to the demand price for amenities can be derived from hedonic prices either with plausible assumptions about the nature of the market and with survey data on household preferences or with a more elaborate econometric study. Such a study would first obtain hedonic amenity prices and second would estimate the amounts of amenities purchased as a function of their prices as well as of the socio-economic characteristics of households.

Notes

[1] A more detailed version of this chapter appears in Abelson P.W.

'The Impact of Environmental Factors on Relative House Prices', Occasional Paper no.7, Bureau of Transport Economics, Australian Government Publishing Service, Canberra, 1977. I wish to acknowledge especially the assistance given by David Hawes, Michael Moore, Murray Aitken, June Crawford and Bernie Ludecke to the research reported in this chapter.
[2] It is, of course, often arbitrary whether we speak of a positive price for amenity or a negative price for disamenity. For example, we may say that a good view has a positive price or a bad view a negative one.
[3] Rosen S. 'Hedonic Prices and Implicit Markets, Product Differentiation in Pure Competition', *Journal of Political Economy* (82), 1974, pp 34-55.
[4] Sydney Area Transportation Study, Base Year (1971) Data Report, vol.1, pp 11-34.
[5] It may be noted that in the field the researchers actually used a five-point scale for traffic levels and a seven-point scale for the quality of the view. However, when the more detailed scale was used in the regressions, the coefficients were not significant.
[6] To be precise, external conditions and area amenities were measured on a five-point scale but there were only a few houses in the very poor category.
[7] All monetary figures are in 1972-73 Australian dollars.
[8] Ball M.J. 'Recent Empirical Work on the Determinants of Relative House Prices', *Urban Studies* (10), 1973, pp 213-33.
[9] The percentages quoted in this chapter are derived where possible from equations with the log of house price as the dependent variable. They are not necessarily the same as would be obtained by dividing the average house price in the municipality by the value of the co-efficient.
[10] Walters A.A. *Noise and Prices*, Clarendon Press, 1974, pp 97-105.
[11] Rosen S. op.cit., p.54.
[12] Freeman A.M. 'On Estimating Air Pollution Benefits from Land Value Studies', *Journal of Environmental Economics and Management* (1), 1974, pp 74-83.
[13] Freeman A.M. op.cit., p.77.
[14] Freeman A.M. op.cit., p.78.

Concluding comment

> Take away number and all is enveloped in blind ignorance
>
> Raban Maur (784-847 AD)

This book has been concerned principally with developing and applying a quantitative method for solving environmental problems. The starting point of our discussion was that every alternative available to a decision maker has an opportunity cost. The decision to build a dam, for example, has a cost in terms of the marketed and non-marketed goods foregone. But equally, the cost of leaving the environment as we find it is the benefit sacrificed in not exploiting it. The use of money as a measure of these costs and benefits should not be controversial since it is simply a practical device which enables us to compare them. The issues of real importance in the evaluation are the amounts of money to be associated with each cost and benefit and the aggregation of these amounts so that the decision maker can determine the most beneficial course for society.

Cost benefit analysis is a systematic and sophisticated attempt to resolve these issues. It is based on the idea that individual preferences matter and that these can be evaluated by analysis of market behaviour along with attitudinal information from surveys. When market prices fail to reflect what individuals are willing to pay for goods and services or the resource costs of producing them, accounting prices are used to correct for market imperfections. Another idea basic to cost benefit analysis is the concept of net present value. This provides a measure of the net worth of a project in terms of its estimated impact on the aggregate value of consumption over time. The net present value can include valuations for many environmental goods, although some non-marketed goods would be considered intangibles. Cost benefit analysis also provides an evaluation framework within which uncertainty and distributional issues can be taken into account.

Nevertheless, as we have often noted, cost benefit analysis has certain important limitations. For a start, its premise that individual preferences matter is a value judgement and opinions may vary as to the extent to which it should be applied (for example, with respect to the treatment of children, of the mentally disturbed, or of foreigners). Secondly, however sophisticated the analysis, it is often difficult to put a value on such things as unpolluted air, beautiful countryside or historical traditions. Questions of life and death raise even more fundamental difficulties. Thirdly, projects which improve the average standard of living may depress the living standards of the poor. Consequently, an estimated positive net present value is only one yardstick of a project's worth; it is neither a sufficient nor even a necessary criterion of that worth.

Some planners feel that these and other criticisms are sufficient to condemn cost benefit analysis, but one must guard against a nihilistic attitude especially if, as seem to be the case, we have no satisfactory alternative to put in its place. In the last resort, all decisions imply that some assessment of costs and benefits is made, however intuitively. What cost benefit analysis does, amongst other things, is to make these assessments explicit, and this is surely a desirable practice.

The other general conclusion of the book which should be emphasised is that there is rarely one simple solution to an environmental problem, like shutting down an airport or stopping all economic growth. The optimal solution nearly always lies in the discovery of the best rate of exploitation or the preferred amount of pollution. Likewise, it is rare that any one policy instrument alone is optimal to achieve an important objective such as pollution reduction. Rather each instrument should be adopted so long as the marginal benefits of using it exceed the marginal costs (allowing if necessary for distributional factors). It is of course a great deal easier to win converts to a cause with all or nothing solutions like 'all uses of nuclear power are wrong' than with the dictum that projects and policies should be implemented to the extent that, at the margin, the costs and benefits are equated. But the latter is the essence of rational choice.

Index

Accounting (or shadow) prices
5, 28, 30-2, 53, 197
Aircraft noise, 143
noise exposure models, 154-8;
noise costs, 158-66;
evaluation of abatement
policies, 166-70
Airport construction and
operating costs, 137-9
Airport peak traffic management, 126-7
Airport study strategy:
objective, 129; selection of
short list sites, 129-30; treatment of aviation services, 130-1;
treatment of airport layout, 131
and the decision process, 149-50
Airport timing, 127-8, 131-2,
145-7
Air traffic forecast, 133-7
Arrow K.J. and Fisher, A.C., 49
Aviation costs, 139-40

Ball M.J., 183
Beaver report, 65
Beckerman W., 25, 62
Benefit cost ratio, 43
Benefit of extra dam capacity,
91-3
Breton A., 67
Buchanan C., 153

Carruthers R.C. and Hensher D.A.,
142
Characterstics determining house
prices, 176-80, 183
Cicchetti C.J. and Freeman A.M.,
48
Civil Aviation Bureau, Japan, 167
Clawson M.J., 122
Collective choice rules, 58, 60,
69-70
Collective decisions, 66-7
Consumer sovereignty, 63-4
Coopers and Lybrand Associates
Ltd., 73
Cost benefit analysis: base case
and, 26, 85; compensation and
willingness to pay values, 33-5,
53; consumer surplus, 37-8;
costs and benefits of a new
airport, 125-6; domestic and
international prices, 29;
external costs, 32-5, 113;
general and relative prices, 28;
limitations of, 71, 197; model
applied to sand mining, 108-10;
objective of, 60-1; principles of
valuation, 27, 30-41; treatment
of uncertainty, 47-9
Cuthbertson B.A., 122

Dasgupta A.K. and Pearce D.N.,
56
Dasgupta P. Sen A. and Maglin S.,
54
Davidson P. Adams F.G. and
Seneca J., 65
Deacon R. and Shapiro P., 67
Department of Environment,
Housing and Community
Development, Australia, 81-2,
86-93, 96-103
Discount rate, 4, 44-7, 85, 98,
110
Discount year, 55, 99-100, 103

Distribution analysis, 5, 50-3, 61, 100-1; airport location and, 132, 147-9; aircraft noise and, 168-9
Downs A., 67

Edwards G.W., 104
Energy resources, 6-8
Environment: definition of, 1; services provided by, 2
Environmental impact statement, 57-8, 62, 71-2, 75-6
Environmental problems, 1-2
Eppalock soil conservation project: description of, 80-1; costs of, 85-7; benefits of, 87-95
Evaluation methods, 57-60; criteria for evaluating methods, 57; philosophy of, 60-2; and decision making, 67-70
Existence benefits, 38, 119
Expected net present value, 48-9

Feldstein M.S. and Fleming J.S., 56
Fishery management, 9-11
Fisher A.C. and Peterson F.M., 7, 23
Fitzgibbon A. and Hendricks H., 121
Flowerdew A.D.J., 140, 142, 152-3
Foley E., 121
Foster C.D., 66
Freeman A.M., 193-5
Fraser Island Environmental Inquiry, 23, 112, 118, 121-2

Galloway W.J., 158
Galloway W.J. and Bishop D.E., 171
Gintis H., 63
Glover J., 64
Goals achievement matrix, 57-8, 62

Harberger A.C., 5, 36, 54-5
Harris S., 121
Harrison A.J., 25
Harrison J. and Grant P., 24
Heath E., 153
Hedonic prices, 174, 192-5
Heggie I.G., 48-9, 54, 56, 152, 171
Held R.B. and Clawson M., 101
Herfindahl O.C. and Kneese A.C., 9, 11, 23, 117, 122
Hills M., 58
Hirsch F., 24
Householder surplus, 34-5, 160-3
Household turnover rates, 162
House price depreciation, 160-3
Hotelling – Clawson method, 115

Implicit prices, 174-5; aircraft noise and, 189-90; road traffic, road widening and, 190; other environmental goods and, 190-2; willingness to pay and, 192-5
Indirect benefits, 27, 118
Individual preferences, 63-7
Industries Assistance Commission, Australia, 121
Intangibles, 26, 47, 68, 95-7
Interdependent benefits, 38, 119
International Civil Airlines Organisation, 166
Internal rate of return, 41-3, 53-4, 59, 69, 97
Irreversibility, 49

Jamaica Bay and Kennedy airport study, 158, 165

Kneese A.C., 20, 23

Lack G.N.T., 153
Land, value of, 31-2, 138
Lave L. and Seskin E., 65
Layard R., 25, 39, 54
Layard R and Walters A.A., 103
Lichfield N. and Chapman H., 72
Lichfield N. and Whitehead M., 68
Little I.M.D. and Mirrlees J.A., 5, 29, 46, 52, 54, 56
Limits to growth, 2

Makower M.S. and Williamson E., 56
Mansfield N.W., 117
Marginal utility of income, 33-4, 36
Material resources, 6-8
Maur R., 197
McColl G.D., 122
McColl G.D. and Throsby C.D., 100
McGowan G.P. and Associates 102
McKern R.B., 121
Merit goods, 61, 67
Mill J.S., 64
Mine management, 11-13
Minford P., 104
Mishan E.J., 28, 63-4, 67, 71, 168
Monte Carlo simulation, 49

Nash C. Pearce N. and Stanley J., 62
Natural amenities, 8, 14-15
Net present value, 9-10, 41-4, 46-8, 50-5, 59, 61, 69, 97, 103, 108, 197
Noise exposure forecast model, 154-8, 161-3, 165-6, 170, 189-90
Noise and number index, 157, 165
Non-convexity, 22
Non-marketed goods, 6, 38-40, 53, 60, 65
Nwaneri V.C., 153

Organisation for Economic Co-operation and Development (OECD), 16
Option values, 38, 48-9, 118, 122-3

Pearce D.W., 23-4, 54
Pigou A.C., 6
Planning balance sheet, 58-9, 61-2
Pollution: expenditure required to reduce pollution, 16; principles of pollution control, 16-20; policies for environmental protection, 20-2

Quandt R.E. and Baumol W.J., 152

Ranger Uranium Environmental Inquiry, 23
Recreation benefits, 114-8
Recycling, 7, 13-14
Reutlinger S., 152
Revealed preference analysis, 39-40, 65-6
Richardson H.W., 25, 61
Rosen S., 174, 193
Roskill Commission, 55, 59, 69, 129-31, 137-9, 145-6, 151-3, 162, 164-5, 172

Sand mining industry: rutile market, 105-6; zircon market, 107; ilmenite market, 107-8; forecasting revenues, 111
Schmalensee R., 56
Second best argument, 111-2
Self P., 58, 71

Secondary benefits, 40-1, 95
Sen A., 65-6
Sensitivity tests, 47, 98-101
Serendipity Inc., 171
Shadow prices, (see accounting prices)
Slater M., 25
Social objectives, 2-6, 9, 22, 60-7
Solow R.M., 11
Standards Association of Australia, 154
Stiglitz J.E., 25
Surface access costs, 140-3
Survey data, use of, 34, 39-40, 64-5, 67
Sydney airport study, 130, 146, 151
Systems analysis, 58-9, 68

Taylor R., 171
Technical progress, 7-8, 22
Tracor Inc., 157-8
Trade off matrix, 57-8
Travel time, value of, 39-40, 66, 142
Travers Morgan R. and Partners, 152-3, 157-8, 163, 172
Turvey R., 173

United Nations Economic Commission for Latin America, 54
UNIDO Guidelines, 46, 54-5
Urbanisation costs and benefits, 143-7
US Department of the Interior, 75
US Flood Control Act, 56

Victor B.A., 25
Victorian Soil Conservation Authority, 83-9, 92, 101-3
Victorian State Rivers and Water Supply Commission, 92

Walters A.A., 71, 151, 161-2, 169, 189
Weinstein M.C. and Zeckhauser R.J., 24-5
Weisbrod B.A., 52
Williams A., 71